Prokofiev

The Complete Series

Bach *Tim Dowley*
Bartók *Hamish Milne*
Beethoven *Ates Orga*
Berlioz *Robert Clarson-Leach*
Brahms *Paul Holmes*
Chopin *Ates Orga*
Debussy *Paul Holmes*
Dvořák *Neil Butterworth*
Elgar *Simon Mundy*
Gilbert & Sullivan *Alan James*
Haydn *Neil Butterworth*
Liszt *Bryce Morrison*
Mahler *Edward Seckerson*
Mendelssohn *Mozelle Moshansky*
Mozart *Peggy Woodford*
Offenbach *Peter Gammond*
Paganini *John Sugden*
Prokofiev *David Gutman*
Rachmaninoff *Robert Walker*
Ravel *David Burnett-James*
Rossini *Nicholas Till*
Schubert *Peggy Woodford*
Schumann *Tim Dowley*
Shostakovich *Eric Roseberry*
Sibelius *David Burnett-James*
Strauss Family *Peter Kemp*
Tchaikovsky *Wilson Strutte*
Verdi *Peter Southwell-Sander*
Villa-Lobos *Lisa Peppercorn*
Vivaldi *John Booth*
Wagner *Howard Gray*

The Illustrated Lives of the Great Composers.

Prokofiev

David Gutman

Omnibus Press
London / New York / Sydney

Cover design and art direction by Pearce Marchbank Studio
Cover photography by Julian Hawkins
Text design by David Morley-Clarke
Printed and bound in the United Kingdom by
Courier International Limited, Tiptree, Essex

© David Gutman 1990
Published in 1990 by Omnibus Press, a division of Book Sales Limited

Hardback
Order No. OP45673
ISBN 0.7119.2082.6

Softback
Order No. OP45681
ISBN 0.7119.2083.4

Exclusive Distributors:
Book Sales Limited,
8/9 Frith Street,
London W1V 5TZ,
England.
Music Sales Pty Limited,
120 Rothschild Avenue,
Rosebery,
NSW 2018,
Australia.
To The Music Trade Only:
Music Sales Limited,
8/9 Frith Street,
London W1V 5TZ,
England.
Music Sales Corporation,
225 Park Avenue South,
New York,
N.Y. 10003,
U.S.A.

Contents

Chapter 1

Russian Overture

Prokofiev was once described by Vernon Duke* as looking 'like a cross between a Scandinavian minister and a soccer player':

His lips were unusually thick . . . and they gave his face an oddly naughty look, rather like that of a boy about to embark on some punishable and therefore tempting prank.

Even today, some 40 years after his death, it is difficult to know quite what to make of Sergey Sergeyevich Prokofiev. As we reconsider what his music means to us, it becomes even more tantalising to find some explanation for our own ambivalent attitudes to it. On one level, Prokofiev's achievement is obvious enough. He contributed to the standard classical repertoire more new music than any other composer of our time: music for the stage, music for the cinema, symphonies, concertos, oratorios and sonatas. Yet, while universally acknowledged as one of the rare twentieth-century composers with a genuine sense of fun, Prokofiev the man is found lacking in those complex, inner qualities we all too readily associate with 'greatness'. Perhaps this should not surprise us. The composer as comic is familiar enough from *Peter and the Wolf, Lieutenant Kijé* and the *Classical Symphony*. But many of those masterpieces which attest to another side of his genius – the First Violin Sonata, the Sixth Symphony, even the epic *War and Peace* – remain comparatively neglected. The immense popularity of a handful of works has tended to submerge much of the best in Prokofiev's vast output.

Born and raised in the Russia of the Tsars, Prokofiev established himself as a bad boy of the musical world in the years up to 1918. After the Revolution he lived abroad, first in the United States, later mainly in Paris. Then came the thirties and, little by little, reconciliation with the new Russia. He spent the last 17 years of

Caricature of Prokofiev by Nikolay Radlov

*the songwriter and composer born Vladimir Dukelsky in pre-revolutionary Russia.

Double-sided processional icon, Novgorod (1531): *recto* – Mother of God of the Sign (Sotheby & Co)

his life in the USSR, stimulated as well as stifled by the cultural policies dictated by Stalin.

It could be argued that Prokofiev's music is more closely bound up with the life of its time than that of his famous contemporaries. It has certainly proved fertile ground for the politically motivated musicologist. All too often the composer has been viewed from the standpoint of ideological warfare, with little obligation to achieve a real understanding. One commentator denounces all that Prokofiev did in the West; another subtitles his account 'A *Soviet Tragedy*'.

Can we detect a vibrant national spirit behind Prokofiev's Soviet phase? Or does the Soviet musician as 'glorifier of Communism' have precious little in common with the nationalist masters of old Russia? Whatever the case, Prokofiev's return to the USSR is itself some measure of his attachment to his homeland. In coming to terms with the man and his music we have to see them against the background of a history and a musical tradition quite different from our own.

As Gerald Abraham writes:

It is hardly an exaggeration to say that until the middle of the eighteenth

8

Double-sided processional icon, Novgorod (1531): *verso* – St Nicholas (Sotheby & Co)

century Russia had almost no live and active musical tradition in the sense of a music handed down over a long period and gradually modified in the process of handing down, freely judged by the community and answering its needs . . .

Russia suffered centuries of exclusion from the common European musical culture in which the Western Slavs participated thanks to their adoption of the Roman form of Christianity. While the Western Church reigned supreme in medieval music, as in arts and letters, the Eastern Church forbade the participation of instruments. Throughout medieval Russia the professional secular musicians were the *skomorokhi*, equivalent to the Western *jongleurs* – wandering minstrels whose accomplishments included juggling. But the Orthodox clergy not only banned the playing of instruments in church; they often succeeded in expelling instrumental performers from the princely courts, so that the *skomorokhi* were reckoned among the dregs of society. It was not until the late seventeenth century that Russian musicians acquired the five-line stave. And well into the eighteenth century, non-liturgical music (other than folk song) was restricted to official acclamations of the monarch and sacred songs for use in the home.

The later course of Russian and Soviet music was the result of something imposed from outside by political factors.

The first important innovations were made in the 1730s by Italians: actors capable of performing a *commedia per musica*, instrumentalists and composers. 'Music' was a foreign cultural notion imposed from the top as a belated consequence of Peter the Great's Westernisation policy. Caring little for music himself, Peter had been content to import a small number of trumpeters and drummers for the new Western-model army. The subsequent musical invasion was sponsored by the Empress Anna. From 1733, the Neapolitan opera composer Francesco Araja (*c.*1700-70) assumed the role of *maestro di cappella*. He stayed for 25 years, contributing little to the music of the Russian people, but conditioning a cultural élite to the enjoyment of a sophisticated Western art form.

Catherine the Great: Empress and librettist (Fotomas Index)

It was not impossible for a wealthy noble to maintain a private orchestra of his serfs:

For sale, a manor serf who plays the violin and knows how to write. Also for sale two English sows and a Danish stallion.

Such advertisements were not uncommon in Russian newspapers of the period. The earliest professional Russian musicians, like the composer Evstigney Fomin (1761-1800) were Italian-trained serfs.

Whether they came to Russia as temporary visitors or to settle permanently, the newcomers wrote operas with Russian texts and sometimes on Russian subjects. Vicente Martín y Soler (1754-1806) composed several – two of them, *The Grief of the Hero Kosometovich* and *Fedul and His Children*, to librettos co-written by Catherine the Great herself.

Domestic music-making in early 19th-century Russia: an anonymous Russian painting (*c.* 1825-50) (Sotheby & Co)

11

The Village Holiday, based on a libretto by V. Maikov, contains the following description of peasants living in the happy state of serfdom:

> We lead a happy life,
> Working every hour;
> We spend our life in the field
> In happiness and joy;
> We labour with our hands,
> And consider it our duty
> To live with such work;
> Paying our quitrent,
> We lead a blissful life
> Under the watchful eye of our landlord.

The influence of court and nobility is much in evidence here; but compare the opening lines of Prokofiev's *Hail to Stalin* (*Zdravitsa*) which, according to his Soviet biographer, Israel Nestyev, 'expresses the joy of free *Kolkhoz* labour':

> Never have our fertile fields such a harvest shown,
> Never have our villagers such contentment known,
> Never life has been so fair, spirits so high,
> Never to the present day,
> Never to the present day grew so green the rye.

Khrapovitzky, Empress Catherine's secretary and her collaborator in the writing of operatic librettos, had written in his memoirs in 1790: 'France perished because of excesses and vices; we must preserve morals.' In 1939, Stalin felt the same and Prokofiev was taking no chances.

After the death of Catherine the Great there was no particular pressure from the monarchy; the main impetus came rather from the aristocracy. While Nicholas I commissioned General Alexey Lvov to write a replacement for *God Save the King*, such genuine music lovers as Count Razumovsky and Prince Nikolai Galitsin commissioned string quartets from Beethoven. Nevertheless, musical life remained limited, resting on no broad national basis. It was not until the 1830s that Russia began to produce musicians with the degree of technical accomplishment taken for granted in the West. The most distinguished of these was Mikhail Glinka (1804-57), whose operas are the foundation stones of classical Russian music.

The old dilettante tradition did not die out of its own accord. It was ended, as it had begun, under imperial auspices, through the work of Anton Rubinstein (1829-94) – an intimate of the well-connected, music-loving Grand Duchess Helena Pavlovna (and,

incidentally, an idol of Maria Grigoryevna Prokofieva, the composer's mother). On Rubinstein's initiative, a Russian Musical Society was founded in 1859, establishing regular series of orchestral concerts in St Petersburg and Moscow, and setting up schools of music: in St Petersburg from 1862, and in Moscow from 1866. The large contingent of foreigners on the original staffs provoked a vigorous reaction from the slavophiles, believing as they did in the inherent superiority of everything Russian. Thanks to Mily Balakirev (1837-1910) and some wealthy supporters, the St Petersburg of the 1860s found itself blessed with two schools and rival series of orchestral concerts. Russian orchestral music, previously almost unknown outside the theatre, poured forth once these opportunities for performance were offered.

The musical flood was accompanied by a philosophical revolution as the idea of 'commitment' took root. The Russian critics of the mid-nineteenth century – notably Belinsky, who first attached social significance to art and literature – set their stamp on the whole subsequent history of the Russian intelligentsia. Russian music was not unaffected.

It was not that such critics thought it was an artist's business to attempt to transform society by means of propaganda, whether direct or indirect. Some Russian writers did believe this, the best example being Chernyshevsky, whose didactic novel, *What is to be done?*, so deeply influenced Lenin. The cultural doctrine set forth in these years was basically this: if you take it upon yourself to speak in public, you must tell the truth as it appears to you, and because all men are social beings, you will, if you speak the truth, inevitably express the social, as well as the individual aspects of contemporary life. This is the artist's inescapable responsibility; if he evades it, he is falsifying reality. The choral spectacle in the operas of Glinka and his disciples is not mere theatrical effect. It represents a genuine desire to create living canvases from the experiences of the Russian people. As the vision faded and the limitations of the political gains of the 1860s became evident, many musicians continued to stand in the forefront of the liberal movement, retaining something of this quest for 'realism' in their art. The cause was most passionately espoused by Modest Mussorgsky (1839-81):

It is the people I want to depict; when I sleep I see them, when I eat I think of them, when I drink – I can visualise them, integral, big, unpainted and without any tinsel.

Perhaps we tend to attribute to Communism much that is really Russian, even nationalist in origin. Were the policies of '*Socialist Realism*' that so affected the latter part of Prokofiev's career anything more than an official attempt to freeze tradition just as the Russian Orthodox Church had managed to do for centuries?

Gerald Abraham again:

Since Communism may be regarded as a species of secular religion – which plays much the same role in the propagation of modern Russian imperialism that Catholicism played in the propagation of Spanish imperialism and Protestantism in that of Anglo-Saxon imperialism – the parallel is quite close.

Although Balakirev's own special passion for social reform withered away, the practical idealism of Russian music proved more durable. It was particularly evident in the aftermath of

'Bloody Sunday', 9 January 1905 [Old style]*, when hundreds of peaceful demonstrators were massacred in St Petersburg's Palace Square. With Prokofiev's studies at the St Petersburg Conservatoire seriously disrupted, the Moscow paper *Nashi Dni* published (on 2 February) an open letter signed by 29 prominent Moscow musicians. These included Sergey Rachmaninov (1873-1943) and Reinhold Moritsevich Glière (1875-1956), Prokofiev's first real teacher:

Only free art is vital, only free creativity is joyful . . . When in the land there is neither freedom of thought and conscience nor freedom of word and print . . . then the profession of 'free artist' becomes a bitter irony. We are not free artists but, like all Russian citizens, the disenfranchised victims of today's abnormal social conditions. In our opinion, there is only one solution: Russia must at last embark on a road of basic reforms . . .

*Russia did not adopt the New Style (Gregorian) Calendar until the end of January 1918; this ended a 13-day discrepancy between Russia and the West which had always obtained under the Tsars.

Yet in 1905, with Prokofiev about to arrive on the musical scene, there was no longer an obvious *creative* path. The young composer would have to establish his own musical identity amidst the chaos of a Russian artistic explosion that predated political revolution by some 25 years. All manner of philosophical questions were being furiously debated in intellectual circles. The attractions of Marxism were lost on those who preached the importance of the individual: that the individual should at all costs pursue his individuality, that the artist had no responsibility other than to his art. Some came to see art as something divine.

The antics of Alexander Scriabin (1872-1915) were a striking manifestation of the current vogue. For Scriabin, as self-centred a composer as ever lived, deliverance was to come not from a revolutionary leader but from a messiah who would unify the arts and provide mankind with a 'new gospel' to replace the New Testament. As for the New Christ, who better than Scriabin himself?

> I am the apotheosis of creation; I am
> the aim of all aims. I am the end of all ends.

The composer apparently saw himself preaching from a boat on Lake Geneva, establishing close links with a radical Swiss fisherman named Otto.

Most of Scriabin's colleagues were less ambitious. Prokofiev's formal Conservatoire training remained, after all, in the hands of relatively unexciting academicians – such men as Nikolay Rimsky-Korsakov (1844-1908), Alexander Glazunov (1865-1936) and Anatol Liadov (1855-1914). Not everyone could be so confident that a 'Promethean' synthesis of cultural endeavour would itself transform the old world. There was bound to be a reaction and, sure enough, with the next generation a novel brand of 'realism' reasserted itself. From about 1910 the stage was set for a new wave of Russian composers with a new outlook. The up-to-date poet-craftsmen could inhabit the *real* world, speaking freshly and vividly, substituting the clarity of statement for the obscurity of allusion. Prokofiev was determined to be one of them.

For audiences stunned by his early appearances as composer-pianist there can have been little doubt about Prokofiev's allegiances. Their outraged ears confirmed the impression of an aggressive modernist. Today, his position is less clear. An innovator who delighted to offend and yet a traditionalist who hankered after simpler, clearer melodies: no wonder Prokofiev has tended to fall between two stools. On the one hand, there is Igor Stravinsky (1882-1971), long established as the cosmopolitan Picasso-figure of twentieth-century music. On the other, Dmitri

Shostakovich (1906-75), open to exploitation by Western musicians in search of a *conservative* model. Prokofiev offers no such possibilities. His work is not held up as a 'lifeline to contemporary music'. By the side of his two great Russian contemporaries (he knew both men well), his progress can seem even more like a perpetual zigzag between incompatible manners and conflicting goals. Even Diaghilev reproached him with a fondness for too many kinds of music: 'In art you must know how to hate, otherwise your music will lose all individuality.' When Prokofiev objected: 'But surely that would lead to narrowness,' Diaghilev hit back: 'The cannon shoots far because it doesn't scatter its fire.' An effective counter, for Prokofiev's dexterity *did* sometimes mask a thinness of emotional commitment, a fundamental musical rootlessness.

More continuity of approach is to be found in the non-dramatic works, as William Austin points out:

. . .Towards the end of World War I, as a deliberate relaxation from the strain of the *Scythian Suite* and *Buffoon*, he composed five of his most charming works – the First Violin Concerto, the *Classical Symphony*, the Third Piano Concerto, and the Third and Fourth Sonatas. During World War II, as if to compensate for *Cinderella*, he wrote five of his hardest, most solid works – the First Violin Sonata, Piano Sonatas 6, 7 and 8, and the Fifth Symphony. Whereas the *Scythian Suite* and *Cinderella* are worlds apart, these ten concert pieces are clearly parts of one world, which during the interval of two decades had developed, as might be expected, toward grander scope and concentrated complexity.

How to break into this musical world and begin to define the Prokofiev style? Prokofiev himself greatly resented the 'grotesque' label so often applied to his work; any 'scherzoish' deviations were, he felt, subordinate to four 'basic lines':

The first was the classical line, which could be traced back to my early childhood and the Beethoven sonatas I heard my mother play. This line takes sometimes a neo-classical form (sonatas, concertos), sometimes imitates the eighteenth-century classics (. . . the *Classical Symphony* . . .). The second line, the modern trend, begins with that meeting with Taneyev when he reproached me for the 'crudeness' of my harmonies. At first this took the form of a search for my own harmonic language, developing later into a search for a language in which to express powerful emotions (. . . *Sarcasms, Scythian Suite,* . . . *Suggestion Diabolique* . . . *The Gambler, Seven, they are seven*, the Quintet and the Second Symphony). Although this line covers harmonic language mainly, it also includes new departures in melody, orchestration and drama. The third line is the *toccata*, or the 'motor', line traceable perhaps to Schumann's Toccata which made such a powerful impression on me when I first heard it (Etudes, op. 2, Toccata, op. 11 . . . the Scherzo of the Second Concerto, the *Toccata* in the Fifth Concerto, and also the repetitive intensity of the melodic figures in the *Scythian Suite, Pas d'Acier* . . . or passages in the Third Concerto). This line is perhaps the least important. The fourth line is lyrical: it appears first as a thoughtful and meditative mood, not always associated with the melody, or, at any rate, with the long melody (. . . *Autumnal* . .), sometimes partly contained in the long melody (. . . the beginning of the First Violin Concerto . . . *Old Grandmother's Tales*). This line was not noticed until much later. For a long time I was given no credit for any lyrical gift whatever, and for want of encouragement it developed slowly. But as time went on I gave more and more attention to this aspect of my work.

Some of the work that preceded Prokofiev's return to Russia shows that his anxiety to keep up with the Stravinskys and *épater les bourgeois* was leading him into a territory which stifled this 'lyrical line', his most original asset as a twentieth-century composer. What, after all, makes his music so unmistakably personal if not his tunes, be they the abrupt melodic squibs of his familiar 'scherzoish' vein or those superb, wide-ranging melodies of his 'epic'/romantic moods?

Prokofiev always maintained that his interest lay not in rhythm but in the invention of good themes; and by good themes he meant melodies that one could recognise as indubitably his own. His style is firmly rooted in the past, although his original use of harmony breathes new life into the old ways. His orchestration, while oddly variable, can impress on account of its acute sense of balance and imaginative texture. Like so many Russian musicians, he chose to work in traditional forms like the symphony and the sonata.

One of Prokofiev's more crucial stylistic innovations was the development of a truly contemporary pianistic style. He was one of the very first to discover the percussive use of the piano and, as

Prokofiev's hands (Novosti)

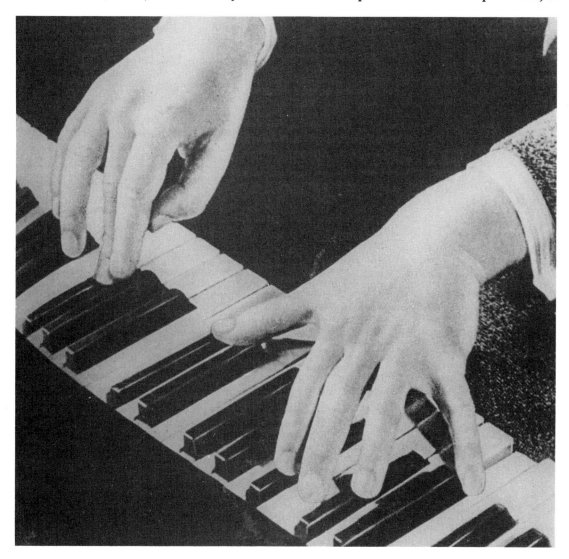

one of its best technicians, he exploited the percussive possibilities early and well. Many of his works in this field have of course become part of the regular piano repertoire. Without being as iconoclastic as Schoenberg, Prokofiev remains a most substantial figure in modern keyboard literature, rivalling Bartók for inventiveness and Messiaen for sheer dazzle.

Whatever its individual characteristics, the music of Prokofiev is deeply rooted in the Russian past, reflecting the heritage of Glinka, Mussorgsky and even Tchaikovsky. His return to a Russia increasingly orientated towards the recreation of a nationalist and 'realist' school on the nineteenth-century model was not, as is still sometimes suggested, a craven flight from failure in the West. It was a means of consolidating his true nature. The 'simplicity' that was required of him in the Soviet Union undoubtedly became too constricting and even distressing towards the end of his life. But Party demands seem to have agreed, more readily than one might assume, with Prokofiev's own simplicity, his genuine patriotism and his willingness to tackle any given task with professional efficiency and enthusiasm. His personal life suffered, but, until 1948, his music did not.

While it is obvious that in Soviet Russia, much bad music has been poured into 'outdated' moulds, it is equally true that a great deal of inferior music has been created in the West by wilful attempts to *avoid* conformity. Any composer starts from conditions as he knows them. What he makes of them must depend on his integrity and creative vitality. Prokofiev lacked neither. As we come to know the composer's personality through his music – in all its bracing humour, tender nostalgia and considerable tragic power – we sense this uniquely personal response to difficult and dangerous times.

Chapter 2

The Prodigal Son

There is a story that Prokofiev's birthplace, the insignificant hamlet of Sontsovka in the Ekaterinoslav district of the Ukraine, was 'lost' for a time by Soviet commentators and cartographers. In line with the post-revolutionary tradition of changing place names, Sontsovka had become Krasnoye. With his customary precision, the composer tells us:

I was born in 1891. Borodin had died four years earlier, Liszt five years earlier, Wagner eight and Mussorgsky ten. There were two and a half years of life remaining to Tchaikovsky. He had completed his Fifth Symphony but had not yet begun the Sixth.
  Alexander III reigned in Russia. Lenin was twenty-one, and Stalin was eleven.
  I was born on Wednesday 11 April [Old style]* at five in the afternoon. It was the one hundredth day of the year.

Although the Prokofievs were by no means at the top of the Russian social tree, Sergey was fortunate enough to be born into an affluent and cultured household. His father, an agricultural engineer from Moscow, had set out for the remote Ukrainian steppe with his young wife in 1878. Offered the chance to manage the vast, sprawling estate of Dmitri Sontsov, a fellow student at the Petrovsko-Razumovskaya Agricultural Academy, Sergey Alekseyevich Prokofiev aimed to put his agronomic ideas to the test on the largest possible scale. Maria Grigoryevna Prokofieva had other priorities. A remarkable, well-educated woman of peasant stock, her devotion to music was to have the greatest influence on the young composer.

The move was, in itself, a success, but the family was all too familiar with tragedy in the years that followed. The Prokofievs lost their first two daughters, Maria and Lyubov, in the 1880s; and when at six weeks little Sergushechka was stricken with

---

*Prokofiev's birth certificate actually gives the date as 15 April.

21

The shape of Russian society in 1900, as caricatured by the Russian Social Democratic Party (Fotomas Index)

dysentery, history threatened to repeat itself. The survival of this third child meant everything to Maria Grigoryevna, and in a very real sense she prepared to devote her life to her son. But first she had to cope with a baby and its disagreeable habits:

I would hit my mother in the face when her pince-nez bothered me, and piercingly shout, '*Makaka!*' – meaning *moloka* [milk].

Thanks to the recent publication of the detailed memoir which Prokofiev started in 1937 and worked on intermittently until his death, we have a remarkably full account of his early life. Regrettably, the chronicle stops short in 1909, just when he really begins to make a name for himself. But the haughtiness often ascribed to him later, his belief in himself, his refusal to conform to imposed disciplines (artistic and otherwise), all this is present in the childhood and adolescence Prokofiev recalls. And even 30 and

40 years on, he was setting down new and fascinating anecdotes. He remembers being kept in a little dress – a reminder of his dead sisters:

Once when my parents took me to church and it was crowded, my mother quietly nudged me up toward the altar so I couldn't be jostled. The priest frowned angrily since girls weren't allowed near the altar. My mother whispered, 'A boy, a boy . . .' And Father Andrei nodded indulgently.

At age three:

. . . I was tumbling about on my father's bed as the family looked on. Then the doorbell rang, signalling the arrival of guests. Everyone hurried to greet them. I went on tumbling about, fell off the bed, and hit my head against an iron trunk. I let out a terrible yell, and everyone came running back.

It was a hard blow. I had a knob on my head throughout my youth, and it didn't go completely away until my thirties. I recall that when I was conducting in Paris as a young man, the painter Larionov touched the knob with his finger and said, 'Perhaps all your talent lies there!'

As an adored only child, Sergey was indulged. This trip to Sevastopol was his first adventure away from Sontsovka:

In Sevastopol my parents were met by their old friends, the Lyashchenkos. Then after hiring two carriages, we all went to Yalta. We stayed in a hotel at the Baidarskiye Gates. While Lyashchenko was eating lunch, I sat next to him. I spat on his bald head and then very seriously spread the saliva around with my finger. When my father noticed my actions, he was filled with consternation. But Lyashchenko said good-humouredly, 'Don't bother him. He's very lovable.'

Lovable or not, the streak of wilfulness is characteristic.

Sergey began to show an aptitude for music quite early: there was always music in the home:

When I was put to bed at night, I never wanted to sleep. I would lie there and listen as the sound of a Beethoven sonata came from somewhere far off, several rooms away. More than anything else, my mother played the sonatas of Volume I.

Next came Chopin's preludes, mazurkas, and waltzes. Sometimes there was a piece by Liszt – something not too difficult. Her favourite Russian composers were Tchaikovsky and Rubinstein. Anton Rubinstein was at the height of his fame, and my mother was convinced that he was a greater phenomenon than Tchaikovsky. A portrait of Rubinstein hung over the grand piano.

In the summer of 1896, the five-year-old confronted his mother

Prokofiev with his parents
(1892) (Novosti)

with a sheet of paper covered with notes and announced: 'I have composed Liszt's *Rhapsody*.'

She had to explain that one couldn't compose a Liszt rhapsody because it was a piece of music that Liszt himself had composed. Also, one could not write music on nine lines without bars, because music was, in fact, written on five lines with bars. All of this prompted Mother to give me a more systematic explanation of the principles of musical notation.

Meantime, I had put together a tune that took on a completely acceptable form. I played it several times, and Mother decided to write it down. No doubt she had some difficulty doing it, since she was new at such an assignment.

A caricature of Anton
Rubinstein (Fotomas Index)

It is hard to imagine a more absurd title than the one I gave this
composition: *Indian Galop*. As it happened, there was a famine in India
in those days, and the adults read about it in the newspapers and
discussed it while I listened.

For the time being, Sergey's musical education remained in the
capable hands of his mother. 'Nothing was done thoroughly,' the
composer declared later. But to have insisted at this early stage on
boring exercises and rigorous practice sessions might have sapped
his youthful enthusiasm. And Sergey was quite precocious
enough. By the summer of 1902, when Glière arrived in Sontsovka

to tutor the boy, he was already the composer of numerous short piano pieces, and two operas! Composition of *The Giant* and *Desert Islands* – 'Why do you have such impossible ideas?' complained his mother – was inspired by a visit to the Solodovnikov Theatre, Moscow (later part of the Bolshoi) in 1899. There, Sergey discovered in rapid succession *Faust*, *Prince Igor* and *The Sleeping Beauty*. He was also encouraged to put on a series of 'wretched' little plays, no doubt sharpening his innate sense of drama and character. At all periods he was to concern himself with music for the stage.

After some rather abortive lessons in Moscow with Yuri Nikolayevich Pomerantsev, another young teacher was invited to put in a three-month stint at Sontsovka. This was Glière. In his reminiscences, he recalls his first contact with the family:

I got off the train at the little station of Grishino . . . with my humble baggage, comprising a huge bundle of manuscript paper and a violin. A two-horse carriage had been sent for me from Sontsovka. The road lay between the magnificent fields and meadows of the 'Black Country', all scattered with flowers. All the way along the road, for a distance of 25 kilometres, I never ceased to admire the marvellous spectacle of the Ukrainian landscape, so rich in colour. At last there appeared on a hill a small manorial hall surrounded with the cheerful greenery of a garden and flanked by outhouses and a large open shed. From the very first moment, I felt at home.

The lessons were a great success and, in June 1903, Glière returned to spend a second summer at Sontsovka.

All Glière's students remember his teaching with pleasure because, like a true pedagogue, he knew how to enter into the mind of his pupil. He did not inflict on him any dry theories which he could and should know for himself, so long as he was not receptive to them. Glière could guess where the interests of his pupils lay and strove to develop them in the right direction . . .

In his free time, Glière was glad to play croquet or chess, or even take up a challenge to a duel with dart pistols – which won me over even more. He always came to see our plays, considering them to be something more serious than a game and seeing in them the embryo of future works for the stage by a composer.

At the same time, Sergey began to be conscious of the importance of his *music*, setting it apart from these other amusements. The passion for chess was one notable exception; it never left him.

Piano lessons played an important part in these early studies but Glière was a composer, not a pianist. He noted the poor technique of his pupil without being able to remedy it. From Glière, Sergey

Opposite
The young Prokofiev at the chessboard (Novosti)

26

A musical autograph from Prokofiev to Glière. The inscription reads: 'With congratulations to dear Reinhold Moritsevich on his wonderful seventieth birthday, in memory of our first meeting in 1902. Here is the first theme of the symphony written at that time under his guidance. S.PRKFV, 1945'

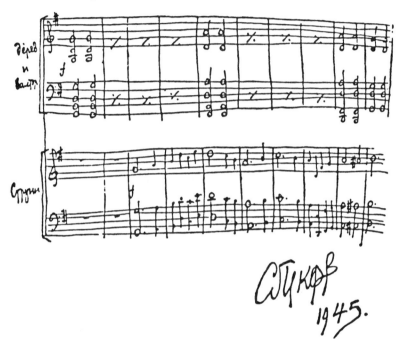

learned especially the rudiments of harmony, form and orchestration. He even completed a four-movement symphony with help.

It is in fact an absurdly titled series of piano miniatures, most of them in simple three-part form, which more clearly hints at the child's potential:

After six years I had written almost 70 of these 'little songs'. Some of them were marches or 'romances', but they were all numbered as 'ditties'. My ear got used to this name, and I no longer noticed how inappropriate it was.

By 1904, quirky harmonies and rhythms have begun to invade the 'ditties', transforming them from naïve 'little songs' into vivid scherzos and dance movements. Later pieces are even laced with the distinctive Prokofiev brand of musical humour.

With the departure of Glière and the onset of the fierce Russian winter, Sontsovka's geographical and musical isolation intensified; Sergey left for Moscow with his mother. Her annual

28

visits to the metropolis rapidly became an important part of his musical education. He was able to play his latest pieces to composer Sergey Ivanovich Taneyev, 'the greatest professor in Moscow', thanks to the success of an initial audition arranged by Pomerantsev. And inevitably the list of works was growing. By 1903, there was yet another opera – *A Feast in Time of Plague*. Prokofiev had only the vaguest recollection of his first meeting with Taneyev but did remember being 'favourably impressed when he immediately picked up a bar of chocolate from the table and offered it to me'.

By 1904, it was obvious that a decision had to be made. On the one hand, for Sergey to develop as a composer he needed more continuous contact with the professional musical world. But it was also time for his general education to become more formal. 'Buttery-smooth' Sergey viewed the prospect of high school, 'where the boys fought and the "newcomers" were hazed', with unconcealed dread. For the Prokofievs it was not quite the usual story of vacillating parents loath to commit their child to a musical career. Maria Grigoryevna was bored and restless at Sontsovka and saw in her son's music a chance to escape to the city. There was 'not altogether harmonious' debate:

One morning when I woke up early (the door between my room and my parents' bedroom was always left open), I heard a stormy discussion, and my Father saying, 'In that case there's nothing for me to do but shoot myself.'

I took him seriously and began to howl. Mother and Father were dismayed. They took me into their bedroom and tried to calm me down. Finally my Father began to cry, too. Then he got up and went to his study.

Eventually the choice was seen to lie between Moscow, where Sergey Alekseyevich's brother and nieces lived, and St Petersburg, where Maria's own 'more interesting' relatives had their home. At length, in the spring of 1904, Sergey was taken to St Petersburg and, on the advice of Glazunov, he applied for entrance to the Conservatoire in that city.

Prokofiev's academic 'baptism of fire' came in September 1904:

The entrance examination was quite sensational. The examinee before me was a man with a beard who had nothing to show the examiners but a single romance without accompaniment. Then I came in, bending under the weight of two huge folders containing four operas, two sonatas, a symphony and a good many pianoforte pieces. 'Here is a pupil after my own heart!' observed Rimsky-Korsakov who headed the examining board.

Confirmation of Sergey's prowess meant that the family was

effectively broken up. Intending to return to Sontsovka for the Christmas and summer holidays, the composer and his mother lived in a rented St Petersburg flat while the Conservatoire was in session. Thus Sergey entered what Igor Stravinsky called 'that horrible musical prison'. He was to spend the next ten years as one of its most unruly inmates.

For the most vivid reminiscences of turn-of-the-century St Petersburg we again turn to Prokofiev's great rival. Prokofiev himself was a natural raconteur, but there were blind spots – probably because he thought so exclusively in terms of music. He was never passionately interested in the art treasures, sights and sounds of the great capitals and has left us no personal description of the city to compare with that of Stravinsky, who loved the place as only an expatriate can:

St Petersburg street noises are especially vivid to me . . . The first such sounds to record themselves on my awareness were those of droshkies on cobblestone, or block wood parquetry pavements. Only a few of these horse carriages had rubber tyres, and these few were doubly expensive; the whole city crackled with the iron-hooped wheels of the others. I also remember the sound of horse-drawn street cars and, in particular, the rail scraping noise they made as they turned the corner near our house and whipped up speed to cross the Krukov Canal Bridge. (Steeper bridges sometimes required the use of extra horses, and those were found at hitching posts throughout the city.) The noises of wheels and horses and the shouts and whipcracks of coachmen must have penetrated my earliest dreams; they are, at any rate, my first memory of the streets of childhood. (The clatter of automobiles and electric trolley cars, two decades later, was much less memorable . . .)

The loudest diurnal noises of the city were the cannonade of bells from the Nikolsky Cathedral, and the noon signal from the Peter and Paul Fortress – a timepiece for the whole populace . . .

A city is also remembered by its odours. In the case of St Petersburg, these were associated chiefly with droshkies. They smelled agreeably of tar, of leather, and of their horses. Usually, however, the strongest odour emanated from the driver himself . . .

One other aroma that permeated the city and, indeed, all Russia, was of the tobacco called Mahorka; it was originally imported by Peter the Great.

I remember St Petersburg as an ochre city (in spite of such prominent red buildings as the Winter Palace and Anichkov Palace), the architecture, as well as the colour, of St Petersburg, was Italian, and Italian not merely by imitation but by the direct work of such architects as Quarenghi and Rastrelli.

Italian stylisation and craftsmanship could be found in any work of the Catherine the Great period, whether in a building, a statue or an *objet d'art*. And the principal palaces were Italian not only in design but in material (marble). Even in the case of the ordinary St Petersburg building stone, which was a local granite or an equally local brick, the outer surfaces were plastered, and painted Italian colours.

The Maryinsky Theatre was a delight to me. To enter the blue-and-gold interior of that heavily-perfumed hall was, for me, like entering the most sacred of temples.

St Petersburg was a city of islands and rivers. The latter were called Neva, mostly – Great Neva, Small Neva, Great Small Neva, Middle Neva. The movements of boats and the life of the harbour are less significant in my recollections than one might expect, however, because of the long, icebound winters.

St Petersburg was also a city of large, open piazzas. One of these, the Champs de Mars, might have been the scene of *Petrushka*.

Another attractive piazza was the Haymarket, where hundreds of wains were stored to supply the city's huge horse population; to walk there was to be reminded of the countryside. But my most animated promenades in St Petersburg were on the Nevsky Prospekt, a wide avenue, three miles long, and full of life and movement all the way. Here were the beautiful Stroganov Palace (by Rastrelli); the Lutheran Church (which Balakirev, a devout Orthodoxist, used to call the upside-down trousers); the Kazansky Cathedral, with its semicircle of columns in

imitation of St Peter's in Rome; the Duma (City Hall); the Gastinny Dvor (Merchants' Court), a block of arcades with hundreds of shops; the Public Library; the Drama Theatre; and the Anichkov Palace, Tsar Alexander III's residence. The Nevsky Prospekt was also the principal arena for amorous assignations, and at night it was full of *grues*, and the officers and students who were their chief customers. A letter of Leon Bakst's to me in Morges in 1915: ' . . . you remember how . . . on a beautiful, white, Russian night, the purple-painted whores yell after you, "men give us cigarettes".'

The Prokofiev memoirs do provide a unique record of Sergey's personal life at this critical time. It is striking how few real friends he had. Only in his remote 'god-forsaken' village could he play with children of his own age. Some 15 years younger than his fellow harmony and composition students, the prodigy of St Petersburg was made to feel very, very small. His over-protective mother encouraged him unrelentingly in his studies but this only contributed to the sense of isolation. Unwittingly perhaps, the mature Prokofiev lets his youthful self emerge as almost impossibly precocious, shy, difficult and sensitive. (Glière remembers him bursting into tears after hitting his mother on the foot with a croquet mallet!) We are even shown the jealous and arrogant young schemer, ready to criticise vehemently the music of others but reluctant to accept the same, even from his professors.

No sooner had classes begun than the first rumblings of revolution were felt at the Conservatoire. By October 1905, the country would be paralysed, its workers, revolutionaries and intellectuals united as never before against the autocratic rule of the Tsar. But Bloody Sunday was a spark which lit many fires. While mutinies broke out in the fleet – the most famous was that aboard the battleship *Potemkin* – there were less dramatic but no less immediate repercussions among the musical intelligentsia.

During the street riots of 1917 a youthful Dmitri Shostakovich was to witness a sight he never forgot. 'They were breaking up a crowd in the street,' the composer told Solomon Volkov, 'and a Cossack killed a boy with his sabre. It was terrifying. I ran home to

Massacre on the Odessa steps; a still from *The Battleship Potemkin*, Eisenstein's film of 1925 (National Film Archive)

tell my parents about it.' Nothing comparable seems to have happened to Prokofiev in 1905. It was the infighting at the Conservatoire which left the most indelible impression:

From Prokofiev to his father at Sontsovka.
St Petersburg, 5 February 1905.

Just imagine! They started a strike at the Conservatory. Today when I went for my harmony lesson I saw that little knots of people had gathered everywhere, students of 16 and 17, shouting and making a lot of noise. The class met anyway, but not even half of the students were there. One of them, Kankarovich, didn't come until after two o'clock instead of at one. He had been at a meeting in the Little Auditorium, where more than 40 people had gathered. They all argued, and made noise, and finally signed their names. The main thing was that they didn't have any aim. [This shows the influence of the talk I heard at home, which I of course repeated. My mother's viewpoint was as follows: since we had left my father in Sontsovka and come to Petersburg so that I could study, the thing to do was study and not become involved in unfathomable matters.]

In general, the students are protesting, for example, the fact that one of their number in a certain class is a soldier who shot at the workers during the disturbances, and that they do not want to have a 'murderer' as a fellow-student. Second that Auer, the professor of violin, is very irritable and is always cursing at the students; that, in their opinion, he dropped one student for no reason at all [he dropped him because he had missed a lot of classes]; that at every lesson he spends ten minutes more with one girl student he knows than with the others. [Auer was very famous and did what he wanted.] Finally, that today one of the attendants behaved rudely, saying they were nothing but 'kikes', that they had killed the grand duke, etc.

My assignments were rather well done, although two unusual mistakes were found: cross-relations.

After the lesson Kankarovich began to make a speech, explaining to Liadov why they called a meeting. In general he talked nonsense. As Liadov put it, these things are family matters that could be settled without a lot of fuss simply by going to the director. And our whole class disagreed with Kankarovich, saying that they were always protesting over trifles, and that we might suffer if the Conservatory were closed: we would lose a year, and we would lose the tuition money we had paid.

On 16 March, the Conservatoire was surrounded by police and more than a hundred protesters taken to the police station. By order of the director, all those detained were expelled. On the very next day, by decision of the Students' Committee, a number of students slipped through the police cordon and created a so-called chemical obstruction by spilling a foul-smelling liquid in the classrooms. A group of teachers then sent A. R. Bernhard a letter demanding his resignation:

. . . recently it has become very plain that there is total dissension between you, the director, and us, the faculty at the Conservatory . . . We trust that the events of the past few days have sufficed to show how right we were in insisting on suspension of classes, and how shameful were the consequences of your manner of acting.

On the basis of the foregoing we have concluded that it is your moral duty to resign as director of the Conservatory.

As tension mounted, it was decided to dismiss Rimsky-Korsakov from the faculty for having defamed the directorate and spoken out in the press. The decision was confirmed by Grand Duke Konstantin Romanov, and on 21 March it was conveyed to Rimsky-Korsakov. Glazunov and Liadov then issued the following statement published in the newspaper *Rus* on 25 March:

Having learned of the dismissal of N. A. Rimsky-Korsakov, Distinguished Professor of the Petersburg Conservatory, we have the honour to inform the Directorate that, to our great regret, we cannot continue our pedagogical activity at that institution after this accomplished fact.

A performance of Rimsky-Korsakov's opera *Kashchei the Immortal* on 27 March became the occasion for a public demonstration and much fiery oratory. Thereafter the composer was put under police surveillance and the Conservatoire building remained closed completely for six months.

The revolutionary spirit was soon making itself felt even in the backwoods of Sontsovka:

On 29 June, while the dedication day of the Sontsovka church was being celebrated, an anonymous letter was nailed to the fence of the big orchard. It was addressed to my father and among other threats stated that it was high time for the landowners and their managers to get out of Sontsovka before they were dealt with in the appropriate manner.

My father was alarmed and called a small meeting of peasants. I don't know what was discussed there but I believe it was all rather peaceable, since the letter was apparently of outside origin and indifference still prevailed in the age-old core of the Sontsovka peasantry . . . But in August, when the mown hay had been piled into high stacks which were often several kilometres distant from Sontsovka, fires began to break out. The peasants were burning out the landowners. Usually this happened around midnight, when I was asleep. I would be awakened by the sounding of the alarm, and in the dark southern night the bright flow of flames could be seen on the horizon. I would feel uneasy and anxious and my parents would send me back to bed, where for a long time I would toss from side to side, unable to go to sleep.

With the concessions of the October Manifesto, signed by the Tsar on 17 October, autocracy sounded the retreat. The peasants had been the decisive factor. It was their methodical seizure of private estates in the autumn months of 1905 which tipped the scales shattering the confidence of the bureaucracy in its power to restore order without making political concessions, and winning from the Emperor the reluctant promise of an imperial duma, or parliament.

The Manifesto was shrewdly devised. Its apparent promise of constitutional government duped liberals and moderates of every shade into shoring up an apparently chastened and yielding government. In fact, the loyalty of army and police enabled the Tsar to regain control once the social revolution began to lose momentum. There was savage repression. And yet it was a strange, contradictory time. The democratic principle once conceded is not easily revoked, and the significance of the limited transformation was not lost on either reactionaries or revolutionaries. The Social Democrats would not confess themselves beaten. For them, revolution and counter-revolution still hung in the balance; and much had been learnt in this first attempt to win power for the Russian masses – a dress rehearsal for 1917.

Chapter 3

Dreams

When Sergey returned to the Conservatoire for the 1905-6 session he found conditions there as chaotic as ever. Rimsky-Korsakov, Glazunov and Liadov eventually reappeared. But even these three most distinguished musicians receive a notably bad press from the Prokofiev memoirs. Although Sergey made strenuous attempts to re-enrol for classes each year, he was sadly disillusioned with the teaching. Only Nikolay Tcherepnin's conducting class emerges with much credit.

The youth seems to have found Liadov vaguely repulsive:

. . . Liadov, absolutely indifferent to his students. I can still see him – the corpulent figure, the swollen eyelids, the bloated face, the short arms with the hands stuffed deep into his trousers pockets – as he swayed on the tips of his high shoes with prunella uppers, waiting for his student to go away and leave him in peace.*

But this account of a Liadov harmony class shows us why so many of Sergey's classmates actively detested *him*!

> From Prokofiev to his father at Sontsovka.
> St Petersburg, 9 February 1905.

Today I had harmony and solfeggio. The solfeggio went off really quite well. My harmony exercises were probably the best ones turned in today. I have begun to keep statistics on the mistakes made in harmony class. It's too bad I didn't before. But first, I didn't know all the other students then; and, second, it never occurred to me. In any case, next year I'll keep account of all the mistakes in counterpoint from the very beginning . . .

Later, Prokofiev reflected:

*Stravinsky found Liadov 'a darling man, as sweet and charming as his own *Musical Snuff Box*'.

I kept those statistics for eleven lessons. Liadov would sit down at the piano, put a copybook containing exercises on the music rack, and play the exercises, marking the mistakes in pencil and from time to time making acid remarks.

I would stand behind Liadov holding a notebook and eagerly jot down each mistake and what it was called. These included parallel and hidden octaves and fifths, cross-relations, bad suspensions, bad passing tones, bad harmonies, bad sequences, incorrect resolutions, etc., totalling nineteen types of mistakes in all.

Back at home I arranged them in nineteen columns, showing the total number of exercises turned in by each student, the total number of mistakes, and the number of mistakes per exercise for each student (in the form of a decimal fraction with an accuracy of one hundredth). In a word, I had an entire book-keeping project at home, not to mention keeping account of the mistakes I myself had made that Liadov had marked in my copybook, since in class I didn't have time to jot down my own mistakes. My classmates at first regarded this project of mine with astonishment, then with hostility. But I never noticed it, having been carried away by the sporting interest of the whole thing, and fearing more than anything else that I would miss a mistake.

At the second lesson Kobylyansky was scathingly criticised by Liadov, who crossed out all manner of things in the pages of his copybook. When he came back from the piano, all red in the face, he asked me in a half whisper, 'What are you jotting down there?'

'I'm keeping statistics on mistakes.'

'What business is it of yours how many mistakes a person makes?' he exploded.

Our talk was interfering with Liadov's teaching. 'Quiet down, gentlemen!' he muttered. And we did. But after class, when Liadov had left, Kobylyansky again went after me.

'I came here to study the theory of composition, and it's nobody's business what kind of mistakes I make in my exercises, or how many I make. I can assure you that it's of no interest to anybody.'

'To the contrary, it's highly interesting! For example, today you brought in (at this point I consulted my notebook) one exercise, and it had eleven mistakes in it. Asafiev brought in six exercises, and there were only eleven mistakes in all six. From this it is quite obvious that your work is six times worse than Asafiev's. In the near future I intend to plot a curve –'

'That's childish and unbearable!' he raged. 'I completely fail to understand how you got into this class, which is intended for adults and not for the adolescent generation.'

'If you would shout less and pay closer attention to your work,' I said didactically, 'both your progress and my statistics would –' I never finished the sentence. Kobylyansky jumped on me, threw me to the floor, and pulled my ears.

Sergey was not blind to the merits of Rimsky-Korsakov's music, but was perhaps too young to derive much benefit from his

experience. The old master's teaching methods did call for some tolerance. If Liadov's classes deadened all enthusiasm, Rimsky's were so large that no one could see what was going on at the piano. According to Prokofiev, he would spend most of each four-hour session correcting students' homework:

One day when he had my assignment on the music rack in front of him, Rimsky-Korsakov turned to me suddenly and asked, 'Why did you give the melody to the oboe here?'

I was stunned by such a point-blank question and said confusedly, 'Because . . . it seemed to me . . . I thought that the timbre of the oboe . . .'

'And why not the clarinet? It looks as though, instead of feeling the tone colour, you were playing "She-loves-me, she-loves-me-not" on your fingers: oboe . . . clarinet . . . oboe . . . clarinet . . .'

He screwed up his eyes and, wrapping one finger of his right hand around a finger protruding from his left hand, he suddenly brought both hands together. And as finger told off finger, he exclaimed, 'Right! The oboe! And so you're in a hurry to use the oboe. But for pity's sake! Is that really acceptable?'

I stood there, overwhelmed by the sudden attack. And I remembered Tcherepnin's saying recently that the oboe has a more distinctive tone than the clarinet, while the clarinet is a more versatile instrument than the oboe.

'I like the oboe,' Tcherepnin continued. 'It has a nasal tone with bright colouration. But Rimsky-Korsakov, for example, prefers the clarinet. He feels that its tone is velvety and softer, so that it blends in with the orchestra better. The oboe doesn't blend in so well, but for that reason it stands out better.'

Rimsky-Korsakov turned the page of my manuscript and again asked me in a disgruntled voice, 'Why do you have a cello playing solo here, instead of all the cellos together?'

I was starting to get cramps somewhere inside because I felt he wasn't so much teaching me as nagging me. I replied bluntly, 'I wrote it for solo cello because I don't like the sound of all the cellos playing in unison.'

He jumped up. 'You don't like it? Why don't you like it?'

'For example, in that Sibelius symphony they all play together for a very long time, and the sound isn't good.' (I don't remember whether that was in the Third Symphony, which I had heard recently, or in another symphony by the same composer.)

'Then why try to learn from Sibelius? And what about *Ruslan* – the second theme of the overture. Perhaps that doesn't sound good, either?'

I looked around in the hope of catching someone smiling as if to say, 'Look, the old man is getting angry.' The other students were standing in a half circle around the piano, and the light was such that I could see their faces clearly. There stood Miaskovsky, and there Zakharov. But no one was smiling. They all wore serious expressions, and I could find no sign of sympathy.

Rimsky-Korsakov picked up my score and passed it back over his shoulder, saying 'Next!'

However, as Prokofiev recalls:

At the next lesson it wasn't I that the lightning bolt struck but . . . Peter Ilich Tchaikovsky. One of the students – I believe it was Asafiev – had brought the score of his First Symphony. Placing it on the music rack in front of Rimsky-Korsakov he asked how the flutes got down to B flat. Rimsky-Korsakov looked at the score, twisted his beard and pulled at it, and then said with a little smile, 'M-m-m, yes . . . Peter Ilich got something wrong here . . . French flutes go down to C. German flutes – the kind we use – go down to B. But no flutes go down to B flat. Of course right here it's not especially important if the flutes don't play the note. But if they can't play it, why write it?'

He was obviously pleased at having found a mistake, and gave a little laugh as he handed the score back to its owner.

Given the 'dry peevish' quality of his teaching, it was fortunate that Liadov's counterpoint class of 1906 served to introduce Sergey to two men who were to become his lifelong friends: Boris Asafiev, later the doyen of Soviet musicology, and Nikolay Miaskovsky:.

Miaskovsky showed up at the Conservatoire in the uniform of a lieutenant in a battalion of engineers.

He was 25, 'a composer with a little beard and a big portfolio'; Sergey just 15. It was perhaps an unlikely friendship. What they had in common was a passionate interest in new music. Both were tremendously excited by Reger's visit of December 1906. (He conducted his Serenade in G major.)

Miaskovsky surprised me one day by producing from his portfolio a four-hand arrangement of the serenade. We sat down and played it then and there. Shortly after that Miaskovsky came to my house to play Beethoven's Ninth Symphony with me. He said no one had ever been able to play it with him to the end. I gave him an album with my latest pieces for piano (I called them 'Little Dogs' now instead of 'Little Songs', because someone had told me that they 'snapped at you'). 'I never suspected what a little viper we had been nursing in our bosom,' Miaskovsky said when he returned them to me a few days later. But from the way he smiled into his moustache I could see that he did not think too badly of them. After that we took to showing one another our sonatas, and sometimes we played duets.

Like Holst and Vaughan Williams, Prokofiev and Miaskovsky built up an extensive correspondence: there survive 312 letters from Prokofiev alone, written over a period of almost 43 years. Miaskovsky's seniority makes him an especially crucial figure in Prokofiev's development. He not only encouraged Sergey in his creative darings but actively promoted his works on the concert stage. With his penetrating critical mind he helped many early listeners, perhaps even Prokofiev himself, to appreciate the true nature of his art. It was to Miaskovsky that Sergey showed his latest pieces, the opera *Undine* and a series of piano sonatas.

'I don't think you ought to bother numbering your sonatas,' Miaskovsky once said to me with a smile. 'The time will come when you will cross out all the numbers and write "Sonata No. 1".' That is exactly what happened, although some of the material from these early sonatas did go into later sonatas (No. 2 after some changes became No. 1, op. 1; No. 3 remained No. 3 even after alterations; Nos. 4 and 6 were lost; No. 5 was incorporated in No. 4, op. 29).

The series of letters from the summer of 1907 shows the burgeoning of Prokofiev's wit and some perceptive and astringent musical criticism. That autumn he wrote in his diary, 'No doubt I'd make a good daily critic – and a real bastard at that.' And of course examples of his whimsical humour abound. [Prokofiev's later annotations punctuate the text.]:

From Prokofiev to Miaskovsky in Oranienbaum. Sontsovka, 26 June 1907.

Esteemed Nikolay Yakovlevich (Dear Kolechka):
I am sending you together with this letter two piano puppies. [The two piano pieces had been sent in a registered parcel at the same time as the letter. I wrote 'together with' because I wanted to express myself with style.] When you analyse them, pay special attention to the themes, which play an important role. Then think about what they should be called. [During later years I often asked Miaskovsky to think up names for my pieces, and in most cases he did very well at this. It is curious that I should have made such a request in my first letter to him.] Especially the second: I would say the idea in it is clearly expressed, but you'll never think up a name for it. [The pieces I sent him on this occasion have not been preserved, but I remember that the first one was tentatively called *Carnival*, and that it contained a theme I later used in my First Piano Concerto.]
You will of course give me the most precise suggestions on those various fine points. How are things going with your symphonic poem on a 'very good' subject? [Apparently I was referring to *Silence*, which Miaskovsky was already planning at that time.] I have completed the first movement of the sonata I showed you at the exam. Probably there will not be any second, third, or fourth movement, and it will remain *à la Miaskovsky*, in one movement: pretty, interesting, and practical.
I recently chanced to write a sonatina in two movements. Writing it was very interesting: I did it as simply as possible, and it came out happily. I am still writing the last part of Act IV of *Undine*, which I gave you in May . . .

Well, so long for the time being. I expect some puppies in return. You have of course forgotten my address. [This wasn't very polite, but someone had once written that to me and I found it rather elegant.] It is: Andreyevka Post Office, Bakhmutsky District, Ekaterinoslav Province.

Best Regards,

S. Prokofiev

From Miaskovsky to Prokofiev at Sontsovka.
Oranienbaum, 12 July 1907. Received 18 July 1907.

Most Beloved Sergey Sergeyevich:

I have been waiting – but in vain, until just now – for an opportunity to respond in worthy fashion both to your letter and (especially, of course) to the puppies you sent me. From the totality of what I have 'created' during this time, I could find nothing that had the slightest little chance of pleasing you [from this it follows that in the spring I was rather critical of the music he had written], so I have decided simply to send you an 'empty' letter without any enclosures – in doing which I am of course showing you the blackest kind of ingratitude. But there it is . . .

Your music gladdened me to the point of clouding my mind. [It was when my father read this that he exclaimed, 'Just look at the kind of letters people are writing now!'] Along with your repulsive (not for me of course) scribbling of the most frightful combinations (especially in the second piece) there are rather convincing moments. And the overall tone, the overwhelming ardour, and that causticity which I am so extremely fond of in you, if one may so express it [Father: 'Come on! Read that again!'], are so vivid that they unquestionably make up for their defects. At the outset I was of course annoyed that I could play only one note with each hand, and at the opposite ends of the keyboard at that. But when I played the pieces at a tempo (half as fast as yours, of course) that enabled me to understand the general tone, I was fully satisfied – especially with the first piece. The second has more mud in it [My father: 'But what strange expressions he uses!'] and is somehow more vulnerable.

So far as the title of the second piece is concerned, I have nothing to say. In general I am not fond of titles, and so I immediately liked the second piece as it was, without any name. *Carnival* is fitting for the first piece: it has a lot of recklessness in it. Perhaps some carnival character would be suitable for the second piece too: its beginning reminds me of Mime and his sobbing. [Obviously Wagner's *Ring* tetralogy was fashionable among us.] . . . I concluded from the notations on the 'things' that they were my property, and hence I shall not return them. If, of course, you do not agree with my conclusion, I shall proceed as you direct me by letter.

All my plans for orchestral diversions have foundered on my profound laziness and sluggishness. I can't get beyond the confines of the piano – and occasionally piano and voice. I constantly muddle along with such trifles as my Third Piano Sonata (in two movements, the first being a small three voice fugue, *Lento*). [He later added two more movements, and the piece became his First Piano Sonata, in D minor.] Also, out of

Alexander Konstantinovich Glazunov (Novosti)

42

sheer idleness, I have thrown together a dozen fragments for piano, some of which are indecently brief (eight bars) and risky. I really can't bring myself to send them along. Last week I set seven poems by Baratinsky to music, but the songs are very ordinary and would be of no interest to you. [They were later published as his Opus 1.]

One of my most piquant amusements this summer has been the study of harmony with Monsieur Kobylyansky, whom Liadov sent me – no doubt in order to exasperate me completely. Every Tuesday he comes to fish out fifths and octaves, play totally nonsensical modulations, and in between listen to heartrending love songs and frivolous things from operettas. There's pleasure for you! In a few days I'm going to Asafiev's to recover. I'll be expecting your sonata and sonatina.

Goodbye for now.

Yours,
N. Miaskovsky.

In 1906, when questioned by Liadov as to his favourite composers, Sergey had singled out Tchaikovsky, Wagner and Grieg. The choice, partly dictated by the desire to appear fashionable, was still conservative enough to satisfy his teacher. His friendship with Miaskovsky marked the beginning of a more regular contact with new music – Reger, Richard Strauss, Debussy – and the downgrading of older models:

No one (especially Miaskovsky) denied the sturdy quality of Glazunov's symphonies and their irreproachable counterpoint. But we wanted something new and unexpected – something that 'took wing'. So it was that at first we were interested in Glazunov and enjoyed playing four-hand arrangements of his music (it was so conveniently at one's fingertips). But finally, while Miaskovsky remained among his followers, I began to get irritated, seeing Glazunov's music as obsolescent and devoid of invention but music that was nonetheless taken as the creativity of a leading composer.

Prokofiev on Rachmaninov:

It seemed to me that in Rachmaninov's music there were certain melodic turns typical of him that were extraordinarily beautiful. But all in all there weren't many of them and once they had been found, they were repeated in other works. As compared to Scriabin, he struck me as a composer who strove less for novelty and harmonic invention. Someone once said (rather venomously) of his melodies that they were mostly written for a voice with a very small range. And yet sometimes he managed to fit amazingly beautiful themes into that small range; for example, in his Second Concerto.

Rachmaninov: an informal study dating from about 1900

What about Scriabin? Stravinsky tells us that Rimsky-Korsakov did not rate very highly the compositional gifts of 'the

narcissus': *'mais, c'est du Rubinstein!'* ('Anton Rubinstein' being at
this time a term of abuse equivalent to *merde*).

But for rebellious youth, Scriabin was a magic name impossible
to ignore. His influence on the ostensibly anti-romantic young
Prokofiev should not be underestimated:

The news that Scriabin had composed a big new symphonic piece stirred
up a lot of interest. Rumour had it that the piece was written for a huge
orchestra and was more avant-garde than *The Divine Poem* . . .

Miaskovsky and I had adjoining seats, and we gulped down *The Poem
of Ecstasy* with great interest, although in some places we were perplexed
by the novelty of the music. We had expected an improvement (so to

44

speak) on *The Divine Poem*, which we knew very well and loved. But both the harmonic and thematic material . . . were completely new.

Basically, Scriabin was trying to find new foundations for harmony. The principles he discovered were very interesting, but in proportion to their complexity they were like a stone tied to Scriabin's neck, hindering his invention as regards melody and (chiefly) the movement of the voices. Nonetheless, *The Poem of Ecstasy* was probably his most successful work, since in it all the elements in his manner of composing were apparently balanced. But it was hard to imagine, at first hearing, just what he was trying to do . . . after the second performance . . . when Scriabin's orchestration, new in its design, had unfolded before us in all the breadth of its sonority, we came away exclaiming 'What a work of genius!' But later, when the intellectual coldness of some of Scriabin's 'flights' became discernible, that opinion had to be downgraded a bit.

By the summer of 1908, Sergey had completed another symphony.

From Prokofiev to Miaskovsky.
Sontsovka, 15 September 1908.

Dear Nikolay Yakovlevich:

Today I completed my symphony. It came out to 131 pages (57+19+55), with enough music for 28 minutes; that is a bit longer than I wanted.

Because of the cholera we shall be a bit late in getting to Petersburg. We are afraid of it, but will set out as soon as it slackens off.

Did you finish your symphony: If not, finish it. If so, don't show it to anyone – wait for me. And *don't so much as mention it to Liadov*, because there's no sense in showing it to him. Glazunov may arrange a performance for us. But Liadov? . . . He'll just revile us.

In fact, the poorly orchestrated Prokofiev work was not a great success and only the *Andante* survives – as part of the Fourth Piano Sonata.

Prokofiev's most characterful music was still to be found in his piano pieces, and he soon had the chance to present a selection to the best-informed audience in St Petersburg. The young composers had managed to worm their way into the very heart of the city's avant-garde – the so-called 'Evenings of contemporary music'. These were weekly concerts, rather shabby affairs much excoriated for their 'excessive' and 'harmful' modernism. But most of the leading critics and musicians of the day attended regularly, eager to catch the first Russian performances of works by Strauss, Schoenberg, Stravinsky and the like. The series had been established as a musical extension of Diaghilev's 'World of Art' movement with its 'art for art's sake' philosophy. Its prominent figures included Vyacheslav Karatygin, Alfred Nurok

45

and Walter Nuvel – modernists all ('impudent and earless', Rimsky-Korsakov called them). While the composer of *Scheherazade* at least attended the Evenings, Liadov sought to avoid exertion of any kind ('every work by Liadov is a precious gem,' said Rimsky, reflecting on the smallness of his output). Prokofiev recalls:

Word of the success of my pieces at the Modern Music Evenings reached Liadov, and in one of his bad moments he asked me, 'Is it true that you have written a piece in which all the voices move in seconds?' and he proceeded to describe seconds in the air by closing and opening his second and third fingers . . . Anyone who dared to depart from the conventional path was bound to incur his wrath. Thrusting his hands into his pockets and swaying back and forth on his soft heelless prunella boots, he would say, 'I cannot understand why you bother to study with me. Go to Richard Strauss, go to Debussy'. He might as well have said 'Go to the devil!' Talking about me to acquaintances, Liadov would gesture hopelessly and say, 'I daresay he will get over it in time'.

Sergey made his public début as composer-pianist on 18 December 1908. He took the audience by storm:

My first number was *Fairy Tale* (later included in op. 3). It was followed by *Snow* (which by now had half melted), *Reminiscence, Elan, Despair,* and *Suggestion Diabolique* (pieces that later made up op. 4), and *Entreaty,* of which not a trace has remained and which I cannot now remember. I played rather well – in any case, jauntily. My success was rather great and, I should say, no doubt unexpected.

The fiery *Suggestion Diabolique* was particularly well calculated to cause a sensation and establish an image with the critics. Unknown boy no longer, Sergey Prokofiev was proclaimed the unintelligible and ultra-modern *enfant terrible* of Russian music. Needless to say, he did his best to maintain the impression.

In the audience for this first concert was Igor Stravinsky who later told Robert Craft:

[Prokofiev's] performance was remarkable – but I have always liked his music hearing him play it – and the music had personality.

The most enthusiastic of contemporary reviews was inevitably the one signed by 'N. Sem' – pen-name of one of the sponsors of the event. This appeared in *Slovo* (20 December). Another positive account, published in the German paper *St – Petersburger Zeitung* for 24 December, was written (as Prokofiev later discovered) by his current piano teacher, Alexander Winkler:

In the second part of the programme, devoted to Russian composers, the talented Conservatory student Prokofiev played several of his own short piano pieces, which met with a favourable reception. Mr Prokofiev is still very young and still in his *Sturm und Drang* phase, while also being under the influence of the very recent Decadent trend in art. But when he has left his developmental phase behind him, we can expect the very best fruits from his unique talent. The pieces this reviewer liked the best – the most interesting harmonically, and most successful structurally – were *Fairy Tale, Reminiscence, Elan,* and *Despair.* The very decadent *Suggestion Diabolique* has the advantage that it was truly created for the piano. [It is impossible to understand what it was that Winkler found 'very decadent' in *Suggestion Diabolique,* a limpid and purposeful piece. But it was significant that this term was promptly applied to everything new, even though it was not at all decadent. And things went on that way for a long time.]*

These first public appearances were crucial for Prokofiev; he realised that it was as an exponent of his own piano music that he might become famous. Not all the reviews were exactly encouraging, but Maria Grigoryevna carefully pasted each and every one of them into a giant scrapbook.

While the charm of some of the early pieces lies in their gentle, pensive lyricism, it is the novel dissonances which really strike home. Prokofiev and Bartók seem to have been working on closely parallel lines at this time. Although a work like *Suggestion Diabolique* is unmistakably personal, no mere rehash of the daemonic Liszt, some have questioned the authenticity of Sergey's particular brand of modernism. 'In 1908,' says Claude Samuel, 'it is above all noisy and sometimes clumsy.' Certain commentators have implied that the impression of newness was less a reflection of the music itself than a tribute to Prokofiev's extraordinarily compulsive keyboard style. Of course, the two were inseparable.

For Sergey Sergeyevich, an interest in the opposite sex was also something new. He met one attractive girl at a piano recital given by Joseph Hofmann late in 1908. Her name was . . .

Katyusha Borshch. I didn't much like it because its sound, although unexpected, was not very pretty . . . My acquaintance with Katyusha Borshch gradually grew, but not to the extent I had hoped for. She proved to be a very talented pianist, but there didn't seem to be much more to her. She didn't know how to talk about music, and in general took little interest in it. She came from a rather uncultivated family and was not remarkable for her good manners. Whenever I took her for a ride in a hansom cab (I sometimes had enough money for such a fling), she liked it but in general she felt drawn, not so much to me as to a different circle of people. Just what kind of circle that was, I never managed to find

*Here Prokofiev seems to be alluding to contemporary *Soviet* attitudes.

out. Even on the basis of friendship, our relations followed a kind of zigzag pattern. Sometimes we would go to concerts together. On other occasions she would say she was busy, and I would go alone, only to be surprised by finding her there in the company of someone I didn't know.

Prokofiev was also friendly with two girl classmates at the Conservatoire, Leonida Glagoleva and Vera Alpers; his friendship with Vera continued for the rest of his life.

From Vera Alpers' diary.
1 December 1908.

I very much like going to the Conservatory. During the time I have spent there I have 'made friends' with Prokofiev. I have frequent, long talks with him. Some of my friends among the girls make fun of me: Ksyushka, Ida, Bessonova, and, in a word, many. At first they said all kinds of bad things about him, but now he has suddenly become good. It's very interesting to talk with him. He behaves well, and is very different from all the Conservatory brats.

Prokofiev has become popular. At one rehearsal for a concert he called attention to my long fingers. He took my hand, studied it, and said it was pretty. I was embarrassed. And when he saw I was blushing, he himself got embarrassed . . . All in all, I don't understand why he attracts me. In the first place, he is frightfully egotistical; in the second place . . . he has many unlikeable things about him in general, but at the same time . . .

At the close of the academic year 1908-9, Prokofiev graduated from the composition course. His marks were not brilliant and the works submitted to the final examining board created a highly unfavourable impression. Liadov complained: 'They're all bent on becoming Scriabins!' Prokofiev was accepted for a short-lived free composition class the following year, but to all intents and purposes this aspect of his musical education was now complete. In his disenchantment with composition teaching at the Conservatoire, his interest in piano performance had grown. 'Technical preparation exceedingly brilliant. Interpretation unique, original, but not always in the best artistic taste' was Glazunov's characterisation of his playing at the public examination in 'special piano' in May 1909. And so the idea arose that he might continue at the Conservatoire with piano and conducting courses.

On his way back to Sontsovka, the 'free artist' visited his first teacher in Moscow. Glière recalls:

Seryozha already looked quite grown up. He had acquired a good deal of self-assurance. His views on modern music were characterised by a deliberate 'radicalism'. He seemed ready to dethrone any generally accepted authority. Nevertheless we parted friends.

Prokofiev spent the summer holidays much as usual – composing furiously. At 18, his working methods were well established. He liked to keep a notebook close at hand in which to jot down ideas as they occurred to him. All his life he hated to let a good tune go to waste. His compositional method had a great deal to do with the skilful joining together of disparate ideas. The familiar tendency to 'step on the throat of his own song', to counter lyricism with irony, was thus reinforced. For Prokofiev, no musical idea had a specific context. He would turn frequently to his earlier compositions, revising them and fabricating new opus numbers in the form of arrangements and transcriptions. Sometimes a completely new work would emerge from the thematic detritus of another. Both the Third and Fourth Symphonies are grounded in music originally intended for the stage.

Of the new works composed during the 1909 vacation, only the Four Etudes, op. 2 remained intact. The Sinfonietta, op. 5 was twice revised, most comprehensively in 1929. The First Piano Sonata, Prokofiev's op. 1 (dedicated to Vasily Morolev, a young chess-playing veterinary surgeon from Sontsovka) was itself a revision of an earlier project and does rather sound it. New music

Prokofiev playing chess with Vasily Morolev (*c.* 1909) (Novosti)

circles were predictably scornful, although it was one of a handful of items eventually taken on by Jurgenson, the Moscow publisher, in 1911. For this work, and 12 smaller piano pieces, Sergey received just one hundred roubles. Perhaps he was unwise to submit the awkwardly four-square Sonata in one movement. It does not achieve the individual voice of the shorter pieces, taking Medtner, above all, as its model. Its importance lies chiefly in the fact that it opens the matchless cycle of nine – a sonata series which (this first instalment apart) displays sufficient unity to make nonsense of chronological development.

While Prokofiev never ceased to compose, the years 1909-14 were also devoted to intensive study of the piano and conducting. His new piano teacher was Anna Esipova, the most distinguished in the Conservatoire. As usual there was trouble. From Winkler and his predecessors, Sergey had acquired a magnificent technique. Yet he lacked any sense of discipline. He played with a remarkable but uniquely haphazard panache, taking great liberties with other composers' scores. 'They say you can't give a piano recital without Chopin,' he said to his friends. 'I'll prove that we can do quite well without Chopin!' Mozart was treated with similar disdain; and if Prokofiev played the Classical repertory at all, it was with his own 'improvements'. Believing that Esipova was trying to 'make everyone fit a standard pattern', he tended to ignore her requests until threatened with expulsion from the class. In fact, the rigours of Esipova's method did much to benefit his playing. Without these four years, neither his pianism nor his compositional style could have matured as they did – the steely brilliance tempered by a fuller awareness of lyricism.

Prokofiev's studies with Nikolay Tcherepnin were much less stormy:

Of all my teachers, Tcherepnin was the liveliest and most interesting musician, although he was entirely made up of contrasts. His talks about conducting were always lively and meaningful, but when he went up to the podium the orchestra fell to pieces under his baton. His talk about the future of music was no less interesting . . . 'In the end,' he said, 'they will write all white and all black notes.' (At this, he would spread his left hand over the white keys of the piano as far as he could, and his right hand over the black keys.) 'Then they will see there's no place to go.' I don't know how right he was, since the development of music doesn't lie merely in the order of written notes. But at the time he struck me as such an innovator that it made my head swim.

Tcherepnin composed in a style actively sympathetic to Scriabinisms. Prokofiev specialist Rita McAllister sees his influence as crucial, fusing with Prokofiev's infatuation with the

Symbolist poets Balmont and Blok to generate music of a mysterious but highly charged, at times positively Straussian, Romanticism. This unfamiliar vein is tapped in the symphonic poems *Dreams* and *Autumnal* (1910), the early one-act opera *Maddalena* (1911-13), many of the songs, and much of the full-scale music drama *The Fiery Angel* (1919-27).

Tcherepnin was influential in other ways:

As [we] were sitting side by side with the score in front of us at one of those endless lessons, rehearsing the student orchestra, he would say, 'Just listen to how marvellous the bassoon sounds right here!' And I gradually developed a taste for the scores of Haydn and Mozart: a taste for the bassoon playing staccato and the flute playing two octaves higher than the bassoon, etc. It was because of this that I conceived or thought up the *Classical Symphony*, although that was five or six years later. Right here I should note that, although I didn't learn all that I should have about orchestration in Rimsky-Korsakov's class, I made up for it in Tcherepnin's class.

Tcherepnin was not slow to pronounce his verdict on Prokofiev the conductor:

You have no gift for conducting; but since I have faith in you as a composer and I know that you will have to conduct your own works on more than one occasion, I shall teach you to conduct.

The death of Prokofiev's father in 1910 meant drastic changes in the life of the apprentice composer. There were to be no more visits to Sontsovka and financial hardship was a real possibility. Naturally, Maria Grigoryevna continued to support her son as best she could, giving him a home in St Petersburg, but he would have to make his own way from now on.

Sergey continued to give recitals. In the 1910-11 season he played twice at the 'Evenings of contemporary music', introducing Russian audiences to the piano music of Schoenberg. 'Homeric laughter broke out in the hall', according to Karatygin. In July 1911, he had his first symphony concerts – second-class affairs in the summer parks of Moscow and St Petersburg far from the academic concert halls. But the critics took note. The jaundiced connoisseur of *Golos Moskvy* reported:

It seems to me a mistake to give so much attention to this callow youth, this musical fledgling – twice in one season. For his own good it would be better to wait. In scope of talent, Mr Prokofiev approximates Kalinnikov [a nineteenth-century Russian more noted for charm than originality]. I believe that he would write in much the same vein, too, were he as sincere as Borodin and other St Petersburgites. But he is affected. He wants desperately to be a modernist, even though modernism does not become him at all.

And in truth, the two works premièred at Moscow's Sokolniki Circle are not among Prokofiev's most distinguished. The 'rather limp' *Dreams* remained unpublished and the Rachmaninov-derived *Autumnal* was revised twice before taking final shape. The performances themselves would not have been up to much:

One of the conductors of the *Dreams* said to me, 'I hope you didn't mind the false notes.' 'My dear fellow,' I replied, 'there wasn't a note in the whole thing that wasn't false. I didn't recognise it as my own at all.'

While the fate of *Maddalena* was being decided at the Conservatoire (in the end it was never produced and had to wait until 25 March 1979 for a first performance*) Prokofiev worked energetically on a First Piano Concerto. The result he considered his 'first more or less mature composition as regards the conception and its fulfilment'. Trenchant, witty and precise, the work condenses the traditional three movements into a continuous (if episodic) structure. The challenging introductory theme functions as a kind of refrain and rounds off the piece with terrific aplomb. The Concerto gives us a good idea of the strengths of Prokofiev's own performing style, 'combining the massive texture of chords and octaves with very difficult "acrobatic" leaps and pearly, étude-like runs' (Nestyev). For Francis Poulenc, a great friend of the composer during his years abroad, the Concerto places its author among the ranks of the musically great as surely as the First Concerto of Beethoven prefigures *his* mature work.

The Moscow première caused a furore. The gutter press declared Prokofiev a madman and demanded that he be put in a 'strait-jacket'. The Concerto was nothing so much as 'musical mud', according to reactionary critic N. Bernstein. Karatygin, Asafiev, Miaskovsky and others were ready to defend the composer in print, but Prokofiev thrived on hostile criticism. Some of his boldest piano pieces followed in 1912, among them the motoric *Toccata*, op. 11 (some way after Schumann), and the first of five *Sarcasms*, op. 17.

Even more than the notorious *Suggestion Diabolique*, the implacable Toccata is a *perpetuum mobile* which never slackens, never misses a semiquaver until just before its 'slambang finish'. (A surviving pianola roll suggests that it may have been beyond Prokofiev's technique.) Miaskovsky was 'absolutely mad' about it.

---

*given on BBC Radio 3 under the direction of Edward Downes, who also completed the orchestration.

The *Sarcasms*, completed in 1914 by which time the influence of Stravinsky can be felt, none the less represent a ten-minute apotheosis of Prokofiev's early 'grotesque' style. However much he hated the label, it was never more applicable. 'All his life Nurok longed for new music and in his old age God sent him Prokofiev,' commented Tcherepnin. Asafiev found the *Sarcasms* 'more taunting, more trenchant than the verses of the early Mayakovsky . . . the horror of them is more terrifying and powerful'. No. 4 is marked *Smanioso* – maniacally; and in no. 5 *Precipitosissimo*, a mocking laughter rushes asymmetrically all over the keyboard.

The wide range of the maturing artist should have been better appreciated with the publication of Ten Episodes, op. 12 – a collation of pieces written between 1906 and 1912.

They have since been smoothed out by the engraver's tool, but when I prepared them for the press, they presented a messy collection, being scrawled on staff paper of odd sizes, partly in ink, partly in pencil.

Prokofiev displays a lighter, wittier, more classical touch than hitherto – heavy-handedness banished in favour of something approaching the poise and discipline of Ravel. The emotional climate is less one-sided. We have that combination of intense vitality and simple lyricism which conveys in peculiarly twentieth-century fashion a nostalgia for, that is finally a reinterpretation of, tradition. (This 'neo-classicism' of Prokofiev's informs much of his later music – not just the pastiche of the *Classical Symphony*.) The Sonata No. 2 in D minor, op. 14, also composed in 1912, consolidates these advances. Marking a step forward into larger musical forms, it too manages to integrate more and subtler contrasts than before.

Prokofiev's largest work so far, the Second Piano Concerto, was completed in the following year. The work we know today as op. 16 is actually a reconstruction made in 1923; the original score had been destroyed in a fire. Yet it remains a problem piece in which the growing refinement of style sits uneasily with some rather superficial virtuosity. If, as the composer claimed, 'charges of showy brilliance and certain "acrobatic" tendencies in the First Concerto' induced him to 'strive for greater depth in the Second', the result is only intermittently successful. The order of movements – slow, fast, fast, fast – is typically perverse. The first two are the most satisfying. In the stormy and memorable *Andantino*, the first subject is clearly related to Rachmaninov, but the second idea and the elaborately hazardous cadenza strike out into the 'grotesque'. The second movement is chock-full of breathlessly effective *scherzando* writing. It is in the last two that an 'updated Lisztian bravura' (Hugh Ottaway) tends to swamp the invention, although Prokofiev's Russian lyricism is also evident in the finale.

The Concerto's Pavlovsk première left the audience in a state of utter confusion. Miaskovsky, who attended the concert, reported that they 'hissed and often did not behave quite "properly"'. 'Here is a new piano star,' began 'Non-Critic' of the *Petersburgskaya Gazeta:*

On the platform appears a youth with the face of a Peterschule student. It is Sergey Prokofiev. He seats himself at the piano and begins to strike the keyboard with a dry, sharp touch. He seems to be either dusting or testing the keys. The audience is bewildered. Some are indignant. One couple stands up and runs toward the exit. 'Such music is enough to drive you crazy!' 'What is he doing, making fun of us?' More listeners follow the first couple from various parts of the hall. Prokofiev plays the second movement of his Concerto. Again the rhythmical collection of sounds. The most daring members of the audience hiss. Here and there seats become empty. Finally the young artist ends his Concerto with a mercilessly discordant combination of brasses. The audience is scandalised. The majority hiss. Prokofiev bows defiantly and plays an encore. The audience rushes away. On all sides there are exclamations: 'To the devil with all this futurist music! We came here to enjoy ourselves. The cats at home can make music like this!'

For N. Bernstein, the work was

a cacophony of sounds that has nothing in common with civilised music . . . Prokofiev's cadenzas, for example, are unbearable. They are such a musical mess that one might think they were created by capriciously emptying an inkwell on the paper.

This was the most famous scandal yet, with Karatygin the only critic to defend the work unreservedly.

The 'futurist' label stuck and Prokofiev was again ranked alongside the poet Mayakovsky. The analogy was not entirely inappropriate. The combination of hyperbolic imagery and gentle lyricism, the striving to counter the 'salon mentality' with an art thunderous, impulsive and earthy, was common to both:

> If you wish,
> I shall rage on raw meat;
> or, as the sky changes its hue,
> if you wish,
> I shall grow irreproachably tender:
> not a man, but a cloud in trousers!

In later years, Prokofiev and Mayakovsky formed something of a mutual admiration society. The poet told Asafiev:

Only Prokofiev's music excites me now. No sooner do the first sounds ring out than life bursts in – not a form of art, but life, a rushing mountain stream, such a torrent that you feel like jumping under it and shouting 'Oh, how wonderful! More, more!'

The year 1913-14 was to be Prokofiev's last at the Conservatoire and he planned a memorable exit. His goal was the much coveted Rubinstein Prize, the highest award offered to a student pianist. He went after it in predictably unorthodox fashion:

. . . instead of a classical concerto, I chose one of my own. While I might not be able to compete successfully in performance of a classical concerto, there was a chance that my own might impress the examiners by the novelty of technique; they simply would not be able to judge whether I was playing it well or not! On the other hand, even if I did not win, the defeat would be less mortifying since no one would know whether I had lost because the concerto was bad or because my performance was faulty. Of the two concertos I chose the First. The Second would have sounded too outlandish within the Conservatoire walls. Besides, the Pavlovsk experience was still too fresh in my memory. Moreover, at my request Jurgenson printed the piano score of the First Concerto in time for the examination. I bought 20 copies and distributed them to all the examiners. When I came out on the stage the first thing I saw was my concerto spread out on 20 laps – an unforgettable sight for a composer who had just begun to appear in print! My most serious competitor was Golubovskaya . . . a very subtle and intelligent pianist. We were extremely gallant and courteous to each other: on the eve of the examination we inquired after the condition of each other's fingers, and in the long hours of suspense while the judges were deciding our fate, we played chess. After a long and stormy session the prize was awarded to me . . .
[Glazunov] lost his temper and flatly refused to announce the results of the voting, which, he declared, encouraged a 'harmful trend'. Since, however, the 'harm' had already been done, there was nothing for it but to read the announcement, which he did in a flat, toneless mumble.

Prokofiev's thoughts returned to this remarkable period when he reviewed the Moscow chess tournament of 1936 for *Izvestia*:

As I watch Lasker, bent in deep thought over the board, I remember how I first made his acquaintance at the tournament in 1914. At the banquet which followed the tournament I received a great many congratulations on having graduated from the Conservatoire and won the Rubinstein Prize. Lasker asked me what the congratulations were about. 'You were awarded the first prize at the chess tournament yesterday,' I replied, 'I received the first prize at a music tournament.' 'I don't know how you play the piano,' said Lasker, 'but I am happy to know that the Rubinstein Prize was awarded to a chess player.'

One of the best descriptions of Prokofiev the pianist comes from Vernon Duke, who was taken to hear the Gold Medallist play his First Concerto in 1914. He remembers:

. . . a tall young man of extraordinary appearance. He had white-blond hair, a small head with a large mouth and very thick lips . . . (Prokofiev was then nicknamed the 'White Negro') and very long, awkwardly dangling arms, terminating in a bruiser's powerful hands. Prokofiev wore dazzlingly elegant tails, a beautifully cut waistcoat and flashing black pumps. The strangely gauche manner in which he traversed the stage was no indication of what was to follow; after sitting down and adjusting the piano stool with an abrupt jerk, Prokofiev let go with an unrelenting muscular exhibition of a completely novel kind of piano playing. The prevailing fashion in those days was the languorous hothouse manner of a Scriabin or the shimmering post-Debussy impressionist tinklings of harp and celesta. This young man's music and his performance of it reminded me of the onrushing forwards in my one unfortunate soccer experience – nothing but unrelenting energy and athletic joy of living. No wonder the first four notes of the concerto, oft-repeated, were later nicknamed '*po cherepoo*' ('hit on the head'), which was Prokofiev's exact intention . . . There was frenetic applause, and no less than six flower horseshoes were handed to Prokofiev, who was now greeted with astonished laughter. He bowed clumsily, dropping his head almost to his knees, and recovering with a yank.

All in all, Prokofiev could feel well pleased with himself. In command of a substantial repertoire of new works, he was looked upon as a leader of the Russian avant-garde. His latest gamble had succeeded brilliantly and now, with the blessing of the Rubinstein Prize Committee, he could set out to conquer Europe.

But this was 1914 and the Great Powers had ambitions of their own.

Chapter 4

The Gambler

From 1914 to 1918, Prokofiev was based in Russia but already the traveller, taking risks to further his career. At 23, and clearly on the threshold of acceptance by the wider Russian musical establishment, he could begin to think big. His London trip of June 1914 set the pattern. The fabulous Ballets Russes would be in London and, with Walter Nuvel for company, an introduction to the world's most fashionable artistic set was assured:

It was indeed a most interesting season: Chaliapin was singing, Richard Strauss was conducting and a wealth of new music was being performed. Diaghilev himself in his frock-coat and top hat, his monocle and white gloves, was a sight worth seeing. Nuvel introduced us and I played him my Second Concerto. An artist who was present exclaimed in French, 'But this is a wild animal!' He apologised profusely when he learned that I understood French.

Despite Prokofiev's tendency to play down the contemporary influences which shaped his art (aided and abetted by persistent Soviet attempts to debunk the Diaghilev legend) all the evidence suggests that the young composer was swept off his feet. Apart from the impresario's own powerful charisma, there was Igor Stravinsky's irresistible music. During his first trip to Europe in the summer of 1913, Sergey had witnessed a number of performances by the Ballets Russes including Ravel's *Daphnis and Chloe* which he mistakenly attributed to Debussy at the time! It was the Stravinsky stage works – *The Nightingale*, *The Firebird* and *Petrushka*, the last of these initially underestimated, to judge from Prokofiev's comments on that earlier Paris season – which left the lasting imprint on his own music. He had apparently been exposed to (and, he later admitted, 'had not understood') *The Rite of Spring* in concert performance. But now Stravinsky's musical revolution seemed to cry out for a response in kind. For the rest of his life, Prokofiev would consider Stravinsky his only rival.

A caricature of Igor Stravinsky
by Mikhail Larionov
(Sotheby & Co)

It is a tribute to both men that their uneasy friendship, formed after that first Prokofiev recital in St Petersburg, December 1908, survived for as long as it did. Lacking a natural basis in religion, politics, or even music, it just tended to fray at the edges a little. When at length Prokofiev returned to Stalin's Russia for good, Stravinsky heard from him directly only once – a telegram of condolence, from Moscow, 11 December 1938, on the death of Stravinsky's elder daughter. But even a few weeks before Prokofiev's own death, a mutual friend received a letter from him inquiring after Stravinsky; the older man was deeply touched.

There is no disguising the fact that Prokofiev was often profoundly jealous of his friend. Secure in the knowledge that he was indisputably the better pianist, he resented the fact that he was unable to score over Stravinsky as a composer. Too many of his own early successes could be put down to the brilliant executant skills of Prokofiev the *pianist*, that tigerish but superficial virtuoso of the image-makers. Stravinsky had a soft spot for the First Violin Concerto, but tended to agree with the columnists. He even ventured to suggest that Prokofiev's innermost being was engaged only when he played chess! The opposite of a thinker in his art, Prokofiev could be 'astonishingly naïve in matters of musical construction'. Diaghilev considered him 'positively stupid', or so Stravinsky alleged. For his part, Prokofiev's affection waned for a time as the vigorous national colour of Stravinsky's art, flaunted in *The Rite of Spring* and *Les Noces*, gave way to a cooler, less engaged neo-classicism. On 4 August 1925 we find Prokofiev writing to Miaskovsky:

58

Stravinsky has written a dreadful sonata, which he plays himself with a certain chic. The music is Bach but with pockmarks.

Two years later, he was fuming over *Oedipus Rex* even though he was involved in preparations for the work:

The libretto is French, the text is Latin, the subject is Greek, the music is Anglo-German (Handel), and the money is American – true cosmopolitanism.

In 1928 he dismissed Stravinsky's *Apollo* as 'a terrible bore'. Among the many instances of strained relations between the two men, the following (documented by Vera Stravinsky and Robert Craft) seems particularly extraordinary:

After a concert in Warsaw, Stravinsky had traced his hand in a woman's autograph album, in his case a not infrequent form of responding to a request for a 'souvenir' . . . Later, when Prokofiev was asked to sign the same book, he inscribed a mocking remark under the drawing. Stravinsky read about this in a Paris newspaper and wrote to Prokofiev on 20 December 1933:

Dear Seriozha,
    I send this clipping, which appeared recently in the Paris newspapers. I suppose that your interpretation of your joke in the album of the Warsaw woman had another character than the one given to it by these

Jean Cocteau's caricature of Stravinsky playing *The Rite of Spring* (1913) (Sotheby & Co)

unknown-to-me slanderers in the newspapers. Surely it cannot have been your intention to laugh at me as a pianist – for, after all, I play only my own compositions – or even as a conductor. My hand, drawn in the album, both plays and conducts, and not so shamefully, I think, that people might make stupid and nasty fun of me. No doubt many people object to my activity as a performer, but it is the only way to avoid the grimaces of other interpreters of my music. Devotedly and with love, Igor Stravinsky.

Prokofiev answered on 21 December:

I much appreciate your indulgence for this affair in the newspapers. It has afflicted me terribly. Now it is time to forget that whole period – when you spoke badly about my music as well as about what I wrote in the woman's album.

Of course, the hard-nosed Stravinsky never did stop speaking badly about Prokofiev's music. As for Seriozha's rapprochement with Moscow (in part, surely, his conscious or unconscious means of escape from a blind alley of Stravinsky-emulation) Igor had it marked down as 'a sacrifice to the bitch goddess, and nothing else'.

And yet, for as long as both men were free to travel, they could still meet for an exchange of indecent stories over dinner.

We even find Prokofiev consulting his friend about driving lessons:

18 rue Troyon, Paris XVII
29 Nov. 1926

Dear Igor Fyodorovich,

Please be so kind as to tell me the address of the company that taught you how to drive an automobile. As it happens we have taken up residence in the neighbourhood and would like to make use of the proximity.

Cordial greetings from us both.

Your
SPrkfv

Sergey Diaghilev, Stravinsky's patron, was always on the look-out for fresh talent, and in 1914 it was Prokofiev's turn to be discovered. Diaghilev's first inspiration was to stage the Second Piano Concerto as a peculiar sort of pantomime, but the idea was quickly dropped. Then, resisting Prokofiev's plan to compose an opera on the theme of Dostoyevsky's *The Gambler* (opera was, he declared, a dying form) he proposed instead a ballet on the fashionable 'prehistoric' theme.

This was Prokofiev's chance to trump the pagan *Rite*, treating

Opposite right
Leon Bakst's portrait of Diaghilev with his housekeeper (1906) (Russian Museum, Leningrad)

similar images in his own way. But it was not until 1921 that a ballet of his was actually staged by the Ballets Russes. This first attempt, *Ala and Lolli*, was a non-starter. Its 'Scythian' scenario was considered too flimsy, cobbled together without conviction.

At this stage of his career, political events meant little to Prokofiev:

Everything in London was so interesting that I was hardly aware of the approaching European war and it was by sheer chance that I returned to St Petersburg a few days before it broke out. As far as conscription was concerned the war did not affect me; as an only son of a widow, I was exempt from service.

According to some accounts, it was only by re-enrolling as a student at the Conservatoire that Prokofiev could be sure of avoiding the call-up. We know that he attended the organ classes of Professor Y. Y. Gandshin and that he re-equipped his own piano accordingly. Nestyev says that it was Maxim Gorky, the most important name in Soviet letters, who arranged Prokofiev's further exemption from military service after the first, February Revolution of 1917. 'We are not so rich that we can shoe the soldiers' boots with gold nails.'

In the autumn of 1914, as a respite from the demands of the Scythian ballet, Prokofiev worked on one of his delightful smaller pieces: *The Ugly Duckling*, a setting (for voice and piano) of Hans Christian Andersen's familiar tale. Was there an autobiographical intention here? Asafiev called it 'a fairy tale about S. Prokofiev as told by himself'. Maxim Gorky also identified the poor duckling, miraculously transformed, with the author of the score. Whatever the case, its warm lyricism, declamatory vocal line and uniquely vivid evocation of childhood show Prokofiev's compositional approach at its most individual.

Less distinctive, in Diaghilev's opinion at least, were the sketches for the unfinished ballet that Prokofiev showed him in Milan in the spring of 1915: 'You must write a new one,' he commented. Prokofiev's Italian concert début – his first engagement outside Russia – received the go-ahead, but the promoter set down his reservations in a letter to Stravinsky:

Grand Hotel, Rome.
8 March 1915.

Dear Igor, Many new questions, but first of all Prokofiev. Yesterday he played in the Augusteum, and with some success, but that is not the point. The point is, he brought me about one-third of the music of his new ballet. The subject is a St Petersburg fabrication; it would have been good for the Maryinsky Theatre ten years ago, but is not for us. The music, as he says, does not look for Russianism, it is just music. Precisely, just music, and very bad. Now we have to start all over again, and for this we have to be kindly with him and keep him with us for two or three months. I am counting on your help. He is talented, but what do you expect when the most cultivated person he sees is Tcherepnin who impresses him with his *avant-gardisme* (*!*) He is easily influenced and it seems to me he is a much nicer person than we suspected he would be after his arrogant appearance in the past. I will bring him to you. He must be changed entirely, otherwise we will lose him forever . . .

In fact the 'replacement' ballet, *The Buffoon* (or *Chout*), turned out to be one of Prokofiev's happiest works. Only the War prevented an early première.

After Stravinsky's departure, Diaghilev and I sat down to examine a collection of Russian folk tales by Afanasyev which Stravinsky had brought and came across a series of tales about a Buffoon. It did not take us long to map out a ballet plot in six scenes from two of these tales, and this time Diaghilev signed a regular contract with me for three thousand roubles. 'Only please write music that will be truly Russian,' he said. 'They've forgotten how to write Russian music in that rotten Petersburg of yours.'

On his return to Russia, Prokofiev noted that his 'stocks . . . had risen', with performances of several recent works in the pipeline. In short, Prokofiev had become fashionable; and, with the younger directors of the Maryinsky Theatre eager to match Diaghilev's theatrical successes on home ground, there was even some prospect of operatic performance. The new conductor of the theatre was Albert Coates.

Coates was not afraid of new music. 'Write your *Gambler*,' he said, 'and we'll stage it.' A more favourable opportunity could hardly be imagined. I reread the story, wrote the libretto and in the autumn of 1915 set about composing the music.

Later that same year, Prokofiev managed to fall out with both Rachmaninov and Medtner. The first incident occurred at a concert in memory of Scriabin. Among other things, Rachmaninov was playing the Sonata No. 5:

When Scriabin had played this sonata everything seemed to be flying upward, with Rachmaninov all the notes stood firmly planted on earth. There was some confusion among the Scriabinists in the hall. Alchevsky, the tenor, whom someone tried to hold back by the lapels, shouted, 'Wait, let me have a word with him!' I tried to be objective and argued that although we were accustomed to the author's interpretation there could obviously be other interpretations. I was thinking of this when I remarked to Rachmaninov after the concert, 'After all, Sergey Vasilyevich, I think you played it very well.' 'Did you think I would play it badly?' replied Rachmaninov with a wry smile, and turned away from me. This ended our good relations. A contributing factor no doubt was Rachmaninov's dislike for my music, which irritated him. Sometime later I had a little tiff with Medtner too. I had hoped that he would play his A Minor Sonata, which I liked. But he had limited himself to one of the more simple sonatas which one could have easily played oneself at home. I told him as much. 'And what do you think of the one I played?' 'That is more suited for domestic use,' I replied. Rachmaninov, to whom Medtner passed on the incident, later related indignantly that Prokofiev divided sonatas into ordinary sonatas and sonatas for domestic use.

On 16 January 1916 Prokofiev unveiled his *Scythian Suite*, a four-movement abridgement of *Ala and Lolli*. Its preparation and reception were not without incidents self-consciously similar to those attending the première of *The Rite of Spring* in Paris, 1913. And much the same could be said of the music itself: Nestyev is decidedly coy when he tells us that the Stravinsky work 'seemingly had some effect' on its style. That said, the *Suite* can still boast a remarkable sense of forward propulsion and an atmosphere all its own. Laboriously scored for an ensemble of 140, it is also a monument to youthful excess.

The musicologist and composer Yuri Tyulin accompanied Prokofiev to the first rehearsals of the new work:

. . . While he was dressing at home, there was a telephone call. I heard him answer: 'Yes, yes, do come. The concert is going to take place. Do you know that the price of rotten eggs and apples has gone up in St Petersburg? That's what they'll throw at me!'

At the rehearsal (in the Maryinsky Theatre) I sat alone in the auditorium, following the score. Prokofiev went up to the orchestra without a trace of excitement, but you can imagine what a great moment it was. He writes in his memoirs that the orchestra hindered his work. In fact, it was far worse: the orchestra tormented him, by openly demonstrating its hostility. There was no room for the two harpists in the orchestra pit, so they sat on the stage and kept asking him questions in an irritated tone. During their pauses they covered their ears with the wide collars (then fashionable) of their dresses. But Prokofiev continued his work with the orchestra with patience and concentration, as if nothing had happened, and came out after the rehearsal, serious but satisfied. 'Everything is all right,' he replied to my anxious question. You could not help but marvel at his self-possession.

Assembled for the première was the city's entire musical élite, but not all of it stayed until the end of the piece. As Prokofiev recalls:

. . . Glazunov, whom I had personally invited, lost his temper again and walked out, unable to endure the sunrise finale, eight bars before the end.

The press seemed to find it incredible that such an 'utterly meaningless' piece could be performed at all. Even the progressive *Muzykalny Sovremennik* carried an openly derisive feature. Comparing Prokofiev's new score with *The Rite of Spring*, the magazine contrasted the style of 'aristocrat and gourmet' Stravinsky, whose works are 'permeated with culture', with the cruder style of young Prokofiev:

He is not troubled by any perceptible spiritual doubts, not encumbered by an overly refined cultural heritage. He is as wholesome as a country boy, and young with that playful youthfulness which feels at home in any circumstances and in any attire so long as it is not tight.

In December 1916, the cancellation at short notice of the Moscow première of the *Scythian Suite* presented Prokofiev with an opportunity for revenge on the critical establishment. Unaware of any change of plan, the critic Sabaneyev proceeded to publish the review he had already prepared, ridiculing the 'cacophonous' music. Apparently, the composer himself had conducted, and 'with barbaric abandon'! Prokofiev lost no time in delivering his counterblow and the disgraced critic was compelled to leave the editorial boards of several newspapers.

The postponement of *The Buffoon* left Prokofiev free to concentrate on *The Gambler* between concerts. Aware that a sensation was expected of him and eager to restore a fluid, theatrical dimension to the form, Prokofiev reacted sharply against operatic convention. In putting together his own text from Dostoyevsky's story, he opted for a supple conversational style, leaving no room for anything as orthodox as an aria to hold up the action. The modernists could scarcely contain themselves at the prospect. 'Stupendous!' wrote Boris Asafiev

. . . but owing to a typographical error the word 'stupendous' appeared as 'stupid'. One day my mother, coming into the room where I was composing *The Gambler*, exclaimed in despair, 'Do you really understand what you are pounding out of that piano of yours?' We didn't speak to each other for two days after that.

Rehearsals began at the Maryinsky in January 1917. In February, they stopped. Political events had infected the disgruntled company with the spirit of revolution. Orchestra and singers flatly refused to perform a work of which they strongly disapproved. The press reported:

The Gambler arrived at English National Opera as recently as 1983.

(1) Graham Clark in the pivotal role of Alexis the tutor (Zoë Dominic)

The prevailing sentiment among the artists is that Prokofiev's opera *The Gambler* should be dropped from the repertory, for while this cacophony of sounds, with its incredible intervals and enharmonic tones, may be very interesting to those who love powerful musical sensations, it is completely uninteresting to the singers, who in the course of a whole season have scarcely managed to learn their parts.

The score has had a chequered career. By the time of the world première, given in French at the Théâtre de la Monnaie, Brussels, in April 1929, Prokofiev had revised it thoroughly, softening the edges in the process. In 1931, he used portions of it to concoct a symphonic suite, but even these *Portraits* gave him trouble. The opera itself had to wait until 1962 for its first British performance – given in Serbo-Croat by a touring company of Belgrade Opera. And until Gennadi Rozhdestvensky's pioneering radio broadcast of March 1963, it was unknown in its native Russia. At least the story has a happy ending. In April 1974, *The Gambler* finally entered the repertoire of The Bolshoi and, in 1983, the production

(2) The cast assembles in the Gambling Room of the Casino (Zoë Dominic)

by English National Opera gave British opera-goers their first real chance to assess one of Prokofiev's most exciting operatic achievements.

Set in the German spa of Roulettenbourg, the drama does have its problems, including a complete absence of genuinely sympathetic characters and an almost relentless cynicism. Nevertheless, Prokofiev builds to a stunning last act in which his 'hero' gambles and breaks the bank.

I make bold to believe that the scene in the gambling-house is totally new in operatic literature both in idea and structure. And I feel that in this scene I succeeded in accomplishing what I had planned . . .

Instead of treating the gamblers and croupiers as a chorus, Prokofiev gives them individual lines and characters. The effect is appropriately feverish: the track of mounting tension will culminate in hysteria and madness. It would be absurd to present a non-political composer as having revolutionary ambitions, but the collective intoxication of Russia on the brink is aptly symbolised in this idiosyncratic score. Prokofiev's *Gambler* holds up a mirror to a society corrupted by the pursuit of easy money and racing toward oblivion.

Prokofiev picked the subject for his next opera while still at work on *The Gambler*. In the artistic ferment of revolutionary Russia, the eighteenth-century Italian playwright Carlo Gozzi had found a kindred spirit in controversial theatre director Vsevolod Meyerhold. His concept of 'abstract' theatre owed a considerable debt to the improvisatory and stylised traditions of *commedia dell'arte*. Among advanced circles, Gozzi's *The Love of Three Oranges* was sufficiently well known to be adopted as the title of an avant-garde magazine; it would have been familiar to the composer even before Meyerhold recommended it as ideal opera material.

The year 1917 was perhaps the most productive in Prokofiev's career. While making a start on the new opera and resuming work on a new piano concerto, he completed a whole series of major compositions: the Violin Concerto, op. 19, the *Classical Symphony*, the Third and Fourth Piano Sonatas, the set of *Visions Fugitives*, op. 22 and the 'Chaldean Invocation' *Seven, they are seven*. 1917 was also the year of Revolutions, and, awkwardly for Soviet commentators, only the last of these works suggests that Prokofiev was taking much notice. No less an authority than the composer himself connects its dark, expressionistic savagery with the events that were shaking Russia, penetrating his subconscious and clamouring for expression.

But *Seven, they are seven* is not a work of celebratory realism. In his capacity as official mouthpiece, Nestyev is affronted by the impropriety:

Is it not strange that so observant an artist, one so thirsty for impressions, was not stirred to the depths of his soul by the romantic revolutionary events of 1917? How could it have happened that he did not hear the true music of the Revolution, that his works bear no trace even of the fiery rhythms of the revolutionary songs which filled the air of Russian cities at that time?

Beneath the propaganda, there is a serious point. The American historian James H. Billington has written of the revolutionary events of 1917-18 as having:

. . . a kind of musical quality about them. Mercier's characterization of the French Revolution 'Tout est optique' might be changed for the Russian Revolution into 'Tout est musique' . . . the so-called 'Eurasian movement' . . . hailed the new Soviet order for recognizing that the individual man fulfilled himself only as part of the 'higher symphonic personality' . . . Nicholas Gumilev wrote a pre-Revolutionary poem bidding the artists of his age 'look into the eyes of the monster and seize his magic violin'. Stringed instruments provide, indeed, the background music for this period of violent change: the gypsy violins of Rasputin's sectarian orgies in imperial palaces . . . the unparalleled profusion of virtuoso violinists in Odessa . . . The consolidation of Bolshevik power . . . provides a kind of feverish crescendo to the music of runaway violins . . .

The poet Alexander Blok asserted 'the artist's *duty* to see the plans, to hear the music blaring in the windtorn air':

Peace and friendship of nations, this is the sign under which the Russian revolution unfurls. This is what the stream roars about. This is the music which he who has ears should hear.

Prokofiev was never much interested in this music. He was preoccupied with his own. Stravinsky more than Lenin was his guru. In *Seven, they are seven*, it is *The Rite*, or more particularly *The King of the Stars*, which clamours for an answer.

Like that Stravinsky choral work, Prokofiev's *Seven, they are seven* is a short 'cantata'* based on a poem by Konstantin Balmont – arch-decadent bogeyman of Soviet literary criticism. And like the tribal elders of *The Rite*, the *Seven* are a pretty unsavoury bunch. Daemonic characters from Chaldean mythology, they 'force open doors and grind men to corn'. 'Divine heavens! Curse them! Curse them! Curse them!' So much for the Revolution.

Prokofiev described in some detail the creation of this, his most experimental work to date. His first step was to block out the design in terms of textures and climaxes without giving much thought to the musical content. Next, reunited with his piano, he endeavoured to 'put meat on the bones . . . at times I began to think I was producing ideas not music'. Finally came the scoring, and the formulation of a multi-layered orchestral texture covering three dozen staves.

Koussevitsky gave the première in Paris on 29 May 1924. As a matter of fact, the 'cantata' was played twice that evening. Prokofiev recalls that the audience was 'somewhat piqued' when the conductor repeated it 'for what he thought would be their greater edification'.

The *Visions Fugitives*, a captivating set of piano miniatures, could scarcely be more different. Although the title is again from Balmont, in some ways it is Debussy rather than Stravinsky who comes to mind:

*Prokofiev protested vigorously when the score was printed with this subtitle in 1922; 'Whoever hit on the idea of calling it a "cantata"? The word "cantata" suggests something draggy and quite at odds with the impetuosity of "Seven".'

In every fugitive vision I see worlds,
Full of the changing play of rainbow hues.

On the whole, the *Visions* represent a 'softening of temper' – as free and experimental as the *Sarcasms* but much more restrained and introspective in character. Clarity and elegance are the keynotes; the harmonic experimentation is more discreet. No. 19 is perhaps the most disquieting. Prokofiev later linked it with his experiences of February 1917:

I was in the streets of Petrograd while the fighting was going on, hiding behind house corners when the shooting came too close. No. 19 of the *Visions Fugitives* . . . partly reflected my impressions – the feeling of the crowd rather than the inner essence of the Revolution.

No. 20 is the most mysterious, concluding the series without resolution.

The Third and Fourth Sonatas are reworkings of material 'from old notebooks', but both may be considered as belonging to the year of Revolutions. The Sonata No. 3 is particularly successful. It consists of a single movement of short duration but considerable scope. The main material takes off energetically, and the second subject, *semplice e dolce*, must be one of Prokofiev's most charming ideas.

While the *Classical Symphony* inevitably falls into a class by itself, it, too, belongs to this group of early masterpieces, showing Prokofiev's invention at its most consistently inspired. The *Classical Symphony* is *so* familiar that its perfect proportions, mastery of irony and unparalleled effervescence can be easily overlooked. Writing in *La Revue de France* in 1927, the composer Florent Schmitt had this to say:

The *Classical Symphony* is an enchantment; a sort of unpublished Mozart, it possesses all his grace, fluidity and divine perfection; and the orchestration streams out in crystal jets. It would be impossible to achieve a pastiche with more ingenuity or science. For in the case of Monsieur Prokofiev, the complete artist, knowledge equals imagination.

Fair enough, but the work is more than pastiche. It is full of those harmonic sleights of hand and uninhibited wide-ranging melodies which by now delineate unmistakably Prokofiev's own creative profile. There is no question of imitating Stravinsky here. That composer had yet to embark on his own very different experiment with the past. Prokofiev's *Classical* finale – in musical terms, an essay in the avoidance of minor chords – was only part of a unique adventure:

I spent the summer of 1917 in the country near Petrograd all alone, reading Kant and working a great deal. I deliberately did not take my piano with me, for I wished to try composing without it. Until this time I had always composed at the piano, but I noticed that thematic material composed without the piano was often better. At first it seems strange when transferred to the piano, but after one has played it a few times everything falls into place. I had been toying with the idea of writing a whole symphony without the piano. I believed that the orchestra would sound more natural. That is how the project for a symphony in the Haydn style came into being; I had learned a great deal about Haydn's technique from Tcherepnin, and hence felt myself on sufficiently familiar ground to venture forth on this difficult journey without the piano.

It seemed to me that had Haydn lived to our day he would have retained his own style while accepting something of the new at the same time. This was the kind of symphony I wanted to write: a symphony in the classical style. And when I saw that my idea was beginning to work, I called it the *Classical Symphony*: in the first place because that was simpler, and secondly, for the fun of it, to 'tease the geese', and in the secret hope that I would prove to be right if the symphony really did turn out to be a classic.

The secret hope was fulfilled. From the time of its first performance, the Symphony won near universal acclaim. And of course it has long been regarded as a classic.

No less outstanding a contribution to the repertoire, the First Violin Concerto was slower to make its way round the world. When first played, in Paris in October 1923, its exquisite lyricism was found insufficiently 'new' to please. The critics were inclined to sneer at such lucidity: the composer Georges Auric found traces of artificiality and 'Mendelssohnism' in it. It was only after the work was taken up by Joseph Szigeti that it began to win the fame it deserved.

Lyrical and virtuoso qualities apart, the First Violin Concerto is remarkable for 'an expressive character that is naturally "romantic" but far removed from a self-conscious Romanticism: a distinction that has much to do with the vein of fairy-tale unreality in Prokofiev's make-up'(Hugh Ottaway). As he shows us in the *Classical Symphony*, Prokofiev can now create an individual sound world with a precise economy of means. The instrumentation here is unusual: the tuba is allotted a prominent part but there is no place for trombones. Lean, translucent textures predominate. The opening melody (conceived as early as 1915) is magical enough, but its reappearance on solo flute (*pp dolcissimo*) with harp, muted strings and lightly running tracery from the soloist is quite ravishing – matched by the more elaborate return at the close of the finale. The second movement, a mercurial *scherzo*, gives the

The composer Georges Auric with napkin: a Jean Cocteau caricature of 1921 (Sotheby & Co)

71

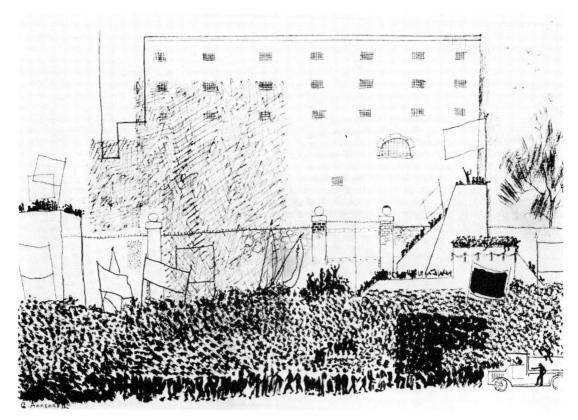

Yuri Annenkov depicts *The Storming of the Winter Palace in Petrograd* (Sotheby & Co)

soloist ample opportunity for display. Throughout, the flow of ideas is so spontaneous that the music seems to create its own form, an alloy of innocence and sophistication.

By September 1917, Petrograd had reached a state of crisis. Toying in the midst of revolution with parliamentary pretensions alien to Russian thought and habit, Kerensky's Provisional Government was pressing ahead with the war against Germany instead of attending to internal reforms. No doubt alarmed by rumours that the city was about to fall to the enemy, Prokofiev left to join his mother in the Caucasus:

From Petrograd came confusing reports about the October Revolution and the formation of the 'Lenin Government', as the Soviet Government was called in the local papers. The news was exciting, but so contradictory that it was impossible to make out what was happening. Kislovodsk was full of Whites who interpreted the events in their own way. I decided to go to Petrograd, although . . . I was told that it was madness to think of travelling. A train with smashed windows arrived and a panic-stricken bourgeois crowd poured out. 'There's shooting in the streets of Moscow and Petrograd. You'll never get there,' people said. It indeed looked as though this was hardly the time for concerts even if one could reach the capital cities . . . Kislovodsk was now a cul-de-sac from which there was no way out.

Boris Kustodiev: *The Bolshevik* (1920) (Tretyakov Gallery, Moscow)

Trapped, without work to look forward to, Prokofiev grew restless. Gradually the idea of going to America took root in his mind: he had already made the acquaintance of a potential patron in farm machinery magnate Cyrus McCormick. Russia was apparently disintegrating. It was his home but was it any place for music? Following Mayakovsky's call to 'push Pushkin off the ship of modernity', the continued use of stringed instruments was not without its critics. (Twentieth-century music, it would be argued, should not be made by 'scraping dried cows' guts with a horsetail hair'.) Then there were the obvious practical difficulties. As composer Alexander Grechaninov recalls:

In the early years of the Bolshevik Revolution, lecture recitals for workers' children were given . . . During intermission we were given herring and black bread to sustain our physical strength. In lieu of an honorarium we received flour, cereals and sometimes, as special premium, a little sugar and cocoa . . .

When H. G. Wells visited Russia, he found Glazunov still director of the Conservatoire but 'pallid and very much fallen away . . . his stock of music paper . . . almost exhausted'.

It should not be assumed that the early Bolshevik leaders were

The power of the Soviets is
commemorated in
St Petersburg porcelain
(Sotheby & Co)

necessarily hostile to Prokofiev's sort of music. They retained the
view that art would be influenced by political and economic
events; it followed that ideological interference was both
unnecessary and inappropriate. Trotsky, for example, did not
believe it possible for a genuinely Soviet culture to emerge until
the period of 'the dictatorship of the proletariat' had ended and
Soviet society had become truly classless:

The cultural reconstruction which will begin when the need for the iron
clutch of dictatorship . . . will have disappeared, will not have a class
character. This seems to lead to the conclusion that there is no
proletarian culture and that there will never be any, and in fact there is no
reason to regret this.

Lenin himself dismissed any ambition to foster such a culture.
If the true Soviet art was to emerge naturally from the synthesis of
all classes, then state interference could only be detrimental to its
development. Music, like the other arts, had to make its own way.
The Party might lead the proletariat but it could not lead the
historical process.

Anatoly Lunacharsky, music-loving first Commissar of
Education and Enlightenment, was certainly no enemy of
'bourgeois culture'. His department aimed to secure the goals of a
new society by encouraging serious artistic enterprise, not by
meddling in the process of creativity.

A certain degree of intervention was of course essential. In
1921, on Lunacharsky's personal orders, the young Shostakovich
was awarded food rations. None the less, many Russian musicians
did choose to emigrate, rejecting any policy of supervision.
Whether they slipped over the border illegally or committed the
lesser crime of requesting an exit visa, such disloyalty was liable to
place them beyond the pale. Igor Stravinsky, above all else a
musician, was strictly speaking an exile from the Tsars. But for
Stalin's ideological henchmen he made the perfect hate-figure – a
virtual Trotsky-image for the arts. Prokofiev (above all else a
Russian?) was clearly more anxious to keep his options open. And,

indeed, for a full 20 years, he was able to carry off something of an East/West balancing act. This might mean breaking with Balmont and his more overtly *White* emigré friends in order to safeguard his position with the *Reds*, but Prokofiev was happy enough. Insisting that he had always intended to return to Russia 'within a few months', he could be warmly welcomed back even after an absence of many years.

However, for Soviet historiography, his 'flight to the West' was still a black mark. As Nestyev puts it:

The decision to leave Russia was a bitter and irreparable mistake for the young musician, for nothing could ever compensate for his prolonged separation from his motherland, which had entered upon the path of revolutionary construction.

Prokofiev would not be allowed to forget this.

A portrait of Lunacharksy by Nikolay Andreyev (1921) (Tretyakov Gallery, Moscow)

When Kislovodsk fell to the Reds in March 1918, Prokofiev was at last able to leave for Moscow, prudently equipping himself with a pass from the local workers' Soviet. The train was fired on only once or twice, he tells us. Determined to resume his foreign travels, his first priority was to attend to money matters. He signed a contract with a favourite interpreter, now doubling as publisher:

. . . I did not have much difficulty in persuading Koussevitsky to advance me six thousand roubles on account of the *Scythian Suite*, *The Buffoon* and *The Gambler*. This was at once a generous gesture and good business, for the rouble was falling rapidly and nobody had any faith in the Kerensky currency, whereas there was a fair chance of my music retaining its value.

Prokofiev's brief stay in the city was also notable for a series of meetings with Mayakovsky and his circle:

. . . our acquaintance deepened; I played for him and he read me his verses, and on parting he presented me with a copy of his *War and the Universe* inscribed: 'To the World President for Music from the World President for Poetry. To Prokofiev from Mayakovsky.'

These two inveterate travellers would meet again, both abroad and in Moscow.

The *Scythian Suite* received many performances prior to Prokofiev's departure; the *Classical Symphony* received only one. But that Petrograd première of 21 April 1918 was important for another reason. Lunacharsky, the agent of his 'release', was in the audience, with Maxim Gorky and Alexander Benois the painter on hand to smooth the introductions.

Prokofiev recalls his encounter with the Commissar:

'I have been working rather hard,' I told him, 'and I would like to get a breath of fresh air.' 'Don't you think we have enough fresh air here now?' 'Yes, but I would like the physical air of seas and oceans.' Lunacharsky thought it over for a few minutes, and then said gaily, 'You are a revolutionary in music, we are revolutionaries in life. We ought to work together. But if you want to go to America I shall not stand in your way.' Thus I missed my chance of becoming part of the life of the new Russia at its very birth. I received a passport for foreign travel and an accompanying document to the effect that I was going abroad on an art mission and to improve my health. There was no indication as to the length of my stay. In vain did one wise friend warn me, 'You are running away from history, and history will never forgive you: when you return you will not be understood.' I paid no heed to these words . . .

By May 7, Prokofiev was en route to Vladivostok. The years of wandering had begun.

Chapter 5

Distant Seas

The journey to Vladivostok was painfully slow (18 days), but otherwise uneventful. I sat in my compartment reading about Babylonian culture and it was only much later that I realised how risky it had been to journey by train across Siberia, then seething with unrest. At one point we were held up for a long time by trainloads of Czechoslovak troops. When at last we were allowed to pass, the Czechoslovak front closed immediately behind us. Beginning from here the postcards I sent my mother at Kislovodsk did not reach her until a year later . . .

On 1 June, I arrived in Tokyo . . . Since several books on modern music had already appeared in Japan and one of them, by M. Otaguro, included a whole chapter devoted to myself, I was given the Imperial Theatre in Tokyo for my concerts. The Japanese did not understand much about European music, but they listened quietly and attentively and applauded the technical passages. The audiences, however, were small and I earned very few yen.

From Yokohama I sailed to San Francisco with a delightful stop-over at Honolulu. In San Francisco I was not allowed to go ashore at first, having come from Russia where the 'Maximalists' (as the Bolsheviks were called in America at that time) were in power – a strange and evidently dangerous lot. After being held for three days on an island and subjected to close questioning ('Have you ever been in jail?' 'Yes.' 'That's bad. Where?' 'Here on your island.' 'Oh, you are joking!'), I was admitted to the United States. By this time I was penniless, but some people I had met on the boat loaned me three hundred dollars, and early in September 1918 I arrived in New York.

IMPERIAL THEATRE, TOKYO

Grand Piano Recital
In his own Compositions

given by

Sergei Prokofieff
The Gigantic Russian Composer & Pianist Virtuoso.

The another Rubinstein Prizz Winner

ON

Saturday, July 6th
Sunday, July 7th
At 1.15 P.M.

Tickets: Yen 3.00
2.50
2.00   *Programme*

With this long and arduous journey behind him, Prokofiev was eager to test the waters of American musical life. 'I found myself in a musical world where everything was excellently organised,' he tells us, 'but utterly different from what I had been accustomed to.' Did Prokofiev really expect his musical career to be 'as smooth-sailing in America as it had been in the latter years in Russia'? The American cult of the interpreter had already relegated the composer to second place. But to be pigeon-holed as a courier for cultural Bolshevism was an additional hazard.

While Prokofiev the pianist was expected to compete in technical virtuosity with the likes of Rachmaninov, his compositions, not infrequently assumed to be part of some vast Bolshevist conspiracy, were treated as mere 'novelties'. At home, he had been inclined to welcome the zanier expressions of critical hostility as a trigger for lively aesthetic debate. In the very different climate of New York, a bad review was a bad review! The weeks passed and Prokofiev found himself trapped in a cul-de-sac of indifference and neglect:

At times, as I roamed New York's Central Park and looked up at the skyscrapers facing it, I would think with cold fury of all the wonderful orchestras in America that cared nothing about my music; of the critics who never tired of uttering platitudes such as 'Beethoven is a great composer' and who balked violently at anything new; of the managers who arranged long tours for artists playing the same old hackneyed programme fifty times over. I had come here too soon: the child (America) was not old enough to appreciate new music.

In the beginning however, things went well enough:

My initial piano recital in New York on 20 November 1918, was, on the face of it, a success. There were many musicians present, and the New York press, whose opinion was decisive in procuring provincial engagements, was on the whole satisfactory. Even its unfavourable comment was served up in a somewhat sensational manner. In appraising my music the critics wrote a good deal of nonsense; for example, the best of them maintained that the finale of Sonata No. 2 made him think of 'a herd of mammoths charging across an Asiatic plateau'. Of my playing they said that it had too little gradation, but that I had 'steel fingers, steel wrists, steel biceps and triceps'. No wonder the Negro lift attendant in the hotel touched my sleeve and remarked with some awe, 'Steel muscles . . .' He evidently thought I was a boxer.

The impact must have been considerable: Prokofiev was immediately invited to make Duo-Art piano roll recordings and a New York publishing house asked for piano pieces. The 'phenomenon from Godless Russia' was reluctant to bind himself to an American contract but he did complete two sets of piano miniatures, *Old Grandmother's Tales*, op. 31 and Four Pieces, op. 32. Together, the Four Pieces constitute an elegant little dance suite, which exemplifies Prokofiev's 'classical line'. The *Tales* on the other hand are nostalgically Russian, with Mussorgskyan touches.

Prokofiev was much disappointed in his meeting with Walter Damrosch, one of the leading American conductors:

'Don't play him the *Scythian Suite*, he won't understand it,' I was

The conductor Walter
Damrosch (EMI)

advised. But even in the First Concerto he did not turn the pages over in
time, and his comment on the *Classical Symphony* was 'Delightful, just
like Kalinnikov.' I went off in a huff, but it turned out that he had
intended this as a compliment; he had toured the whole of America with
Kalinnikov's symphony.

Prokofiev had better luck in Chicago. Two concerts given by
Frederick Stock on 6 and 7 December (the programme included
the First Piano Concerto and the *Scythian Suite*) were so successful
that the directors of the Chicago Opera offered to produce one of
his stage works. The full score of *The Gambler* was still in Russia,
but the composer had not abandoned his *Love of Three Oranges*
project:

I put the idea to Campanini. 'Gozzi!' he cried. 'Our dear Gozzi! But that

79

is wonderful!' We signed a contract in January 1919. The opera was to be ready by the autumn.

In New York, meanwhile, Prokofiev appeared under the well-meaning but ineffectual baton of Modest Altschuler, founder of the Russian Symphony Society in that city:

The press unanimously tore our performance to pieces – the orchestra, Altschuler, and myself as well.

It was sometime after this debacle that Prokofiev met his future wife, the strikingly beautiful Carolina Codina. There has always been a certain mystery about Lina's origins. Indeed, her background alone might have been sufficient to intrigue the composer. Born in Madrid in 1897, her father was Spanish; her mother, of Alsatian/Polish descent, was born in Voronezh, south of Moscow. When the family moved to the States and Lina began her professional singing career, she took her grandmother's name, Llubera, as a stage name, and, eventually, as a surname. That Prokofiev felt for Lina more than a casual passing affection can be inferred from *The Love of Three Oranges*. In Prokofiev's opera, Gozzi's Princess 'Violetta' has been renamed: it is the Princess 'Linetta' who emerges from the first orange.

Lina was Prokofiev's constant companion during some of the most discouraging months of his career to date:

In March I fell ill with scarlet fever and diphtheria combined, plus an abscess in my throat that very nearly choked me. 'I thought you were dying, so I sent you some roses,' one American lady later confessed to me, obviously a little sorry that she had taken all that trouble for nothing. When I recovered, I could barely wait for the doctor's permission to get back to work. I had slowed down a little before my illness, but the fever seemed to have cleansed me and I returned to work with renewed vigour. By June the music was all composed. The summer was spent on orchestration. By 1 October, the score was ready, exactly as the contract stipulated. The theatre had spared no expense; the sets had been ordered from Anisfeld. Everything was going splendidly when Campanini died suddenly in December, and the theatre, being afraid to continue with the production without him, postponed it until the following season. I was left high and dry without the opera and with no concerts to speak of.

An unseemly wrangle over financial compensation resulted in a further postponement.

The complications were typical of Prokofiev's operatic career. He shared with Tchaikovsky a lifelong passion for opera. But if Tchaikovsky's operatic genius is still insufficiently prized, many of Prokofiev's efforts in the field have only recently come to light.

English National Opera's first production of *The Love of Three Oranges*. A scene from the revival of August 1970: Heather Begg as Clarissa, Eric Stannard as Leandro, Robert Lloyd as the King of Clubs (Donald Southern)

Three operas, *Maddalena* (1911-13), *Khan Buzay* (1942) and *Distant Seas* (1948), were abandoned unfinished. Three more, *The Fiery Angel* (1919-27), *War and Peace* (1941-52) and *The Story of a Real Man* (1947-48), were denied complete staged performances in his lifetime. Of the remainder, only *The Love of Three Oranges* was an immediate success. The initial Chicago production of December 1921 was followed by stagings world-wide: at New York (1922), Cologne (1925), Berlin and Leningrad (1926). And although the work was not introduced to British audiences until the Edinburgh Festival of 1962 (courtesy of Belgrade Opera), it has since been given at Sadler's Wells Theatre, in a BBC television production and, most sensationally, at Glyndebourne.

For Nestyev, *The Love of Three Oranges* is 'a work of limited appeal' that offers further evidence of nihilism in its 'rejection of the principles of classical operatic form'. The opera may not be a flawless masterpiece; yet the structural problems which remain unsolved were created by the composer's scarcely unprecedented attempt to devise a dramatic form appropriate to the subject matter. He follows closely the text and spirit of Gozzi's play, and the result is a kaleidoscopic theatrical extravaganza rather than convincing drama or even conventional comedy. Some very familiar music accompanies the many dances, processions and pantomimes: Prokofiev drew upon these sections for his orchestral suite of 1924, which includes the celebrated *March*.

81

Most of what is sung, in his typical declamatory style, is too closely allied to the stage action (and to individual sight-gags) to survive outside the theatre. As for hidden meanings, Prokofiev himself was insistent: 'All I tried to do was to write an amusing opera.' It succeeds best if translated into the language of the audience and played very much for laughs. In English-speaking countries, *The Love of Three Oranges* is still sometimes given in French – an unhelpful convention, given that all Prokofiev's librettos were originally written and set in the Russian language. (The French translation is by the composer and Vera Janacopoulos.)

The starting-point of the central fairy-tale is the melancholia of a young Prince, son of the King of Clubs. He will be cured, if only he can be made to laugh. Two wicked conspirators, the Prime Minister Leandro and the King's niece Clarissa, set out to ensure that he never recovers. The jester Truffaldino is summoned to organise festivities to amuse the Prince, but all his efforts fail until Fata Morgana, Leandro's witch-protectress present in disguise, totters over in undignified fashion. Enraged by the Prince's hysterical laughter, she curses him with a consuming love for three oranges which he must pursue to the ends of the earth. After various adventures, the oranges are successfully retrieved from under the nose of sorceress Creonta's enormous cook (amusingly cast as a *basso profondo*). One of the oranges contains the Princess Ninetta, with whom the Prince falls in love and eventually marries. There are many hazards still to be overcome – Ninetta is promptly turned into a rat – but all complications are resolved in the end.

In addition to the 'real personages' of the story, we are privy to a world of magic: the ineffectual Celio, sorcerer to the King, set against a number of obstructive demons. A third ingredient, a sort of disparaging commentary, is provided by the chorus. Its various pressure-groups comment, criticise and disrupt – 'a critical "conscience" for composer and audience,' suggests Donald Mitchell.

The conceit of a play within a play whose spectators interfere with the inner action whenever so disposed had an obvious appeal for Prokofiev. He could suggest serious morals without explicitly committing himself, and make fun of them (and anything else) at the same time. While the score abounds with his usual sly turns of wit and deceptive harmonic quirks, the scheme does have its disadvantages. The emphasis on dramatic *non sequitur* and the slender opportunities for characterisation impose heavy demands on purely musical invention. With everyone singing in much the same idiom and differences between the fabulous and the earthly effectively ironed out, there can be little light and shade. At his best, notably in Act 3, where his heroine *and* his lyrical powers put in a belated appearance, Prokofiev manages to avoid the barren patches.

The text maintains a farcical tone throughout. The Prince declares his love to Ninetta crying:

> There was no power to keep me
> From my ardour to be near you.
> I was not afraid of dreadful Creonta,
> I overcame the hideous Cook,
> I escaped the huge brass spoon,
> I worked my way into the hot kitchen.
> No, no!
> My love is stronger than Creonta, hotter than the kitchen,
> Before it the Cook grew pale and the spoon dropped.

Elsewhere, the humour is sometimes a trifle unsubtle. The bass trombone produces a not unrealistic 'fart' on behalf of the fanfaring stage trumpeter.

In the autumn of 1919, the Jewish 'Zimro' ensemble arrived in America. The group comprised a string quartet, a clarinet and a piano. All the musicians had been fellow students of Prokofiev's at the Conservatoire.

The official purpose of their concert tour was to raise funds for a Conservatoire in Jerusalem. But this was merely to impress the Jewish population of America. Actually they barely made enough to keep themselves alive. They had a repertoire of rather interesting Jewish music for diverse combinations of instruments: for two violins, trio, etc. They asked me to write them an overture for a sextet, and gave me a notebook of Jewish themes. I refused at first on the grounds that I used only my own musical material. The notebook, however, remained with me, and glancing through it one evening I chose a few pleasant themes and began to improvise at the piano. I soon noticed that several well-knit passages were emerging. I spent the next day working on the themes and by evening I had the overture ready. It took ten more days to whip it into final shape.

Dashed off by the hard-up composer in record time, the *Overture on Hebrew Themes*, op. 34 was, in his own words, 'quite a success'. (Its freshness is dimmed in the congested orchestral version of 1934.)

Early the following year, Prokofiev embarked on a concert tour of Canada:

A very amusing thing happened in one small town. Before I left for this town my New York manager had warned me to be sure to collect my fee in advance, otherwise I might not be paid. When I arrived and made this stipulation to the local concert manager, he shrugged his shoulders but promised to attend to the matter. The concert hall was tremendous and tickets were sold at twenty-five cents, chiefly to students. Before the concert began, the manager came into the dressing room carrying a small valise. 'Students pay for their tickets in silver,' he said. 'I shall have to pay you the same way.' He handed me twenty-five huge silver dollars, one hundred fifty-cent pieces and one hundred quarters. I stuffed them into my pockets until I felt as if I had a hundred poods of silver on me. A terrible thought occurred to me: What if my pocket seams gave way in the middle of the recital and a heap of coins spilled on to the floor. I would be the laughing-stock of all the Americans! 'I shall try to change the rest of the silver for you by the intermission,' the manager said. But I never saw him again and I returned to New York with only one-third of the receipts due me.

Out of sheer escapism – there was little prospect of performance – Prokofiev had begun work on another opera, *The Fiery Angel*. But he was still practical enough to want to further his career. With Diaghilev's Ballets Russes back in business, Prokofiev set his sights on Paris. His links with the American continent would continue unbroken: he still had the production of *The Love of Three Oranges* to attend to and, of course, there was Lina; until 1938, he would undertake extended concert tours all over the United States. But Europe seemed the more promising base. He decided not to go back to Russia for the time being. The young Soviet Republic was virtually cut off from the world by the Western blockade. And the young Soviet composer was no doubt reluctant to return home a failure.

Prokofiev arrived in Paris in April 1920 and immediately he renewed his association with Diaghilev and Stravinsky, securing an introduction to the Paris art world. He met Pablo Picasso. He also met Maurice Ravel:

It was at a musicale attended by Stravinsky, Ansermet and some other prominent musicians. A little man with sharp, distinctive features and a mane of hair beginning to turn grey entered the room. It was Ravel. Someone introduced me to him. When I expressed my pleasure at the opportunity of shaking hands with as distinguished a composer as himself and called him *maître* (a form of address commonly used in France in addressing noted artists) Ravel snatched away his hand as if I had been about to kiss it and exclaimed, 'Oh, please do not call me *maître*.' He was an extremely modest person.

I do not doubt for a moment that Ravel was perfectly aware of his great talent, but he hated any sort of homage and did whatever he could to avoid all attempts to honour him.

Some time after his arrival in France, Prokofiev was joined by his ailing mother. Later, Lina was able to stay for a while. Much

Prokofiev and Lina: two
portraits by Natalia
Goncharova (Sotheby & Co)

encouraged, Prokofiev rented a small house near Mantes-La-Jolie. Here he could work undisturbed and take care of Maria Grigoryevna whose sight was failing rapidly. With *The Buffoon* scheduled for the next summer season of the Ballets Russes, he embarked on a thorough revision. Only the very beginning of the ballet was to be left intact, with its whistling and rattling sounds, as if someone were 'dusting the orchestra' before the performance.

In the autumn, Prokofiev returned to the United States. 'Composer Stravinsky and *pianist* Prokofiev' ran the caption of one photograph in *Musical America*. It is not difficult to imagine Prokofiev's reaction to publicity of this sort. In December, he toured California and wrote the *Five Songs without Words*, op. 35 for Nina Koshetz, the Russian soprano.

When *The Buffoon* opened in Paris on 17 May 1921, it was the novelty of the season. In London, it created more of a scandal:

On 9 June the ballet had its première in London. At the dress rehearsal, held the day before the opening, I stopped the orchestra at one point noticing that something was wrong. The next moment Diaghilev came

85

Mikhail Larionov: caricature
of himself, Prokofiev and
Diaghilev attending a
rehearsal of *The Buffoon*
(1921) (Sotheby & Co)

Mikhail Larionov: designs for
The Buffoon

(1) The Buffoon, his wife and
two of the other seven
buffoons, sketched as early as
1915 (Sotheby & Co)

up to me his face contorted with rage, and hissed, 'I have gathered the cream of London society for you and now you have ruined the whole impression. Now, please continue and do not stop on any account.' The public received the ballet very well, but press comment was most unfavourable, quite abusive in fact. The English are supposed to be very polite, but that certainly does not apply to their music critics. English critics are the most impolite in the world, with the possible exception of the Americans. Even as experienced a person as Diaghilev once lost his patience and committed an unheard-of breach of etiquette: he did not send an invitation to the leading music critic of *The Times*. The point was that if a critic is invited he is expected to express his opinion and is at liberty to praise or not as he sees fit, but if he buys a ticket and abuses the performance he may be sued for damages. The London musical world is more conservative than the Parisian, the British are slow to accept anything new, but once they have accepted it they are less apt to change their minds so quickly.

With *The Buffoon*, it was not so much the element of mockery in the music as the sadistic oddities of the plot which reinforced Prokofiev's reputation as master of the grotesque. The ballet is set in a Russian village. The Buffoon and his wife have a scheme to extract money from their neighbours: he will pretend to murder her and then 'revive her corpse' by beating it with a 'magic whip'. Seven other Buffoons are sufficiently impressed to purchase the whip. But, having murdered their seven wives, they discover that the whip has lost its magic powers. To escape retribution, the Buffoon disguises himself as his 'sister'. The aggrieved Buffoons then carry her off; she is to be their new cook. Soon a rich merchant arrives to look for a wife. Rejecting the Buffoons' daughters, he opts instead for the cook. In the merchant's bedroom, the Buffoon/cook evades discovery by substituting a goat for himself, and, in the ensuing confusion, the unfortunate animal is killed. Later the Buffoon reappears, this time demanding payment for his sister!

Ala and Lolli had been modelled on *The Rite of Spring*; *The Buffoon* is inclined to ape *Petrushka*, which allows for tunes. For this reason alone it is the more inventive of the two scores. Although there is some loosely written connective tissue, Prokofiev's harmonic resource is at its most delightful throughout and the orchestration glitters, sharp-edged and distinctive. Why then should *The Buffoon*, so recognisably music for dancing, be less popular than many of Prokofiev's other ballets? The audiences of 1921 had Larionov's cubist sets, costumes and choreography to object to, but Prokofiev's music is itself such clearly focused theatre that its bleak stage-history seems unaccountable.

Nestyev hurls some of his most fallacious invective at *The Buffoon*. The score is concise, amusing and strikingly melodic.

The Soviet writer misrepresents it as 'fundamentally pessimistic',
'a striking expression of . . . nihilistic grotesquerie'. Prokofiev
himself protested:

Be kinder about *The Buffoon* . . . Folk tales are often wicked, you cannot
blame me for that. And in view of its musical qualities, *The Buffoon*
should be recommended to the reader.

In the spring of 1921, the celebrated artist Henri Matisse
sampled Diaghilev's latest production at the rehearsal stage.
Impressed by Prokofiev's music, he executed a fine portrait of the
composer for inclusion in the programme booklet. Unfortunately,
the original was left behind in Diaghilev's hotel room and never
found. Some years later, an unsuccessful attempt was made to
persuade Matisse to design the sets for *The Prodigal Son*.

After 'the excitement of the theatre', Prokofiev retired to
Etretat. Here, he resumed work on an old project, the Third Piano
Concerto:

Much of it had already been composed at various times over a long
period. As far back as 1911, while working on the First Piano Concerto,
which like the First Violin Concerto was conceived originally as a
concertino, I had planned a large virtuoso concerto. I made very little
progress with this work, however, and only one passage of parallel
ascending triads was preserved. This I now inserted at the end of the first
movement of the Third Concerto. In 1913 I had composed a theme for
variations which I kept for a long time for subsequent use. In 1916-17 I
had tried several times to return to the Third Concerto. I wrote a

(3) Design for Scene V, set in
the Merchant's bedroom
(Sotheby & Co)

The Buffoon: photograph of
the final scene in the original
production of 1921

Matisse's portrait of Prokofiev
(the original is lost)

beginning for it (two themes) and two variations on the theme of the
second movement. At about the same time I contemplated writing a
'white quartet', i.e. an absolutely diatonic string quartet that would be
played only on the white keys of the piano. The quartet was to have
consisted of two movements, a slow first movement in sonata form and a $\frac{3}{4}$
finale. Some of the 'white' themes were composed in St Petersburg, some
on the Pacific Ocean and others in America. However, I found the task
too difficult. I was afraid it would prove too monotonous, and now in

1921 I decided to split up the material: the subordinate theme became the theme of Renata in *The Fiery Angel*; the principal theme I used for the monastery; the first and second themes of the finale went into the finale of the Third Concerto. Thus, when I began working on the latter, I already had the entire thematic material with the exception of the subordinate theme of the first movement and the third theme of the finale.

The result? One of Prokofiev's most attractive and popular scores – a conventional three movement design which belies its patchwork origins.

The Third is generally considered the most successful of Prokofiev's five piano concertos. Its solo part fairly bristles with the customary pianistic innovations, but this time the orchestra emerges as an active and responsive partner. The Concerto successfully 'accommodates nearly all the Prokofievs we have ever known' (Hugh Ottaway), and many of the great virtuosi have included it in their repertoires.

In Brittany, Prokofiev renewed his acquaintance with the émigré poet Balmont, setting five new poems in the summer of 1921. The song cycle, op. 36 was dedicated to Lina. Balmont responded in an unusual way – with a sonnet on the Third Piano Concerto:

> An exultant flame of a crimson flower,
> A verbal keyboard sparkling with flames
> That suddenly leap forth in fiery tongues.
> A raging stream of molten ore.
> The moments dance a waltz, the ages a gavotte.
> Suddenly a wild bull, startled by foes,
> Bursts his chains, halts, his horns poised to strike.
> But once again the tender sounds call from afar.
> From tiny shells children fashion a castle.
> An opaline balcony, beautiful, finely wrought.
> But all is dashed by a foaming wave.
> Prokofiev! Music and youth in bloom,
> In you the orchestra yearns for summer's ecstasies
> And the indomitable Scyth strikes the tambourine-sun.

In October, Prokofiev left for America – his third visit. The Chicago première of *The Love of Three Oranges* had been long delayed, and Prokofiev was keen to supervise all aspects of the production.

The singers were good, the settings superb, but the stage director, Coini, was a colourless personality: he was one of those professionals who know a hundred operas by heart but have nothing new of their own to offer. At first I merely grumbled at his lack of originality, but after a while I went back-stage and explained the parts to the singers myself, and instructed the chorus right on the stage. Once, when I got excited and made a mistake in English, one of the members of the chorus said, 'You needn't bother trying to talk English to us, half of us here are Russian Jews!' Finally Coini lost his temper. 'Who is in charge here, you or I?' he demanded. 'You are,' I replied, 'but you are here to carry out my wishes.'

Well received in Chicago, the opera provoked a hostile response in New York. Critics carped at the cost of the production ('130,000 dollars, that is about 43,000 dollars an orange') and they slated the music. The new piano concerto provoked similar responses from the rival cities. Prokofiev was still hoping that Chicago Opera might produce *The Fiery Angel* when, in the spring of 1922, Mary Garden, his supporter in the company, resigned her directorship. 'The American season, which had begun so brilliantly, completely fizzled out,' writes Prokofiev. 'I was left with a thousand dollars in my pocket, an aching head, and a longing to get away to some quiet place where I could work in peace.'

In March 1922, Prokofiev returned to Europe and set up his first real home in four years. Along with his mother and the poet Boris Verin, he rented a house in the village of Ettal, near Oberammergau in the Bavarian Alps. He continued to give concerts and prepared a number of his recent scores for publication, but most of his energies were now devoted to the composition of his latest and strangest opera.

The action is set in a surrealistic sixteenth-century Germany where black magic and the Inquisition thrive but the scientific spirit is also stirring. Ruprecht, a soldier who has seen service in the recently discovered New World, is disturbed by the hysterical crying of a strange and beautiful girl. He soothes her and she tells him her name – Renata – and her story. From childhood, she had been visited by an angel called Madiel, but when she grew up and begged him to love her as a human being he turned on her in anger and disappeared. Later, she believed she had rediscovered him in the guise of Count Heinrich, with whom she lived for a time. He has now deserted her. (The role of Renata is crushingly difficult and demands a singing-actress of the first rank.) Ruprecht, captivated, tries to make love to her, but Renata fights him off – she is wholly dedicated to her angel and his human manifestation.

Ruprecht's fate is now caught up with Renata's obsession. For her he explores various magical means of recovering her angel. For her he challenges Heinrich to an impossible duel in which he is almost killed. At length, Renata abandons him to enter a convent. In the final scene, he is a mute witness as the Inquisitor's questioning rouses her old passion which then infects the other nuns. The opera ends with Renata proclaimed guilty of carnal intercourse with the devil. She must be put to death. Her fiery vision will be consummated at the stake.

What was the composer intending to say in this raw, seething opera? No one seems to know for sure. Doomed attempts have been made to interpret the drama in intellectually respectable terms, to claim that it is in fact making some kind of statement about good and evil, about sacred and profane love, the battle of the sexes, or perhaps the relationship between Man, God and the Devil. Is it an account of Renata's schizophrenia or simply some sort of '16th-century *Carmen* with supernatural trimmings'? (Jeremy Noble) What are we to make of the participation of Faust and Mephistopheles – characters who had fascinated the composer from childhood?

On one level, *The Fiery Angel* is probably an attempt to trump the expressionist music drama. The importance of diabolic possession in its scenario sets up strong links with a German Romantic tradition stretching back to Weber's *Der Freischütz*. Prokofiev's discovery of the original novel, by Symbolist poet Valery Bryusov, coincided with a preoccupation with magic, metaphysics and also Christian Science. Composition of the opera must have satisfied a powerful inner need to project the mystic, anti-rational side of his creative personality. At the same time, for a composer who loved theatrical tricks, the magic setting offered a chance for knocks on the wall, skeletons that talk and a convent full of hysterical nuns.

Prokofiev began a third version of *The Fiery Angel* after the Metropolitan Opera in New York had indicated an interest in staging it (1930). Would the opera's total impact have been better controlled with its five acts reshaped as three? We shall never know. It was the second version that eventually reached the stage – that of La Fenice in Venice – following a posthumous première on French radio under Charles Bruck (25 November 1954). The revision must have been abandoned at the time the composer decided to return to Russia. He can have had few illusions about the prevailing Soviet attitude to this sort of 'decadent farrago'. Current attempts at ideological rehabilitation turn on representing *The Fiery Angel* as an anti-clerical satire.

The work received a first British stage presentation, thanks to the initiative of the New Opera Company, at Sadler's Wells Theatre on 27 July 1965. But even today, this almost excessively vital operatic score remains less accessible than the Third Symphony which Prokofiev drew from similar material in 1928.

While Prokofiev was hard at work on *The Fiery Angel*, Lina was studying opera in Milan, and the relatively short distance to Ettal made it possible for them to see each other often. In the summer of 1922, Lina made her Milan début as Gilda in *Rigoletto*. Prokofiev

gave a piano recital there, followed by a joint concert with Lina singing some of his songs. Together, they returned to Ettal via the Austrian Tyrol. Lina soon discovered the extent of Sergey's current extra-musical interest in her. Romance aside, there was astronomy, botany and, naturally, chess. Lina's initial introduction to the game was happy enough, but further progress in solving chess problems sometimes led to tears.

Until the late 1960s, one of the most impenetrable mysteries in Prokofiev's life was that surrounding the date of his marriage. The 'cosmopolitan' Lina gets scarcely a mention in Nestyev's biography of the composer. It has been the lot of those considered *persona non grata* in the Soviet Union to vanish, virtually without trace, from the chronicles of the living and the dead. Nevertheless, the date of their wedding has now been established as 29 September 1923. The permit from the Department of Justice in Munich for a civil ceremony to be performed at Ettal cost the composer one million inflation-ravaged marks.

In the spring of 1923, Prokofiev received his first official invitation to return to Russia. A series of concerts with the Leningrad Philharmonic was proposed. Miaskovsky, Meyerhold and other friends had kept him well briefed on developments at home. Despite the privations, musicians were continuing to work, compose and innovate. A characteristically futuristic development was the first demonstration, in August 1922, of the *Thereminovox*, an electrical instrument invented by engineer Leon Theremin. Also typical of its period, the *Persimfans*, the First Symphonic Ensemble, an orchestra without conductor inaugurated in Moscow in February 1922. Its ideological significance lay in its emancipation from the imposed authority of the symphonic boss who wields the baton without doing any playing himself. By 1923, some of Prokofiev's own recent works had begun to appear on Soviet concert programmes. In February 1926, *The Love of Three Oranges* began a run of 49 performances in Leningrad.

The offer was undeniably attractive, but Prokofiev turned it down, unwilling to desert what looked like a promising European career. There were other factors in this decision. For the time being, Prokofiev had his blind mother to look after. And, by the time of her death (in December 1924) the birth of a son, Sviatoslav, meant new ties with the West. Still the composer was careful to keep his options open. At no time did he consider cutting himself off from the new Russia with its new audience for his work.

Chapter 6

PRKF – Buffoon about town

Perhaps because of certain anomalies in the idiom of his music, its mixture of sophisticated elements with a sort of home-grown innocence, of steely dissonance with almost tender lyricism, perhaps also because of his personality, Prokofiev must have found the Paris of the early 1920s a difficult world to conquer, to shock or to amuse.   (Rita McAllister)

Unlike Stravinsky, Prokofiev never became truly Parisian. France was never for him a second mother-country. Its capital was simply a logical point of attachment for the aspiring composer and his family. With a formidable backlog of compositions awaiting first performance – the First Violin Concerto, *Seven, they are seven*, the revised Second Piano Concerto among them – Prokofiev and Koussevitsky could afford to treat Paris to a whole spate of premières in 1923-4. Audience reaction was decidedly mixed.

The composer unveiled a more recent composition in March 1924: the Fifth Piano Sonata, op. 38. Substantially revised at the end of his life and reissued as his op. 135, the Sonata's basic character belongs nonetheless to 1923, a period during which Prokofiev is often said to have been under the influence of 'bourgeois modernism'. As if to prove the contrary, the Fifth is a C major sonata of considerable charm, the 'classical line' everywhere apparent. Although Prokofiev later confessed himself unhappy with certain intricacies of style (Nestyev gleefully discerns elements of 'a cold, formal speculation' in the piano writing) the success of the piece 'lies precisely in its calculated artlessness and pastoral elegance' – qualities unlikely to appeal to Parisian sensation-seekers.

And so Prokofiev found himself out of sympathy with the sophisticated high-jinks of French musical life. He had no time for jazz. Stravinsky, still the most fashionable of all musical figures, was, he felt, bewitched by 'pseudo-Bachism'; and the contempt he registered on encountering the music of Milhaud, Poulenc and the other members of the group known as Les Six was dispelled only

Koussevitsky, Prokofiev's most consistent champion on the podium (RCA)

when he found himself face to face with them at the bridge table. In time, he came to appreciate the affecting as well as amusing qualities in the music of Francis Poulenc. That said, his friendship with the composer of *Les Biches* was scarcely based on a shared approach to composition. As Poulenc himself recalled, there were two factors:

First, we each of us had a liking for the piano – I played a lot with him, I helped him practise his concertos – and then something else that has nothing to do with music: a liking for bridge . . . Usually we spent our evenings playing. Music was an extra. If I arrived early, we'd have a cold dinner and play music for four hands . . . There . . . That's the point where my friendship with Serge crystallised.

It was after a particularly close game that Poulenc addressed the score of his *Concert champêtre* to Prokofiev with the inscription, 'To Serge Prokofiev, with very few trumps in my hand'. Poulenc knew that his friend would sooner enjoy his company at the bridge table than hear his music performed in the concert hall:

. . . No, no, no, our relations boiled down to bridge, the piano and friendship. For example, he came to spend a weekend in the country at Noizay (it was in June 1932, before he left for America), and I remember his last weekend in my house. He'd brought a huge tin of caviar. Sauguet was there, so was Auric. We were all musicians, and of course it's a moving memory for me because they were all happy relationships, you understand . . .
And it was a big tin, God knows. There must have been as much for the kitchen as there was for the guests' table!

Poulenc was a great admirer of Prokofiev the pianist:

He played on a level with the keyboard, with an extraordinary sureness of wrist, a marvellous staccato. He rarely attacked from on high; he wasn't at all the sort of pianist who throws himself from the fifth floor to produce the sound. He had a nervous power like steel, so that on a level with the keys he was capable of producing sonority of fantastic strength and intensity, and in addition . . . the tempo never, never varied. I had the honour of rehearsing all his concertos before his departure for America . . . We rehearsed in the Salle Gaveau. It was June 1932, we began . . . in shirtsleeves . . . afterwards, we took our shirts off . . . and in the end we were bare-chested . . . as if we were in Deauville. Prokofiev's rhythm was relentless and sometimes, in the Fifth Concerto, when a very difficult passage cropped up, I'd say to Serge: 'That's the orchestra, I'm doing what I can.' He'd say to me: 'Never mind, don't alter the tempo . . .'

A week or so later Prokofiev was gone:

We were coming out of the Salle Gaveau where we'd just been rehearsing. Serge got into the bus and said to me: 'A bientôt.' He waved to me with his hand. I shouted out: 'Write to me . . .' And I never received anything . . . He went back to Russia and I never had anything more from him. Two or three times – I hope he was told – I passed on a friendly message to him. One day I met one of the leaders of Soviet music in Brussels where he happened to be at the time. I said to him: 'Listen, since you're so kind to me, I'm going to ask you to do something for me. See Prokofiev and tell him I'm still fond of him, I still admire him.' Did he pass on the message? I haven't a clue . . .

Another close confidant of these years was the Russian émigré musician Nicolas Nabokov:

For four or five years in succession our relationship consisted [of] playing to one another our new music and that of others, and of bitterly criticising and violently reacting to all the things we liked and disliked. There were long telephone conversations about nothing and everything, about the most recent concerts, and Meyerhold's *Inspector-General*, about Stravinsky's *Apollo*, and about the best restaurants in Paris, and all this was in the particular atmosphere of suspense and gaiety of which the Ballets Russes at that time was a symbol.

From about 1930, Prokofiev was in the habit of making a daily circuit of the Invalides. Although, like all Prokofiev rituals, the walk was strictly timetabled, there would be time enough for a lively denunciation of French musical life:

We passed in front of the old cannons that stand in front of the Place des Invalides. Prokofiev stopped and pointed at one of them. 'See how angry it looks,' he remarked. 'This is the way I feel when I go to one of these Parisian concerts. All these countesses, princesses and silly snobs make me angry. They act as if everything in the world was invented to amuse *them*. And . . .' his voice got harsh and irritable, 'look what all their *salonarisme* has done to French music. There hasn't been a first-rate French composer since the time of . . . Chabrier and Bizet. Because the French composers have been busy entertaining and "tickling the ears" of their princesses, countesses and marquises.'
'But Sergey Sergeyevich,' I tried to interject.
'I know, I know,' he cut me off, 'you like everything French. You even like that old crank Satie. And I know what you think about his followers. You think they are important. Well, they're not. They're pure mush. The only one in France who knows what he's doing is Ravel. All the rest are hopeless.'
'But what about . . . Debussy?' I said timidly, as we were turning into the rue Valentin Haüy.
'Debussy!' he smirked. 'Debussy! You know what Debussy is: it's *stouden* (calf's head or feet in aspic) . . . it's jelly . . . it's absolutely spineless music.' His voice grew excited and loud: 'No, I can't share

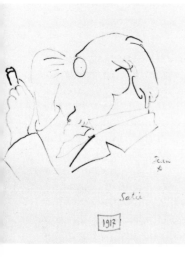

Jean Cocteau's portrait of 'that old crank' Erik Satie (Sotheby & Co)

98

anyone's admiration for Debussy. Except perhaps,' and he grinned again, 'it's very "personal" jelly and the jellymaker knows what he's doing. You know –' But he interrupted himself abruptly and raised the glove-covered index finger of his right hand. We had stopped in front of his house. He looked at his watch and beamed: 'Wonderful!' he said. 'Twenty-six minutes and twenty seconds. Excellent time. Won't you come up and have lunch with us, Nika?'

Prokofiev's circumstances might change, but not his commitment to music, or rather to *his* music. For Nabokov he seems to have been in all respects the rigorously methodical man his manuscripts suggest:

In the purely grammatical writing of his music Prokofiev was always more meticulous than any other composer I knew. The calligraphy of his manuscript is not so astonishing in its perfection as that of Stravinsky (Stravinsky's scores look like illuminated manuscripts), but when his manuscript reaches the publisher it is completely free of mistakes. Prokofiev is very precise about his metronome markings, the opus number and the dates of his compositions. All the little systems which he has devised are generated by the same kind of practical-mindedness which one finds in his music.

. . . I remember two May weeks in Paris during the Thirties when a group of twelve of us would sit down and play [bridge] every day from three in the afternoon until two in the morning in Prokofiev's crowded and smoky apartment . . . Prokofiev had devised a system of graphs for this tournament. Those graphs showed the relative position of every player at every phase of the game.

A similar impulse led Prokofiev to the playful, space-saving device of dropping all vowels, especially when drafting a speech or writing a postcard. 'A postcard of his would start "Dr frnd," and . . . end "Yrs, Srg Srgvtch Prkfv".'

Of course, Prokofiev's passion for honesty, efficiency and order had its less endearing side. As in youth, he could be surpassingly rude:

Once in a concert hall in Paris a fairly well-known composer came up to him and introduced himself. The man in the usual superlative manner of French bores started his 'my deep and inexpressible admiration for your work, dear master . . . what an infinite pleasure to meet you.' Prokofiev stared at the man with cross bull eyes and grumbled: 'On my part there is *no* pleasure,' and turned away.

Another time after a concert he told a famous singer, who had just performed a few of his songs, that she did not understand anything about his music and had better stop singing it. He said it in the presence of a large group of startled onlookers and in such a boorish way that he brought the poor fat lady to tears. 'You see,' he continued reprimanding her, 'all of you women take refuge in tears instead of listening to what one has to say and learning how to correct your faults.' In the touchy milieu of professional musicians, critics and composers, behaviour like this hardly produces a friendly reputation. As a result few composers had so many quarrels, feuds and lawsuits and made so many enemies as Prokofiev.

One summer, Nabokov made the mistake of accompanying the Prokofievs on what is called in France *le tour gastronomique*:

. . . The tour had been long and tiring, partly because most of the day was spent in first ordering meals, then eating them and then attempting to digest them; but also because the Prokofiev *ménage* had hourly squabbles (often ending with tears) about what to do next. While Lina Ivanovna wanted to stop in every village, visit every cathedral, château and museum, her husband wanted to go from one three-star restaurant to the next one in the town he had scheduled as our next stop . . . He was not a bit interested in museums, châteaux and cathedrals and when compelled to join us in what he called our 'phony gravedigging ritual' he looked bored and gloomy. The only thing he could find to say looking at Chartres Cathedral was: 'I wonder how they got those statues up so high without dropping them.' But when he had a large, fancy menu in his hand his mien would change, he would brighten up and start ordering for each one of us the *plat du jour* or the *spécialité de la maison* with the concomitant *vin du pays*.

My exhaustion from the trip was further enhanced by Prokofiev's abominable driving. It was, I think, his first prolonged driving experience and he drove slowly, overcautiously, and shook us up whenever he had to shift gears or stop. Consequently we crept along the roads of France in his tiny new four-seater at the rate of twenty miles per hour. He had computed every particle of our time at this average rate of speed and planned all our stops in advance. Everywhere we went we had to arrive on the dot of x o'clock and leave the same way . . .

We were told that we would leave Domrémy at 9.30 am ('and not a minute later'). But Lina Ivanovna and I wanted to visit . . . the Domrémy Museum and the Basilica. We met at 8.30 and started our tour while Prokofiev was still shaving. We went from one hideous memorial of Joan of Arc to the next until we reached the monstrous Basilica which was built after Joan's beatification . . .

When we left the crypt of the Basilica it was 9.35 am. Anticipating a scene we ran back to the inn. Prokofiev stood in front, his face blue with rage. At his first angry bark Lina Ivanovna burst into tears. This made him madder and the ensuing barks grew louder and more intense. He turned the heat on me. 'What kind of behaviour is this?' he shouted. 'Who do you think I am? I'm not your lackey to wait on you. You can damn well get your bag and go by train.' The outburst lasted for at least a quarter of an hour while the porter went on calmly packing our bags into the car.

When we finally drove off, Prokofiev and I sat in total silence in the front seat. His lips pouted. They were thicker and sulkier than ever. He

Natalia Goncharova: sketch for a programme cover for the Ballets Russes (Sotheby & Co)

Mikhail Larionov: project for a poster advertising Les Ballets de Monte-Carlo (1920) (Sotheby & Co)

looked positively grim, and from the back seat of the car came the ill-controlled sobs of his spouse. After about an hour of this business I turned to Prokofiev and said: 'Sergey Sergeyevich, either we stop this scene at once or let me out in the next village and I'll go by train.' At first he did not answer. Then in about five minutes he smiled awkwardly and said quietly: 'Yes, it does look funny, doesn't it? Two grown-up people sit in front with sour faces and a third is bleating away in the back.'

But Prokofiev's boorishness, his roughness, the rudeness of his temper had also another side – and that side contributed to constant, true friendship. Prokofiev, by nature, cannot tell a lie. He cannot say even the most conventional lie, such as 'This is a charming piece,' when he believes that the piece has no charm. Nor would he, when one showed him a new piece of one's music, shirk the responsibility of critical judgment and remain silent. On the contrary he would say exactly what he thought of it and discuss at great length its faults and its qualities and give valuable suggestions as to how to improve the piece. Thus to those who were ready to take his occasionally gruff manner and accept the frankness of his opinion he became an invaluable friend.

101

André Derain: poster for the
Ballets Russes de Monte-Carlo
(1932) (Sotheby & Co)

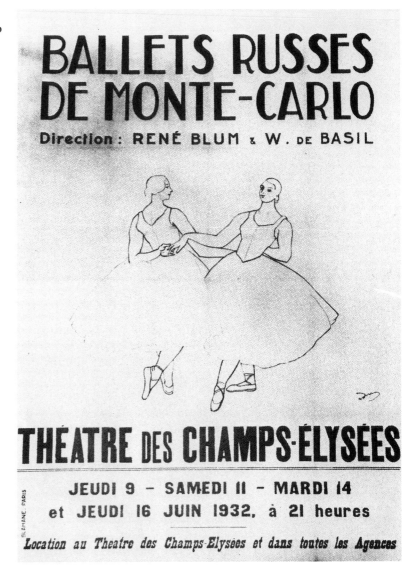

Prokofiev could be just as frank with his own music. Such was
the fate of the Second Symphony, first performed under
Koussevitsky's direction on 6 June 1925. Prokofiev had laboured
through the autumn and winter months of 1924 to make the work
as 'hard as iron and steel', as sensational as *Pacific 231*, Honegger's
locomobile hit of the season. Now he observed self-critically:

Neither I nor the audience understood anything in it . . . It was too
thickly woven. There were too many layers of counterpoint which
degenerated into mere figuration, and although one critic did comment
admiringly on the septuple counterpoint my friends preserved an
embarrassed silence. This was perhaps the first time it occurred to me
that I might be destined to be a second-rate composer.

102

The fear was well-founded. One present-day critic sees the Symphony as evidence of a 'marked deterioration in Prokofiev's standards and ambitions, . . . the work of a highly talented composer who has completely misjudged his capabilities.'

The Symphony's oddly balanced two-movement structure was allegedly modelled on Beethoven's Piano Sonata No. 32 in C minor, op. 111, but the formal parallels are superficial. Prokofiev's aim was not structural innovation but novelty value pure and simple. Deliberately dissonant and 'difficult', the piece was supposed to shore up his increasingly threadbare radical image. Unfortunately, the smart Parisians were not taken in and it flopped.

Perhaps the modernity of the Second was bound to be purely speculative. Even so, the orchestration does seem needlessly grotesque. It is almost impossible to disinter the main themes of the first movement from the prevailing din. The music grinds along at a seemingly constant, self-defeating *fortissimo*. Its angular melodic lines are balletic rather than symphonic, its progress remorseless and yet curiously arbitrary. The second movement, a set of free variations, is rather more characteristic. If the treatment is sometimes over-reminiscent of several Stravinsky ballets, the theme itself is utterly personal in its cool lyricism. It comes from the never completed 'white' (i.e. white note) quartet that Prokofiev was sketching in the summer of 1918, chiefly while waiting to receive his US visa in Tokyo.

No doubt recognising the quality of such ideas, Prokofiev long had it in his mind to revise the Symphony. Towards the end of his life he set about recasting it into three movements; he even assigned op. 136 to the project. But as with so many of his plans, he never managed more than a few sketches on paper. It is up to today's increasingly catholic audiences to reassess the work. Francis Poulenc always had a good word for it:

. . . I like the Second Symphony very much, the one where there's such a huge number of double-basses because it's a symphony dedicated to Koussevitsky, who was a double-bass player himself.

In order to earn some money while working on the Symphony, Prokofiev accepted a commission to write a ballet score for the roving Romanov ballet troupe. The company wished to present a sequence of short ballets accompanied by chamber ensemble.

I proposed a quintet consisting of oboe, clarinet, violin, viola and double-bass. The simple plot from circus life, entitled *The Trapeze*, served me as a pretext for composing a chamber piece that could be performed as pure music. This explains the impractical rhythms . . . which gave the choreographers a great deal of trouble. Nevertheless the *Trapeze* ballet ran in several cities in Germany and Italy with some success.

Composed, like the Second Symphony, 'in a spirit of quest', the Quintet, op. 39 similarly fails to convince. The style is quirky even for Prokofiev, an uneasy mélange of clearly defined melodic motifs and (densely) complex harmonic language. Despite (or perhaps because of) the richness and originality of its instrumental fabric, the piece is not much performed even today.

No doubt Prokofiev would have been thrown into deep despair had not Diaghilev approached him with a new commission. The composer was taken aback:

'But I cannot write in the style you approve of,' I said, hinting at the rather banal stuff Auric and Milhaud were composing for him. 'You must write in your own style,' Diaghilev replied and suggested that I write a ballet on a Soviet theme. I could not believe my ears. It was as if a fresh breeze had blown through my window . . .

It was decided to invite Yakulov as the artist; he had recently exhibited in Paris with great success.

Sitting in a tiny café on the banks of a river half an hour outside of Paris, Yakulov and I roughly sketched several draft librettos. We assumed that the important thing at this stage was not to provide mere entertainment but to show the new life that had come to the Soviet Union, and primarily the construction effort. It was to be a ballet of construction, with a wielding of hammers big and small, a revolving of transmission belts and flywheels, a flashing of light signals, all leading to a general creative upsurge with the dance groups operating the machines and at the same time depicting the work of the machines choreographically. The idea was Yakulov's who had spent some years in the Soviet Union and described it all most vividly.

Georgy Yakulov: designs for *Le Pas d'Acier*

(1) Working drawings for the set (Sotheby & Co)

(2) Costume designs for three dancers (Sotheby & Co)

(3) More costume designs. The text reads: '. . . Spectacles with electric lightbulbs. The index finger pulls the trigger, at the report the frightened speaker falls. The book is on rubber. The bulbs flash on and off alternately, one red the other blue and green . . .'
(Sotheby & Co)

105

As for the music, it marked, so Prokofiev tells us, a deliberate turning away from modernism, a challenge to the frivolities of French taste. In fact, it owed more to the machine music of the French avant-garde than anything specifically Soviet. Diaghilev found it authentically 'constructivist' which was enough. He had a name for this latest extravaganza: he proposed calling it *Le Pas d'Acier* – something variously translated as *The Tread*, *Leap*, *Pace*, *Step*, or worst of all, *Trot of Steel*!

In December 1925, Prokofiev and his wife returned to the United States after a four year interval:

I gave fourteen concerts, seven of them (in five cities) with the Boston Symphony Orchestra which Koussevitsky had been conducting for two years. I played the Third Piano Concerto. Six concerts were sponsored by the *Pro Musica*, a society of modern music which was founded by a Frenchman named Schmitts, with branches in several cities. My wife Lina took part in these concerts. She sang songs by Miaskovsky and Taneyev as well as my own. I also played Miaskovsky's *Whimsies*. In one provincial town the members of the society (there were three hundred of them) expressed the desire to shake hands with us. The ceremony proceeded thus: a member of the society would approach the secretary and say, 'I am Mr Smith.' The chairman would say to me, 'Let me introduce you to Mr Smith.' I would shake hands and say, 'Happy to meet you Mr Smith!' Whereupon Mr Smith would say, 'Happy to meet you Mr Prokofiev!' and pass on to my wife. In the meantime Mr Jones would be approaching in the same manner and so on, three hundred times!

Despite the distractions, Prokofiev continued to work on the orchestration of *Le Pas d'Acier*:

Since the branches of the *Pro Musica* society were scattered all over the United States, from New York to San Francisco, and a good deal of my time was spent in railway carriages, I endeavoured to utilise the time by scoring my ballet. The shaking of the car made it difficult to write the score, so I decided to do all the preliminary work en route, not only choosing the instruments, but scoring each bar complete in every detail, including the instrumentation of chords, bowing, accents and nuances. In this way all that remained was the mechanical job of copying on to the orchestral score what had been sketched out in pencil on the piano score. At first it seemed impossible to map out all the instruments on the piano score, but after a little practice I learned to do this without much difficulty. Moreover, between the braced staves there was always an extra stave on which one could insert the additional voices or accents, and if there was not enough room I would make a note and carry over the extra passages or complex string chords on to a separate stave.

In later years the transcription into full score was usually left to

(4) A model of the set
(Sotheby & Co)

an amanuensis and a number of authorities imply that musicologist. Pavel Lamm did more than merely transcribe. Certainly, it is unclear whether Prokofiev himself ever saw a complete full score of his *Ode to the End of the War*. There are several queries in the published edition (1969) marked 'for the composer's approval' with nothing in the composer's hand. Of course he *may* have approved these passages verbally.

Prokofiev's American tour was followed in 1926 by another trip to Italy:

After a matinée recital in Naples, Maxim Gorky came to see me and carried me off to his place for dinner . . . He was in good form, and I spent a most pleasant evening in his company.
. . . The big palazzo-type house in which Gorky lived at the time struck me as being chill and uncomfortable in spite of the Italian climate; and hardly fitting for Gorky, who when I asked after his health, replied, 'One of my lungs is gone altogether, and only half of the other one is left.'

By the summer of 1926, Prokofiev's new Diaghilev ballet had been rescheduled for production the following year. But, with his 'old' opera, *The Fiery Angel* recently accepted by Bruno Walter for performance in Berlin, there was plenty to do. Enthusiastically, Prokofiev set about reworking one of his own favourite scores. (He

107

Maxim Gorky: a photograph of 1928

was not to know that the performance would be postponed indefinitely.) He also came up with the bizarre *American Overture*, op. 42.

The story of this overture is as follows: my contract with the American pianola company was still valid, but by now player pianos had gone out of style, and the company began to switch over gradually to other lines; among other things it was building a concert hall in New York. Instead of playing a new batch of pieces for recordings (which could have been done in London) the company asked me to write an overture for the opening of the new hall. I eagerly seized on the idea, for I much preferred composing to making recordings.

Despite the *Overture*'s comparatively simple harmonic idiom, its nursery rhyme melodics and oddball scoring make for something refreshingly 'different'. Prokofiev later wrote an alternative version for symphony orchestra – more practical, less bonily distinctive.

Towards the end of the year, Prokofiev was again corresponding with the Soviet concert authorities. This time, he was determined to make an extensive tour of what he still regarded

108

as his homeland. But what kind of reception could he expect?

The magnificent flowering of Russian poetry which had begun in the 1890s, the bold advances in painting and sculpture, in literature, in the theatre and the ballet – this unique amalgam, so far from being arrested by war and revolution, had continued to derive vitality and inspiration from a vision of a new world. Despite the conservative tastes of Lunacharsky and his colleagues, anything that could be represented as a slap in the face to bourgeois taste was in principle approved and encouraged. The Russia of the early 1920s experienced a genuine renaissance, with much cross-fertilisation between novelists, poets, artists, musicians, historians, critics and scientists.

And yet all this unorganised revolutionary activity was viewed with suspicion by proponents of the kind of collectivist, proletarian aesthetic apparently repudiated in 1917. The critic Averbakh was soon to lead his ideological zealots against something variously described as unbridled individualistic literary licence, 'formalism', decadence, aestheticism or simply 'kowtowing to the depravities of the West'. In no time at all the artistic hothouse was besieged.

The aesthetic debate within Russian music gradually polarised between the Russian Association of Proletarian Musicians, founded in 1924, and the Association for Contemporary Music; its Moscow branch was founded in 1923. In numerous policy statements, RAPM demanded 'the extension of the hegemony of the proletariat to music'; the creation of 'music reflecting the rich, full-blooded psychology of the most advanced, sensitive and understanding class – the proletariat'; the rejection of 'contemporary bourgeois music incompatible with the proletarian spirit'; the prohibition of 'extremist innovations', and the assimilation of those 'masters of the past whose music embodied proletarian ideals'. The ACM, on the other hand, urged Soviet composers to learn from the 'full-blooded virile, sane, lucid, deeply emotional' music of Alban Berg. New music, claimed ACM, was closer in spirit to the proletarian century than the great music of the past:

What is closer to the proletariat, the pessimism of Tchaikovsky, and the would-be heroic spirit of Beethoven, a century out of date, or the chiselled rhythm and the excitement of *Rails* by Deshevov? During the performance of Beethoven, the workers were utterly bored, and patiently, with polite endurance, waited for the music to end. But music by contemporary Soviet composers aroused a contagious emotion among the audience . . .

RAPM agreed with the modernists only in their opposition to Tchaikovsky. There was nothing more damaging than the

109

advocacy of modernism as 'consonant with the epoch' except perhaps the performance of 'the erotic dance music of contemporary capitalist cities': 'The foxtrot subordinates the human body, the human will and thought to a mechanical movement. Such is the rhythm and pulse of capitalist society.' Even Gorky drew parallels between the decadence of jazz and the decay of capitalism in an article, 'The Dance of the Fat Men'.

Political meaning was also discovered in 'light' music, such as Albert Ketèlbey's *In a Persian Market*. According to G. Krasnukha:

The aim of the British composer is to convince the listener that in the colonies, and in the semi-colonial regions, people are happy; beautiful princesses bask in the sunlight; beggars and caliphs enjoy life together . . . When disorders flare up, why, this is the work of malefactors and Komintern agitators.

Lunacharsky had remained a loyal adherent of Prokofiev's throughout the early period of criticism of émigrés. In June 1926 he cautioned, 'Stravinsky has, in a significant measure, already fallen into the clutches of glittering artifice. Prokofiev, in order fully to develop, must return to us before the devil of Americanisation overwhelms him.'

Prokofiev rehearsing with Oistrakh (Novosti)

The musicological manoeuvres of the twenties paralleled crucial struggles in the upper echelons of the Party. It is easy to pour scorn on debates which revolved around such questions as whether counterpoint in music tends to inculcate a collectivist or an individualistic ethos, but something serious was at stake: the right to compose in idioms which inevitably seemed 'highbrow and alien' to large sections of the Soviet public (including most of the political leaders who, in the end, could settle aesthetic controversy by decree).

On 18 January 1927, Prokofiev stepped on to Russian soil for the first time in nine years. The tour lasted for three months. Everywhere he was received as a celebrity:

. . . on the 19th, I arrived in Moscow. How can I describe my feelings on returning to my native land! I was met by the Persimfans people and driven in a car with frost-coated windows straight to the Metropole Hotel where I found many old friends awaiting me . . .

. . . With L. M. Tseitlin, the moving spirit of the Persimfans, I went to a rehearsal of the orchestra. As we approached the hall I heard the March from the *Three Oranges* being played. 'They are taking it a little too slow,' I said, thinking they were rehearsing it. But it turned out that the orchestra was playing the March in my honour.

. . . The programme of the first concert, held on 24 January 1927,

A poster announcing a chess match between Oistrakh and Prokofiev. The conditions were of a peculiar type: whoever won the contest would join the audience; the loser was obliged to give a concert.

МОСОБЛАСТКОМРАБИС

КЛУБ МАСТЕРОВ ИСКУССТВ

9
НОЯБРЯ

ШАХМАТНЫЙ МАТЧ
ДАВИД   СЕРГЕЙ
ОЙСТРАХ-ПРОКОФЬЕВ

УСЛОВИЯ МАТЧА:

Открытие матча 9 ноября 1937 года в 9 часов вечера

Isaac Rabinovich: costume designs for the Bolshoi Theatre production of *The Love of Three Oranges* (1927)

(1) The Cook (Bakhrushin Museum, Moscow)

consisted of the *Buffoon* Suite (ten numbers), the Third Concerto and the suite from the *Three Oranges*.

The reception I was given in Moscow was tremendous. For an encore after the Third Concerto I played Miaskovsky's *Whimsies*, but knowing that the author was present I lost my nerve and muffed it so badly that he hardly recognised his own work. Altogether two symphony programmes (in the second I played the Second Piano Concerto) and two piano recitals had been prepared for Moscow. Each programme was given twice, making a total of eight concerts.

At the rehearsal of each new piece the musicians expressed their enthusiasm, but after the *American Overture*, op. 42, they preserved an awkward silence: they did not understand it. Neither did the public.

Prokofiev gave 21 concerts in all. Here, the violinist David Oistrakh recalls the 'sensational' impact of his visit to Odessa:

The recitals were given in the Odessa Opera House, and the large hall

(2) Costume designs for two characters (Sotheby & Co)

was filled to overflowing long before the concert began. Practically every musician in town, all the veteran music-lovers and a host of young people came to hear the famous composer. The concert was a resounding success. For some reason I felt as excited as if I were the hero of the day. The impression made on me, not so much by the music, which by that time I had learned to understand and appreciate, as by the performance, was unlike anything I had ever experienced. What struck me about Prokofiev's playing was its remarkable simplicity. Not a single superfluous gesture, not a single exaggerated expression of emotion, no striving for effect.

. . . After the recitals there was a banquet for Prokofiev at which local musicians gave renderings of his music. I was chosen to play the *Scherzo* from his Violin Concerto. I was naturally much thrilled at the prospect of meeting the composer in person, and it was with mingled feelings of happiness and shyness that I, then a lad of eighteen, awaited the day of the performance. At last it came. Little did I suspect how sadly it was to end for me.

The cream of Odessa public was assembled in the Scientists' Club where the banquet for Prokofiev was to be held. In the place of honour right in front of the platform sat the composer himself. As I played I observed his face grow darker and darker. When I had finished, the audience applauded, but not Prokofiev. Instead he stepped on to the stage, paying no heed to the hubbub in the hall, sat down at the piano and, turning to me with the words: 'Young man, you don't play it right at all,' proceeded to show me how the piece ought to be played. My debacle was complete.

Many years later when I knew Prokofiev quite well I reminded him of the incident and of his Odessa concert tour in general. To my surprise he remembered everything down to the smallest detail, including the programme and the number of encores, and Chishko, the Ukrainian composer and singer with whom he performed *The Ugly Duckling* at the banquet, and 'that unfortunate young man' whom he had given 'a fine drubbing', as he put it. His genuine embarrassment and distress when I told him that I was that young man showed me how warm and human he could be.

The unprecedented success of the tour posed an obvious question: might Prokofiev make immediate plans for taking up permanent residence in Soviet Russia? There is no doubt that the composer was deeply touched by the warm welcome extended to him by his countrymen. He sensed that he was potentially the most important of Soviet composers, that, here, no Stravinsky was going to take his place. Old friends and younger colleagues made much of the material facilities offered to musicians by a beneficent state. And there was as yet no monolithic authority to condemn works which did not conform to an official dogma.

In answer to Diaghilev's enquiries, Prokofiev provided a detailed survey of 'the young Soviet composers I have spoken to you about' in his letter of 21 September 1928:

. . . Shostakovich, Mossolov and Popov are prominent above the general level of talent . . . the most eminent is Shostakovich, whose Symphony Bruno Walter has conducted with success and Stokowski intends to conduct in America.

. . . I personally heard only his Piano Sonata from his earliest compositions, vivid and definitely talented, not without my influence.

. . . Of these composers, I think I would put my money on Popov, in spite of the fact that Shostakovich has been able to make himself more prominent. Besides, Shostakovich's difficult character forces one to be careful when doing business with him . . .

It is intriguing to speculate that we might still have seen a Shostakovich ballet performed by the Ballets Russes if Diaghilev had lived.

Chapter 7

The Return of the Prodigal

Prokofiev left Moscow filled with vivid impressions and new ideas, but he was reluctant to sever his ties with the fashionable West. On 29 May he attended a party given by the celebrated patroness the Princesse de Polignac at which he and Stravinsky accompanied on two pianos an otherwise full-scale performance of *Oedipus Rex*. Rehearsals for *Le Pas d'Acier*, his 'Bolshevik ballet', had begun in earnest.

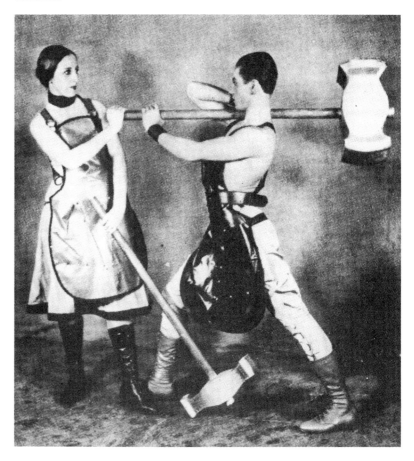

Lubov Tchernicheva and
Serge Lifar in *Le Pas d'Acier*

The ballet had its première in Paris on 7 June 1927. Like all Diaghilev productions it was magnificently staged and was a great success. 'A queer production,' the French press commented, 'beginning with the title and ending with the music and the choreography. Can it possibly be intended to replace *A Life for the Tsar?*' The whiteguard press scoffed at this 'prickly flower of proletarian culture'. Stravinsky was disgusted by the hammering on the stage. But the youth were in ecstasies. On 4 July the ballet opened in London. The theatre was full of lords and ladies and a dazzling display of diamonds. 'The packed hall rocked with applause,' wrote the newspapers. . . . 'Prokofiev deserves to be famous. As an apostle of Bolshevism he has no peer! Prokofiev travels through our countries but refuses to think as we do.'

Soviet reactions were distinctly cool. Unkind commentators dismissed the show as a box of 'urbanistic tricks':

Prokofiev had never seen or known at first hand the Soviet reality . . . and the deeper meaning of the revolutionary movement signified for the creators of *Le Pas d'Acier* nothing but a noisy, picturesque brawl, a mob of ranting, confused tub-thumpers, the rumble of a steam engine – all things which in no way differed from the mechanical subjects of urban art, so dear to the bourgeoisie. The vision of Soviet life was discredited in the eyes of the West, in spite of all the goodwill of the composer.

Having orchestrated the revamped *Fiery Angel*, Prokofiev looked over the manuscript of an earlier opera retrieved from the library of the former Maryinsky Theatre. This was *The Gambler*. Prokofiev and Meyerhold hoped for a Soviet première: Meyerhold had even been in Paris to discuss the possibility of staging it as a follow-up to Leningrad's successful *Love of Three Oranges*. However, in the light of RAPM's disapproval, the project stood little chance of succeeding in Leningrad. Soviet interest waned. The première was assigned to Belgium.

On 14 June 1928, Prokofiev was able to hear at least a portion of *The Fiery Angel* when Koussevitsky directed a concert performance of Act 2. The composer had been about to make a suite out of it. Now he decided that such strong thematic material merited the full symphonic treatment. The result, the Third Symphony, op. 44, was first performed under Pierre Monteux on 17 May 1929.

Fiercely self-critical after the failure of the Second, Prokofiev was far happier with the Third. More ambitious too. He had after all chosen to dedicate it to a confirmed symphonist, his old friend Nikolay Miaskovsky. And in 1933, he decided to introduce it to the Russian public.

As for my concerts in Moscow and Leningrad, I was delighted by the reception given my Third Symphony. I believe that in this symphony I

Georges Rouault: designs for
The Prodigal Son

(1) A sketch for Scene 1
(Sotheby & Co)

have succeeded in achieving greater depth of musical idiom. I do not want Soviet audiences to judge me only by the March from the *Three Oranges* and the Gavotte from the *Classical Symphony*. But the difficulty is that as soon as one begins to talk a little more seriously one's language is bound to become more difficult to grasp. All the more gratifying for me was the Soviet audience's attitude to this symphony.

Prokofiev regarded the Third as one of his strongest works, but despite the evocative inner movements – expertly proportioned and faultlessly scored – there are problems. The first movement is undeniably brash and lacking in cohesion, while the finale is chronically over-scored and out of proportion with the rest of the work (it lasts only six minutes, despite being padded out with material from the earlier movements).

In spite of its faults, the Third does provide a foretaste of Prokofiev's great Soviet symphonies. And, Rita McAllister points out, its drama and intensity are the only hints to the listener of its operatic origins. The identification of specific musical episodes with scenes and characters from *The Fiery Angel* does not really enhance our understanding of what Prokofiev intended as a *symphonic* drama:

I should like to point out . . . that the tendency to regard my Third Symphony as a programme work simply because it contains material from the opera *The Fiery Angel* . . . is erroneous. The leading themes of *The Fiery Angel* were composed as symphony music long before I began work on the opera and when I subsequently used them for the Third Symphony they merely returned to their native element without, as far as I am concerned, being the least tainted by their temporary operatic sojourn.

In the autumn of 1928, Diaghilev again surprised Prokofiev with an unorthodox commission. This time he asked for a ballet on a biblical theme: the parable of the prodigal son. In the interests of dramatic cogency, the plot was modified to give a closer focus on the Prodigal himself. The detailed scenario was mapped out by Boris Kochno.

. . . the prodigal son leaves home, goes on the spree and falls under the spell of a beautiful maiden. At last, robbed and destitute, he crawls home to his father who welcomes him and forgives him. It was a brief plot in three scenes, but it contained all the necessary elements. This made the job both easy and pleasant. When Diaghilev called me up in November to ask how the work was progressing I was able to tell him that the rough draft of the piano score was ready. He was amazed. 'What, already!' he gasped. 'Then it cannot be good.' But when he heard the music he was satisfied.

Prokofiev's co-workers were less productive. Amid a welter of backstage intrigue, jealousies professional and personal conspired to sabotage the production altogether. When the designs by Georges Rouault failed to materialise, Diaghilev was obliged to gain access to the artist's Paris apartment and spirit the appropriate sketches away. Meanwhile, Serge Lifar was unhappy with his leading role. As Victor Seroff describes the events of 21 May 1929, it was touch-and-go to the very end:

Lifar, sulking, took to his bed, telling Diaghilev's cousin that he refused to go to the theatre. 'I don't feel I'm in sympathy with the part of the Prodigal Son, and I'm afraid I may turn it into a failure. I can't understand how they want me to treat the part. Let them act it themselves. I can't and I don't want to, and prefer to stay at home.'
Although mute with terror, Diaghilev's cousin fortunately remained

(2) Drop curtain

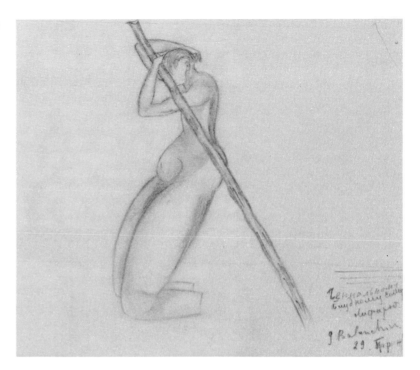

Balanchine's portrait of Serge
Lifar in *The Prodigal Son*
(Sotheby & Co)

with Lifar, occasionally glancing nervously at his watch. He pleaded
with him, but to no avail. Lifar would not get out of bed, not even when
he was told that it was ten minutes past eight, just a few minutes before
curtain time.

Then according to Lifar, in a flash he saw his own life, starting – as any
good psychiatric patient does – long before he had left Russia; his life
with Diaghilev, who 'lavished on him love, tenderness, and care,
becoming his spiritual father'; and still later, his growing into an artist
through this association, etc., until suddenly he saw himself as the
Prodigal Son. Lifar leapt out of bed to run to the theatre in order not to
desert his 'spiritual father'.

Prokofiev, completely unaware of all these shenanigans, had calmly
taken his place at the conductor's desk and waited in silence for the extra
fifteen minutes caused by Lifar's delay before he raised his baton for the
beginning of his ballet.

Despite the problems, *The Prodigal Son* was a considerable
success:

I conducted the orchestra, following Stravinsky who conducted his own
ballet, *Renard*. Rachmaninov sat in the front row and condescendingly
applauded a few numbers. The public and press were most enthusiastic.
I was not altogether satisfied with the choreography; it did not always
follow the music. Having been occupied with *The Gambler*, I was too late
in contacting the producers to be able to change anything. I had a clash
with Diaghilev on this score. Stravinsky, too, had been having some
trouble with him.

120

Prokofiev was wrong about the choreography. Balanchine's ballet has continued in the repertoire, being produced by the Royal Ballet from 1973 with Rudolf Nureyev in the title role. But he was right about the music. *The Prodigal Son* is a significant score which foreshadows the richer lyricism of the mature Soviet ballets without sacrificing the propulsive drive and sardonic humour of earlier works. Refreshingly cool and transparent in texture, it shows Prokofiev back in control. Nestyev sees the

Rudolf Nureyev in the Royal Ballet's production of *The Prodigal Son* (Anthony Crickmay)

Siren's music as a prototype for the greatest Prokofiev heroines: Juliet, Cinderella and Natasha (in *War and Peace*).

By this time neither Stravinsky nor Prokofiev was talking to Diaghilev. 11 June 1929 and Stravinsky writes to Ernest Ansermet:

> . . . the other day, Prokofiev and Païchadze* were served with a summons to appear in court this Wednesday (tomorrow) to respond to charges formulated in the complaint of 'Boris Kochno' (i.e., Diagh.). He is suing both of them for having published *The Prodigal Son* (entitled *The Prodigal Child* on the published score) without the permission of the author of the scenario, despite the existence of an agreement between Prokofiev and Kochno that joins them together as collaborators.
>
> Both Païchadze and Prokofiev are accused of having murdered the 'book', that masterpiece of literature (in the complaint Kochno calls himself a 'man of letters'), by publishing the titles in a form that renders the meaning of this 'work' completely different from what Kochno had conceived, etc. etc. (I must admit that Païchadze and Prokofiev did not put Kochno's name on the score.) In short, yesterday they consulted a lawyer who, unfortunately, foresees trouble, because, as a preventive measure, the document threatens the confiscation of all ballet editions by Prokofiev.
>
> There, *mon vieux*, is what's happening with these gallant gents of the Ballets Russes, so genteel, and so devoted to the cause of art! . . .

Little more than two months later, the news came from Venice. Diaghilev was dead. One of the threads that bound Prokofiev to the West was broken.

On 23 October 1929, we find Stravinsky writing that 'Prokofiev and I have been given an order by Koussevitsky for the composing of (I don't remember what sort of) things for the Boston Philharmonic'. The occasion was in fact the 50th anniversary celebrations of the Boston Symphony Orchestra, and Stravinsky went on to supply one of his most profound works, the *Symphony of Psalms*. Prokofiev's own contribution was the Fourth Symphony; its first performance was given under Koussevitsky's direction on 14 November 1930.

Seroff's assertion that the composer decided *against* reusing old material in this work – i.e. that he meant (symphonic) business – is the very opposite of the truth. Pages from *The Prodigal Son* are in fact transplanted much as they stand, and not merely in the second and third movements as Prokofiev maintained. Immensely attractive in context, they tend to sound rather insipid here. The slow movement, drawing on the final scene of the ballet, contains some of the most serenely lyrical music in the Prokofiev canon. But there is no conflict, no drama, no real sense of direction. For

*director of the *Edition Russe de Musique*, Prokofiev's publisher.

once, Nestyev's jibes, the references to 'lifelessness' and 'insufficient contrasts', seem apt. The work contains a succession of beautiful tunes; the rest is padding.

Today, the Fourth is most often heard in an ill-conceived revision of 1947. In its original form, the Symphony was a refreshing change from the overscored frenzy of the Second and parts of the Third, a change welcomed by composer Henri Sauguet:

The work is remarkable for its modesty . . . The composer has allowed the very lovely music to express itself quite naturally, without constraint, without any external strivings after colour, picturesque motifs, scholarly developments – in fact without any regard for any kind of modernism or aestheticism.

There are obvious pointers to the development of a smoother, more settled style.

After the cancellation of a Russian trip planned for 1928, Prokofiev was unable to visit Moscow until November 1929. There were to be no concert engagements on this occasion; Prokofiev had recently injured his hands in a car accident. Instead, there would be time to hear more new Soviet music, time also to experience at first-hand the workings of a Soviet musical establishment unlikely to be so welcoming second time around. The cultural situation had been allowed to deteriorate along with much else.

For some years the Trotskyite 'left' had been proposing its scenario of rapid industrialisation and 'permanent revolution' as an alternative to the dominant platform of 'socialism in one country'. As understood by the 'right' group headed by Bukharin, Tomsky and Rykov, this, the official line, entailed a programme of gradualism in industrial growth and agricultural collectivisation, stressed the alleviation of the harsher aspects of dictatorship, and favoured such revision of foreign policy as might secure strengthened ties with (and economic concessions from) the Western democracies. Now, Stalin was turning on his former allies, stigmatising them as a 'Right Opposition'. Only the label, 'socialism in one country', was retained. The policy pursued was designed to secure Stalin's dictatorship through intensified industrialisation and the coercive collectivisation of the peasantry. This programme, put into effect as the First Five-Year Plan in 1928, had repercussions in every sphere of Soviet life.

In an article entitled *Lenin's Political Testament*, published in *Pravda* on 21 January 1929, Bukharin made his final open attempt to oppose the new line. He argued that Lenin's ultimate position was essentially one of tolerance, that socialist systems could be

The first Five-Year Plan
achieved in four years by a
benevolent Stalin, against
whom the forces of reaction
rage in vain (Fotomas Inex)

built only through a long process of 'peaceful organisation and cultural work'. Coercion constituted a further revolution and was not implicit in Leninism.

Nevertheless, the artist had an obvious propaganda role at a time of internal unrest and industrial transformation. As the lenient New Economic Policy was replaced by the hard-driving Five-Year Plan, so the Party's Central Committee adopted a militant attitude to the arts. In 1929, Lunacharsky, the symbol of enlightened arts policy, was replaced by a Party functionary, Andrey Bubnov, with no musical connections. Preference was now to be given to Communist writers whose literature served the Party's political aims more directly. Justification for the new line was found in certain of Lenin's aesthetic commentaries; the particular insistence on party spirit was extrapolated from a single article of 1905. When the Russian Association of Proletarian Writers moved into a favoured position, its smaller musical counterpart assumed new powers. Soviet commentators prefer to forget that, following a call for consolidation in *Pravda*, RAPM acquired a monopolistic position between 1929 and 1932, enabling

124

Mayakovsky, Shostakovich, Meyerhold and Rodchenko during rehearsals for *The Bedbug* (Moscow, 1929). Meyerhold would have preferred a Prokofiev score.

it, for example, to interfere in the curriculum of the Moscow Conservatoire. As composer Vissarion Shebalin complained:

My pupils who studied with Shekhter (a prominent proletarian musician) bring me three or four bars of some clumsy melody. Then the discussion starts whether these three or four clumsy bars reflect the experience of the proletariat at the time of the Kronstadt uprising.

After years of committed Soviet culture-mongering, Mayakovsky confronted the proletarian philistines, the NEP profiteers and the Party hacks in his devastating (1928) satire, *The Bedbug*. In this piece of dialogue, householder Oleg Bard has pounced on the piano keys; the wedding usher looks over his shoulder, threateningly:

Why do you play only on the black keys? I suppose you think black is good enough for the proletariat. You play on all the keys only for the bourgeoisie, is that it?
Please, citizen, please! I'm concentrating on the white ones!
So you think white is best? Play on both!

Prokofiev in 1930 (Novosti)

I *am* playing on both!
So you compromise with the Whites, opportunist!
But, comrade . . . the keyboard is . . .
Who said 'broad'? And in the presence of the newlyweds! Take that!
(*Hits him on the back of the neck with guitar*)

Prokofiev's visit of 1929 was not without its bitter controversies:

The Bolshoi decided to stage *Le Pas d'Acier* which had been performed three times in Moscow on the concert stage. However, after some rather sharp criticism by members of RAPM, the Bolshoi Theatre changed its mind, and I had to content myself with the foreign productions for the time being. An excellent production was given in 1931 in the New York Metropolitan Opera with Stokowski conducting. It was thrilling to see a tremendous red flag flying on the stage of this most bourgeois of bourgeois theatres.

Prokofiev here glosses over what amounted to a campaign against him. He was reviled in some quarters as 'an enemy of Soviet culture', his ballet dismissed as a 'flat anti-Soviet joke, a

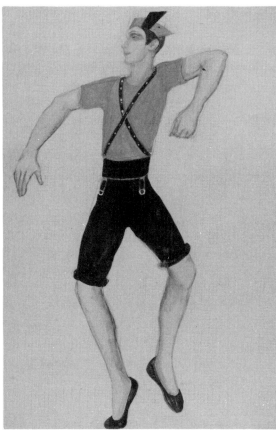

Natalia Goncharova: two costume designs for Serge Lifar in *Sur le Borysthène* (Sotheby & Co)

counter-revolutionary, and all but Fascist work'. The severity of the attacks can only have made him think twice about returning to the Soviet Union on a permanent basis.

At the beginning of 1930, Prokofiev resumed his travels with an extended tour of the United States, Canada and Cuba. His work was now better known in America, and his 'reception both by the public and by the press was quite serious this time'. The Library of Congress even asked for a string quartet, the concluding *Andante* of which reveals his growing inclination toward a typically 'Russian' melodic style – a development welcomed by Miaskovsky:

. . . there is true profundity in the sweeping melodic line and intensity of the Finale. This movement strikes deep . . . How marvellous it would be if this tendency in him were to become firmly fixed.

In the summer of 1930, the Paris Opera commissioned a new ballet from Prokofiev. His collaborator, Serge Lifar, had no particular plot in mind, so the composer set to work without one. That the action should take place on the Dnieper was decided only

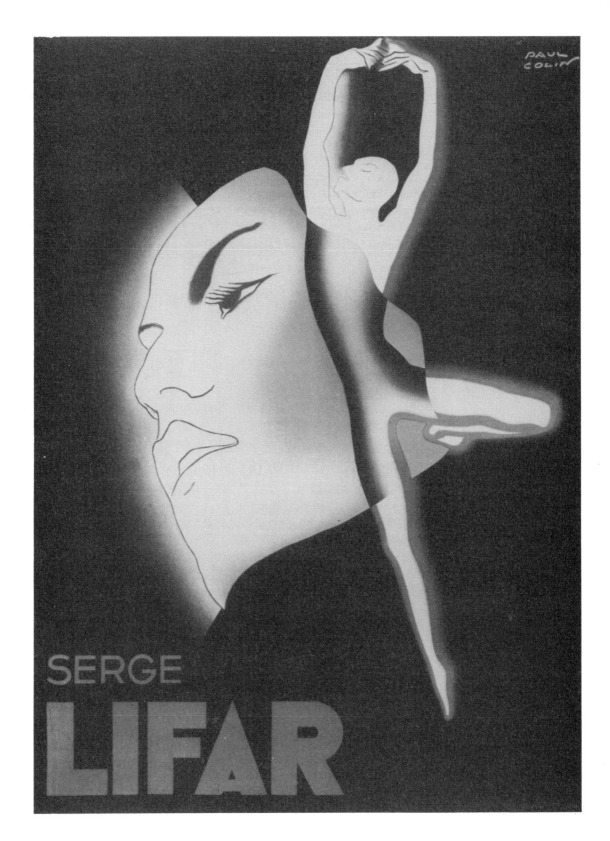

late in the day. Later still, when it was realised that the French would have difficulty in pronouncing the word 'Dnieper', the Slavic name of the river was replaced by its ancient Greek equivalent and the ballet retitled *Sur le Borysthène*.

The production – sets by Larionov, costumes by Goncharova – opened on 16 December 1932. It closed after only a few performances. Prokofiev tried to rationalise his failure:

Considering ten years elapsed before my early, lyrical music was noticed, I presume this ballet's turn will come some day, too.

Unfortunately, the score still sounds pallid – a diffuse rerun of *The Prodigal Son* with the tunes taken out.

16 December 1932 was also the official opening of a society called 'Triton', formed in Paris for the performance of new chamber music. The members included Honegger, Milhaud and Poulenc, as well as Prokofiev, whose Sonata for two violins received its Western première on this occasion:

Fortunately the ballet came on half an hour later, and so immediately after the sonata we dashed over to the Grand Opera – musicians, critics, author all together.

Few sonatas for two violins can claim much charm or depth, but Prokofiev offers something of both in his op. 56.

Having composed little for the piano for some years, Prokofiev received an unusual commission in 1931:

I wrote a Piano Concerto (No. 4) for the left hand at the request of the Austrian pianist Wittgenstein, who had lost his right hand in the war. He was concentrating all his energy on developing his left hand and building up a concert repertoire. In the latter respect he was not very successful. Richard Strauss had written some symphonic études for an orchestra with quadruple woodwinds. 'How can I with my one poor hand hope to compete with a quadruple orchestra!' Wittgenstein said in despair. 'But it is not for me to tell Strauss how to orchestrate . . . ' Ravel composed a concerto beginning with a tremendous cadenza for the left hand. Wittgenstein was furious. 'If I wanted to play without the orchestra I would not have ordered a concerto!' he said. He demanded that Ravel rewrite the piece. But the conductors supported the composer and insisted that the concerto be played exactly as Ravel had intended. I sent Wittgenstein my concerto and received this answer: 'Thank you for your concerto, but I do not understand a single note and I shall not play it.'[*]

Prokofiev intended to recast the work for two hands, but he never realised the project and it was not until 1956 that the first

[*]Prokofiev tells a good anecdote but misrepresents Richard Strauss and Ravel.

129

performance was given by Siegfried Rapp in Berlin. The Fourth was revealed as a precise, entertaining score, modest in scale but with no shortage of keyboard pyrotechnics and plenty of light and air in the orchestral texture. Although the third movement *Moderato* shows Prokofiev in Stravinskyan mood, the expressive world of the second, a sombre *Andante*, is thoroughly his own. The miniature final *Vivace* provides one of Prokofiev's most effective pay-offs. A brilliant summary of the essentials of the opening movement, it runs for less than a minute and a half.

Soon after completing the Fourth Piano Concerto, Prokofiev threw himself into the composition of a Fifth:

If we discount the Fourth Concerto for left hand, more than ten years had passed since I had written a piano concerto. Since then my conception of the treatment of this form had changed somewhat, some new ideas had occurred to me (a passage running across the entire keyboard, with the left hand overtaking the right; chords in the piano and orchestra interrupting one another, etc.), and finally, I had accumulated a good number of vigorous major themes in my notebook. I had not intended the concerto to be difficult, and at first had even contemplated calling it 'Music for Piano with Orchestra', partly to avoid confusing the concerto numbers. But in the end it turned out to be complicated, as indeed was the case with a good many other compositions of this period. What was the explanation? In my desire for simplicity I was hampered by the fear of repeating old formulas, of reverting to the 'old simplicity', which is something all modern composers seek to avoid.

Did Prokofiev himself sense an emotional thinness in the flashing outlines of the Fifth? For many listeners, his old *joie de vivre* seems to be stiffening into meretricious acrobatics – a sign of 'the crisis inherent in this composer's later modernism' (Hugh Ottaway). Even Miaskovsky found the 'first and third movements not very pleasing'.

Prokofiev played the Fifth Concerto for the first time on 31 October 1932, with the Berlin Philharmonic Orchestra under Furtwängler. Also on the bill was Berlioz's *Harold in Italy* with the composer Hindemith as viola soloist. Stravinsky was among the luminaries in the audience and Prokofiev reports that 'the concert went off very well'. However, for some years no pianist would touch the brilliantly accomplished five-movement Concerto with its reputation for (brilliantly accomplished) brittleness. Then, in February 1941, the 25-year-old Sviatoslav Richter prepared the work. The first run-through took place at the home of the pianist and pedagogue Heinrich Neuhaus. (Richter's accompanist was Anatoly Vedernikov.):

Prokofiev arrived with his wife and the room filled with the strong scent of Parisian perfume. He straightaway began to tell some unbelievable

Opposite
In June 1932, Prokofiev was in London to record his Third Piano Concerto with the LSO under Piero Coppola; Lawrance Collingwood produced for HMV (EMI)

stories about the life of gangsters in America. They were told in Prokofiev's inimitable style – businesslike and with humour. We sat at a small table under which our legs didn't fit and drank tea with the invariable Neuhaus slices of ham. Then we played.

Prokofiev was pleased and, standing in front of us behind the two pianos from where he had conducted, he pulled two chocolate bars out of both pockets simultaneously and presented them to us with a grand gesture. There and then we agreed on the dates of the rehearsals.

Late in 1932, Prokofiev was back in the USA for his sixth concert tour:

. . . In New York Bruno Walter played the *Portraits* from *The Gambler* which he had conducted with some success in Leipzig and Berlin. The performance was excellent but the reception was poor. As I was coming out of my box after the performance, a splendid specimen of the prosperous American came out of the next loge and remarked in a loud voice to someone inside: 'I'd like to meet that guy. I'd tell him a thing or two about his music!' I hastily withdrew.

By the mid-1930s, Prokofiev was making ever more frequent tours to Russia, gradually entrenching himself in Soviet musical life. No doubt urged to settle more permanently by the 'highest authorities', he had the use of a Moscow apartment from 1933. In the same year, he even agreed to teach a few post-graduate composition students at the Moscow Conservatoire – very much the done thing for the Soviet composer. ('Prokofiev's remarks were friendly, specific, and to the point,' recalled Khachaturian; other students remember him as haughty and aloof.) Following the dissolution of RAPM, Prokofiev had been received with respect and sometimes with affection. Could he afford to remain, as Rachmaninov and Stravinsky had done, an émigré in the West? 'To be Russian was, in itself, no longer chic' (Rita McAllister), and his musical career was stagnant, at least in the sense that his style was no longer considered trend-setting.

Seroff, in his biography of the composer, describes a conversation with Prokofiev in 1932 which implies that his mind was already made up. The French critic Serge Moreux reports Prokofiev as saying in 1933:

The air of foreign lands does not inspire me because I am Russian and there is nothing more harmful to me than to live in exile . . . I must again immerse myself in the atmosphere of my homeland . . . I must hear Russian speech, and talk with the people dear to me. This will give me what I lack here, for their songs are my songs . . . I'm afraid of falling into academicism. Yes, my friend, I am going home.

Other sources disagree. Prokofiev may well have been undecided about his future in these years, just as he had been in 1918-22.

Inevitably, Nestyev plays up the evidence of a creative crisis. And there is at least some suggestion of a growing dichotomy in his work. Such basically disparate offerings as the *American Overture*, the Fifth Piano Concerto and the piano pieces opp. 45, 54 and 62 seem to follow on from the Second Symphony and the Quintet in their pursuit of a rationalised European style. Other works, like *The Prodigal Son* and the String Quartet, sound more distinctively 'Russian'.

On a personal level, Prokofiev was homesick. He had his family – a second son, Oleg, was born in 1928 – but his closest friends remained in the USSR and he missed their advice and support. Even now, the political dimensions seemed unimportant. It was Russia that beckoned him, not the Soviet régime nor Marxism. Nicolas Nabokov explains:

Prokofiev accepted the Russian Revolution in its 'totality' and saw in the new Russia the logical consequence of the old one, the result of a century-long process of emancipation. He was . . . a sincere and *instinctive* Russian patriot, . . . a person whose political thinking never developed and who, not unlike many American artists, believed that his main job was to do his own work and leave political matters and entanglements to others. At the same time he felt very strongly his profound association, or rather his organic tie, with Russia, with the Russian people and Russian culture. Despite his long years abroad and his position as a famous composer in the Western world, he remained essentially Russian, in his habits, his behaviour, and his art.

When the early plans of the Soviet government concerning the future of Soviet music became known, . . . Prokofiev welcomed the official edict as a realisation of some of his own ideas about the function of music. 'I always wanted to invent melodies,' he often remarked, 'which could be understood by large masses of people – simple, singable melodies.' This he considered to be the most important and difficult task of the modern composer.

Or, as Prokofiev confided to Vernon Duke after the decision was made:

Here is how I feel about it: I care nothing for politics – I'm a composer first and last. Any government that lets me write my music in peace, publishes everything I compose before the ink is dry, and performs every note that comes from my pen is all right with me. In Europe we all have to fish for performances, cajole conductors and theatre directors; in Russia they come to *me* – I can hardly keep up with the demand. What's more, I have a comfortable flat in Moscow, a delightful *dacha* in the country and a brand-new car. My boys go to a fine English school in Moscow . . .

The process of return was a gradual one. Not until spring 1936

Two stills from *Lieutenant Kijé*, Alexander Feinzimmer's film of 1934.

(1) N. Chaternikova as Countess Gagarine, with Sophie Magarill as her Lady-in-Waiting (National Film Archive)

was Prokofiev permanently resident in Moscow. Until then, his 'home' was still Paris. His family lived there, all his belongings were there and most of the music he wrote between 1932 and 1936 was composed there. What changed first were the sources of the Prokofiev commissions. Before long, his large-scale pieces were being written to Soviet order.

Some Prokofiev thoughts on the future of Soviet music were contained in an article published in the 16 November 1934 issue of *Izvestia*:

The question of what kind of music should be written at the present time is one that interests many Soviet composers today. I have thought a good deal about this during the past two years and I believe that the following is the correct solution. What we need is great music, i.e., music that will be in keeping both in conception and technical execution with the grandeur of the epoch. Such music would be a stimulus to our own musical development; and abroad too it would reveal our true selves. The danger of becoming provincial is unfortunately a very real one for modern Soviet composers. It is not so easy to find the right idiom for this music. To begin with, it must be melodious, moreover, the melody must be simple and comprehensible, without being repetitive or trivial. Many

134

(2) Mikhail Yarshin as
Tsar Paul I
(National Film Archive)

composers have difficulty in composing any sort of melody; all the harder
is it to compose a melody that has a definite function. The same applies to
the technique and the idiom: it must be clear and simple, but not banal.
We must seek a new simplicity.

At the same time, Prokofiev in 1934 was still dividing his work
into two distinct categories of music: one for 'connoisseurs' and
another for average listeners; on the one hand, 'great music',
capable of 'posing problems even to leading musicians', and on the
other, 'serious light music', comprehensible to the masses coming
into contact with art for the first time.

Falling naturally into this second division, the music for
Lieutenant Kijé occupies a special place in Prokofiev's output. It is
his first Soviet commission and the first time he had worked for the
cinema. As 'a fable on the generative power of language',
Lieutenant Kijé the film has been seen as 'a remarkable working
model of Formalist literary theory'. Needless to say, what
attracted Prokofiev to the project was the gently satirical humour
of Yuri Tynyanov's original story. Its mainspring is well known:
the inadvertent transformation of an ink blot into an officer, one
Lieutenant Kijé.

135

Heine Heckroth: designs for Fokine's *Lieutenant Kijé* ballet of 1942

(1) Six backcloth designs for light projections
(Sotheby & Co)

Kijé may owe his birth to a clerical error, but the eccentric Tsar Paul I assumes that he does indeed exist and demands to know all about him. Since the Tsar cannot be wrong, the resourceful military must invent a life for their officer. Thus Kijé starts his career by being sent into exile in Siberia. Later, as he rises through the ranks and is married, his bride punningly explains to the wedding guests that Kijé has no 'presence', to account for his invisibility during the ceremony. At length, the elusive hero is killed off. Alexander Feinzimmer's film looks less creaky than one might expect, a stylised comedy with Prokofiev's evocative music closely integrated into its structure.

By 8 July 1934, Prokofiev had worked the fragmentary vignettes of his film score into a 'delightfully frivolous' (Rita McAllister) five-movement suite. One of his most popular compositions today*, it is also one of the most accomplished.

Ravel liked to distinguish between instrumentation and orchestration, the one being simply the craft of spreading the notes so that the result sounds acceptable, the other involving that subtle alchemy by which two or more sounds fuse to become something quite new. In *Lieutenant Kijé*, Prokofiev displays an acute awareness of the expressive potential of orchestration. The

*though rarely heard in its alternative version with baritone soloist.

136

(2) Two costume designs
(Sotheby & Co)

Kijé combination of pawky humour and sentimental, distinctly Russian nostalgia could scarcely fail with melodies like these. But the piquant colours certainly help. Bells, percussion, piano and harp propel the famous *Troika*, with cornet, piccolo, tenor saxophone and tuba animating other key passages. The sound remains transparent throughout. '*Kijé* is a devilish job,' Prokofiev remarked in a letter to friends, 'but what gay music!'

Less inspiring music in a vaguely similar vein was the orchestral suite *Egyptian Nights*, op. 61. Prokofiev pieced this together in the summer of 1934 using incidental music commissioned by Moscow's Kamerny Theatre. A. Y. Tairov's dramatic extravaganza, with a text drawn from Pushkin's *Egyptian Nights*, Shakespeare's *Antony and Cleopatra* and Shaw's *Caesar and Cleopatra*, opened in April 1935. The run was short.

In the nature of a summing up of his Paris period, Prokofiev also composed a number of more exploratory works in 1933-34. These included the piano cycle *Thoughts*, op. 62, the *Symphonic Song*, op. 57 and sketches for the Cello Concerto, op. 58, commissioned by the distinguished émigré cellist Gregor Piatigorsky. Feigning ignorance of the cello literature, Prokofiev was shown some of the outstanding works of the repertoire. 'You should not keep this stuff in the house. It smells!' he told Piatigorsky, but completed his own score in 1938. In fact, the Cello Concerto is rarely heard today; Prokofiev reconstructed it as an 'appreciably "healthier"' *Sinfonia Concertante* in 1950-2. (For some years he refused to change a note, railing at Nestyev in 1941: 'Be more careful with the Cello Concerto: it is very close to the Second Violin Concerto. The indifference to it is mere stupidity.')

The première of the *Symphonic Song* in Moscow on 14 April 1934, was a notable disaster. According to Miaskovsky: 'There were literally three claps in the hall.' Soviet audiences would never accept such gloomy abstractions, warned the journal *Sovetskaya Muzyka*:

Prokofiev's *Symphonic Song* does not sing; it is not a song at all in our sense of the word . . . We regard it as a symphonic monologue for the few, a sad tale of the decline of the fading culture of individualism.

Prokofiev's 'Westernised' outlook would have to change.

Later in the year, there was talk of the Kirov Theatre staging a new, full-length Prokofiev ballet. With recent failures in mind, the composer cast about for a relatively 'safe', lyrical subject:

Shakespeare's *Romeo and Juliet* was suggested. But the Kirov Theatre backed out and I signed a contract with the Moscow Bolshoi Theatre instead. In the spring of 1935 Radlov and I worked out a scenario, consulting with the choreographer on questions of ballet technique. The music was written in the course of the summer, but the Bolshoi Theatre declared it impossible to dance to and the contract was broken.

There was quite a fuss at the time about our attempts to give *Romeo and Juliet* a happy ending – in the last act Romeo arrives a minute earlier, finds Juliet alive and everything ends well. The reasons for this bit of barbarism were purely choreographic: living people can dance, the dying cannot. The justification was that Shakespeare himself was said to have been uncertain about the endings of his plays (*King Lear*) and parallel with *Romeo and Juliet* had written *Two Gentlemen of Verona* in which all ends well. Curiously enough, whereas the report that Prokofiev was writing a ballet on the theme of *Romeo and Juliet* with a happy ending was received quite calmly in London, our own Shakespeare scholars proved more papal than the pope and rushed to the defence of Shakespeare. But what really caused me to change my mind about the whole thing was a remark someone made to me about the ballet: 'Strictly speaking, your music does not express any real joy at the end.' That was quite true. After several conferences with the choreographers, it was found that the tragic ending could be expressed in the dance and in due time the music for that ending was written.

Prokofiev carried out large-scale revisions to his 'undanceable' music in the months that followed, but it was to be some years before *Romeo and Juliet* was seen in Russia. (The first two orchestral suites and the ten piano pieces arranged from it were received favourably in 1936 and 1937.)

A more immediate success was the Second Violin Concerto, op. 63 – a work similar in idiom, finished at about the same time as the ballet:

In 1935, a group of admirers of the French violinist Soëtans asked me to write a violin concerto for him, giving him exclusive rights to perform it

Asociación de Cultura Musical

MADRID

AÑO 15   1935·1936   Concierto 3

SERGE
PROKOFIEFF
PIANISTA

ROBERT
SOETENS
VIOLINISTA

Lunes 18 de Noviembre de 1935

for one year. I readily agreed since I had been intending to write something for the violin at that time and had accumulated some material. As in the case of the preceding concertos, I began by searching for an original title for the piece, such as 'concert sonata for violin and orchestra', but finally returned to the simplest solution: Concerto No. 2. Nevertheless, I wanted it to be altogether different from No. 1 both as to music and style.

. . . The variety of places in which that concerto was written is a reflection of the nomadic concert-tour existence I led at that time: the principal theme of the first movement was written in Paris, the first theme of the second movement in Voronezh, the orchestration I completed in Baku, while the first performance was given in Madrid, in December 1935. This was part of an extremely interesting concert tour which I made together with Soëtans through Spain, Portugal, Morocco, Algeria and Tunisia. Besides my own compositions, we played Debussy and Beethoven sonatas.

Despite Prokofiev's desire to compose something 'altogether different from No. 1', his Violin Concerto No. 2 clearly belongs in the same 'line' as the work written 18 years before. There is the same generous lyricism, the same unforced variety of mood, the same exquisite balance maintained between violin and orchestra. The formal plan, while perfectly assured, might seem a shade earthbound by comparison. But then, for all its fine pointing, the Second is a more comfortable work than its predecessor. Whether or not the sombre opening evokes Nestyev's 'image of the snow-covered plains of Russia', the seductive, insinuating second theme is undoubtedly 'one of the mature Prokofiev's most felicitous melodic revelations'. This idea bears a close resemblance to some of the love music in *Romeo and Juliet*. The radiant, *arioso*-like *Andante assai*, more sustainedly tranquil than the younger Prokofiev would have allowed, is balanced by a spiky finale, 'Prokofiev's version of the peasant rondo familiar from a number of the best-known violin concertos of the nineteenth century' (Hugh Ottaway).

Soviet commentators were impressed:

It was significant that he should return, after so many years, to writing for the solo violin. Seemingly convinced of the utter futility of formalist experimentation, he renewed his youthful striving to express genuine human emotions, choosing for this effort one of the most singing of all musical instruments.

(Israel Nestyev)

With *Romeo and Juliet* still under wraps, the 'romantic' new Concerto could be taken to mark an appropriate *volte-face* in Prokofiev's creative life, the return of the prodigal.

Chapter 8

Hail to Stalin

On 15 May 1936, with the arrival of his wife and family in Moscow, the transition was complete. For the time being at least, Prokofiev was satisfied with the new arrangement.

The last twenty years of his life, spent 'at home', were not cloudless: there were failures, brutal disappointments, and unjustified criticism. But there were also warm response, sincere admiration, and that intangible flow of inspiration filtered through people and landscape, language and tradition. Here, his music acquired a quality of lyric expansiveness, of deepened humanism that created a new bond of communication with his audiences. (Boris Schwarz)

Ilya Ehrenburg tells us how Prokofiev was overwhelmingly saddened by the dreadful years of political persecution, but his attitude was always the same: 'Today one must work. Work's the only thing, the only salvation.'

Prokofiev's return was considered a milestone in the development of Soviet music. It could scarcely have been otherwise. Following the dissolution of RAPM and the subsequent establishment of the Union of Soviet Composers, the administration of musical life was effectively controlled by central government. Composers were officially encouraged to look to the folk traditions of the past, to pay heed to the social content of their music and its appeal to the general populace. And here was Prokofiev 'the Westerniser' apparently choosing to throw in his lot with the new directives. He was not alone in failing to grasp their significance.

The new slogan for the arts was 'Socialist Realism', a term allegedly coined by Stalin himself at a meeting of writers in Maxim Gorky's flat in October 1932:

If the artist is going to depict our life correctly, he cannot fail to observe and point out what is leading it towards socialism. So this will be socialist art. It will be socialist realism.

What could this exclusively literary dogma mean for the Soviet musician? During their last talk in Moscow, Prokofiev asked Gorky what sort of music one should write now:

'You ought to know that yourself,' he replied with a smile. I said, 'Everyone says that music ought to be vigorous and optimistic to match the spirit of the new life.' 'Yes,' he added, 'but it must be warm and tender too.'

And so Prokofiev stumbled into the third revolution, a cultural revolution of isolationism and chauvinism, as decisive in its way as the first Bolshevik revolution of 1917, and the second, collectivisation revolution of 1928. This too had its (tenuous) links with Marx.

Like many of their contemporaries, Marx and Engels had a distinct bias in favour of 'realistic' art, although their emphasis upon the social relevance of literature did not amount to an advocacy of explicit messages. They recognised that an imaginative grip on life in all its contradictions and an ability to present credible and individualised characters will always be more important than abstract rhetoric, noble sentiment and well-intentioned preachiness. An artist's intuition will always transcend his politics. Shakespeare is unmistakably a greater writer than Schiller. Marx dismissed the idea that the art of a decadent epoch must also be decadent, pointing out that when people speak of ideas that revolutionise society they should be aware of the fact that within their 'old' society elements of a new one are constantly being created.

'Socialist Realism' was put forward as a 'refinement' of this 'realistic' art. The great nineteenth-century novelists, it was argued, were 'critical' realists who, whatever their conscious ideology, could not help but reveal in their works the vices of contemporary society. However, as bourgeois artists, they were in no position to escape from their milieu and were drawn inescapably toward fatalism and despair. For the Soviet artist, the impasse had been overcome. Socialism offered the positive way forward, with 'Socialist Realism' the *progressive* art of a *progressive* society.

Inevitably in an era of transition there was going to be tension between 'Realism' and its 'Socialist' modifier: the former calls for the portrayal of life as it really is, while the latter points toward life as it ought to be. But then Soviet art has never been content with a mere reflection of reality. It must be instrumental in ideological remoulding. It must display *partiinost, klassovost* and *narodnost* (loosely: party spirit, class consciousness and 'peopleness').

To justify this cultural strategy, the Stalin régime drew

selectively from the Lenin legacy. The principle of *narodnost* derives from Lenin's apparent exhortation to the educated upper stratum to sacrifice its personal artistic preferences upon the altar of revolutionary priority:

Should we serve exquisite sweet cake to a small minority while the worker and peasant masses are in need of black bread?

Never mind that Lenin anticipated a levelling up, through the development of a mass cultural consciousness, rather than any levelling down of cultural standards. He had been insistent on this; the masses were not to be fobbed off with 'spectacles' and 'circuses' or the so-called 'proletarian culture':

For art to get closer to the people and the people to art we must start by raising general educational and cultural standards . . . [The people] are entitled to real, great art. That is why we put foremost public education . . . on the biggest scale.

Stalin's unremitting animosity to formal experimentation may also be traced to Lenin. But Lenin called himself a 'barbarian' and joked of his incomprehension of modern trends, making it clear that on this matter at least his opinions were not to be taken as authoritative directives:

We won't be able to keep pace with the new art; we'll just have to come trailing behind.

As Lunacharsky recalled in 1933:

. . . since dilettantism had always been hateful to him and alien to his nature he did not like to make any statements on art . . . I repeat, Vladimir Ilich never made guiding principles out of his aesthetical likes and dislikes.

Whatever its exact origins, 'Socialist Realism' would not easily translate into musical terminology. The Composers' Union contributed the following guidelines in 1933. As Boris Schwarz has remarked, they 'make up in belligerence what they lack in clarity':

The main attention of the Soviet composer must be directed towards the victorious progressive principles of reality, towards all that is heroic, bright and beautiful. This distinguishes the spiritual world of Soviet man and must be embodied in musical images full of beauty and strength. Socialist Realism demands an implacable struggle against folk-negating modernistic directions that are typical of the decay of contemporary

143

bourgeois art, against subservience and servility towards modern bourgeois culture.

Ideally in this new world, the musician was supposed to look at contemporary problems from the perspective of a Utopian future, portraying today's defects as positive forces which actually serve to push society toward the ultimate goal of socialism.

That it is impossible to give a programmatic explanation of every symphonic composition, to describe musical 'meaning' in terms of concrete, verbal imagery was reluctantly accepted. And yet Soviet aestheticians, trying to find how close is a musical work to the precepts of approved doctrine, have felt obliged to regard verbal and musical forms of expression as closely linked. The methodological gap was filled by one of Prokofiev's closest friends from his Conservatoire days, the musicologist Boris Asafiev.

Basing his ideas on Marxist-Leninist dialectics, Asafiev developed a theory of musical 'intonanzias' or intonations. In *Intonanzia*, his key work of 1947, he likened musical expression as a manifestation of thought to the intoning of the human voice in speech. Just as the rise and fall of vocal pitch reveals hidden nuances of emotion, so music must express its true 'meaning' through associative intonations.

These musical intonations may act as carriers of meaning on a variety of levels. In their simplest form, they constitute a transmutation of some common experience of life into musical phraseology. Hence certain decisive musical gestures are often said to resemble martial bugle calls. But it is only by retaining some deeper, essential quality of the original sound-source that the composer is able to touch the hearts and minds of men; in this way, the use of stylised fanfares can give rise to the more general 'musical imagery' of heroism and patriotism.

Today's Soviet musicologists would maintain that the semantics of musical expression are far more than merely illustrative, but operate at the most profound level of human and social consciousness. Each historical epoch has its own norms and habits on the basis of which any new composition will be judged. These must stem from an 'intonational dictionary' in which life experiences and aspirations are inseparably linked with musical expressions and idioms. In the early 1930s, the slogans were still rudimentary and the issues may well have seemed academic to Prokofiev. It was not until he had made his decision and begun committing himself and his family to a more genuinely Russian life that the régime made its requirements known in unmistakable, practical terms.

In January 1936, Stalin attended a performance of Shostakovich's *Lady Macbeth of Mtsensk* – an opera already two

144

СУМБУР ВМЕСТО МУЗЫКИ

Об опере «Леди Макбет Мценского уезда»

Вместе с общим культурным ростом в нашей стране выросла и потребность в хорошей музыке. Никогда и нигде композиторы не имели перед собой такой благодарной аудитории. Народные массы ждут хороших песен, но также и хороших инструментальных произведений, хороших опер.

Некоторые театры как новинку, как достижение преподносят новой, выросшей культурно советской публике оперу Шостаковича «Леди Макбет Мценского уезда». Услужливая музыкальная критика превозносит до небес оперу, создает ей громкую славу. Молодой композитор вместо деловой и серьезной критики, которая могла бы помочь ему в дальнейшей работе, выслушивает только восторженные комплименты.

Слушателя с первой же минуты ошарашивает в опере нарочито нестройный, сумбурный поток звуков. Обрывки мелодии, зачатки музыкальной фразы тонут, вырываются, снова исчезают в грохоте, скрежете и визге. Следить за этой «музыкой» трудно, запомнить ее невозможно.

Так в течение почти всей оперы. На сцене пение заменено криком. Если композитору случается попасть на дорожку простой и понятной мелодии, то он немедленно, словно испугавшись такой беды, бросается в дебри музыкального сумбура, местами превращающегося в какофонию. Выразительность, которой требует слушатель, заменена бешеным ритмом. Музыкальный шум должен выразить страсть.

Это все не от бездарности композитора, не от его неумения в музыке выразить простые и сильные чувства. Это музыка, умышленно сделанная «шиворот навыворот», — так, чтобы ничего не напоминало классическую оперную музыку, ничего не было общего с симфоническим звучаниями, с простой, общедоступной музыкальной речью. Это музыка, которая построена по тому же принципу отрицания оперы, по какому левацкое искусство вообще отрицает в театре простоту, реализм, понятность образа, естественное звучание слова. Это — перенесение в оперу, в музыку наиболее отрицательных черт «мейерхольдовщины» в умноженном виде. Это левацкий сумбур вместо естественной, человеческой музыки. Способность хорошей музыки захватывать массы приносится в жертву мелкобуржуазным формалистическим потугам, претензиям создать оригинальность приемами дешевого оригинальничанья. Эта игра в заумные вещи, которая может кончиться очень плохо.

Опасность такого направления в советской музыке ясна. Левацкое уродство в опере растет из того же источника, что и левацкое уродство в живописи, в поэзии, в педагогике, в науке. Мелкобуржуазное «новаторство» ведет к отрыву от подлинного искусства, от подлинной науки, от подлинной литературы.

Автору «Леди Макбет Мценского уезда» пришлось заимствовать у джаза его нервозную, судорожную, припадочную музыку, чтобы придать «страсть» своим героям.

В то время как наша критика — в том числе и музыкальная — клянется именем социалистического реализма, сцена преподносит нам в творении Шостаковича грубейший натурализм. Однотонно, в зверином обличии представлены все — и купцы и народ. Хищница-купчиха, дорвавшаяся путем убийств к богатству и власти, представлена в виде какой-то «жертвы» буржуазного общества. Бытовой повести Лескова навязан смысл, какого в ней нет.

И все это грубо, примитивно, вульгарно. Музыка крякает, ухает, пыхтит, задыхается, чтобы как можно натуральнее изобразить любовные сцены. И «любовь» размазана во всей опере в самой вульгарной форме. Купеческая двуспальная кровать занимает центральное место в оформлении. На ней разрешаются все «проблемы». В таком же грубо-натуралистическом стиле показана смерть от отравления, сечение почти на самой сцене.

Композитор, видимо, не поставил перед собой задачи прислушаться к тому, чего ждет, чего ищет в музыке советская аудитория. Он словно-нарочно зашифровал свою музыку, перепутал все звучания в ней так, чтобы дошла его музыка только до потерявших здоровый вкус эстетов-формалистов. Он прошел мимо требований советской культуры изгнать грубость и дикость из всех углов советского быта. Это воспевание купеческой похотливости некоторые критики называют сатирой. Ни о какой сатире здесь и речи не может быть. Всеми средствами и музыкальной и драматической выразительности автор старается привлечь симпатии публики к грубым и вульгарным стремлениям и поступкам купчихи Катерины Измайловой.

«Леди Макбет» имеет успех у буржуазной публики за границей. Не потому ли похваливает ее буржуазная публика, что опера эта сумбурна и абсолютно аполитична? Не потому ли, что она щекочет извращенные вкусы буржуазной аудитории своей дергающейся, крикливой, неврастенической музыкой?

Наши театры приложили немало труда, чтобы тщательно поставить оперу Шостаковича. Актеры обнаружили значительный талант в преодолении шума, крика и скрежета оркестра. Драматической игрой они старались возместить мелодийное убожество оперы. К сожалению, от этого еще ярче выступали ее грубо-натуралистические черты. Талантливая игра заслуживает признательности, затраченные усилия — сожаления.

---

years in the repertoire. When Soviet musicians opened their copies of *Pravda* on the morning of 28 January, there, in the left hand corner on page 3, was a three column denunciation of the opera entitled 'Chaos Instead of Music'. Its author may have been Andrei Zhdanov, Leningrad's new Party boss and Stalin's spokesman on cultural policy in the Central Committee. Shostakovich is said to have detected the hand of the 'leader and teacher' himself:

From the first moment, the listener is shocked by a deliberately dissonant, confused stream of sound. Fragments of melody, embryonic phrases appear – only to disappear again in the din, the grinding, and the screaming . . . This music is built on the basis of rejecting opera . . . which carries into the theatre and the music the most negative features of 'Meyerholdism' infinitely multiplied. Here we have 'leftist' confusion instead of natural, human music . . . The danger of this trend to Soviet music is clear. Leftist distortion in opera stems from the same source as the leftist distortion in painting, poetry, teaching, and science. Petty-bourgeois innovations lead to a break with real art, real science, and real literature . . . All this is coarse, primitive, and vulgar. The music quacks, grunts, and growls, and suffocates itself, in order to express the amatory scenes as naturalistically as possible. And 'love' is smeared all over the opera in the most vulgar manner. The merchant's double bed occupies the central position on the stage. On it all 'problems' are solved . . .

The apparent correctness of its ideological stance in exposing the shallowness of petty-bourgeois morality was not enough to save *Lady Macbeth*. The message was clear. The forms of Russian life may now have been socialist, but the content of the 'new' culture was to be retrogressive, puritanical and nationalistic. 'Socialist Realism': the aesthetic was vague, and now its very vagueness humiliated the artist, encouraging the debilitating phenomenon of anticipatory self-censorship. To avoid controversy, it was best to maintain a steady flow of melody, risking few, if any, departures from a basically nineteenth-century harmonic scheme. Safest to adhere to an unadventurous, old-fashioned idiom, especially when writing not an accompaniment to an ideologically vetted text but a purely instrumental piece. Inevitably a mood of forced optimism tended to prevail.

Shostakovich's predicament was acute, Prokofiev's less so. The two composers had much in common, although, it now appears, they were never close. Official Soviet pronouncements on the matter must be taken with a grain of salt, the more so since the publication in the West of Solomon Volkov's controversial memoir. For the Shostakovich of *Testimony*, Prokofiev was not 'the inspiring example' of Soviet lore but 'a chicken in the soup' with 'the personality of a spoiled *Wunderkind*'. There was friction:

Prokofiev and I never did become friends, probably because Prokofiev was not inclined towards friendly relations in general. He was a hard man and didn't seem interested in anything other than himself and his music. I hate being patted on the head. Prokofiev didn't like it either, but he allowed himself to be quite condescending to others . . . He had two favourite words. One was 'amusing' which he used to evaluate everything around him. Everything – people, events, music. He seemed to feel that 'amusing' covered *Wozzeck*. The second was 'Understood?' That's when he wanted to know whether he was making himself clear. These two favourite words irritated me . . .

Prokofiev and I could never have had a frank talk, but I feel that I know him, and I can imagine very well why that European man preferred to return to Russia. Prokofiev was an inveterate gambler and, in the long run, he always won. Prokofiev thought that he had calculated perfectly and that he would be a winner this time too. For some fifteen years Prokofiev sat between two stools – in the West he was considered a Soviet and in Russia they welcomed him as a Western guest.

But then the situation changed and the bureaucrats in charge of cultural affairs started squinting at Prokofiev, thinking 'Who is this Parisian fellow?' And Prokofiev considered that it would be more profitable for him to move to the USSR. Such a step would only raise his stock in the West, because things Soviet were becoming fashionable just then, they would stop considering him a foreigner in the USSR, and therefore he would win all around.

By the way, the final impetus came from his card playing. Prokofiev was deeply in debt abroad and he had to straighten out his financial affairs quickly, which he hoped to do in the USSR. And this was where Prokofiev landed like a chicken in soup. He came to Moscow to teach, and they started teaching him. Along with everyone else he had to memorise the historic article in *Pravda*, 'Muddle [Chaos] Instead of Music'. He did look through the score of my *Lady Macbeth*, however. He said, 'Amusing.'

The mature Shostakovich was not unmoved by Prokofiev's fate, recognising that he too was forced to 'swallow many humiliations'. But he was indifferent to his compositions and what he termed their 'superficial random effects'. In his own work the influence of Mahler had pushed Prokofiev into the background long ago.

Though relatively unaffected by the campaign against musical 'formalism' thanks to his unique position in musical life, Prokofiev himself was well aware of the dilemma: 'Formalism is sometimes the name given here to that which is not understood on first hearing,' he quipped. Willing to learn but equally willing to criticise, he had always been cool to a certain stale Russian traditionalism whose personification he saw in Glazunov. Now, with the disappearance from concert programmes of progressive music from the West, he continued to resist the descent into provincialism:

In . . . music . . . I have striven for clarity and melodiousness. But at the same time I have not tried to get by with hackneyed melodies and harmonies. This is what makes it so difficult to compose clear music – the clarity must be new not old.

There survives a manuscript synopsis (written in Prokofiev's familiar abbreviated form without vowels) of a speech to activists of the Composers' Union, Moscow (9 April 1937). Here, at the height of the Yezhov purges – 'the wild and indiscriminate mowing down of individuals and groups, later of whole peoples' – Prokofiev continues to outline a frank aesthetic programme. Insulated by his own very personal lagging of arrogance and naïvety, he condemns 'uncultured comrades' for their false interpretation of 'formalism', disdain of real skill and willingness to pander to under-developed tastes:

We are striving ahead in all spheres of the Soviet economy . . . Why then do our comrade musicians imagine that they alone can feed on yesterday's bread and rotten beef?

All the same, Prokofiev turned his attention to musical miniatures and incidental music in the wake of the *Lady Macbeth* affair. Having failed to secure a production of *Romeo and Juliet*, he played safe by releasing a series of short, deliberately approachable works, many of them designed for children. These included the twelve easy piano pieces of *Music for Children*, op. 65 (seven of them orchestrated in the 1940s to form the symphonic suite *A Summer's Day*), two of the *Three Children's Songs*, op. 68, and, of course, *Peter and the Wolf*.

Peter and the Wolf is one of those Prokofiev works which is so

Peter and the Wolf: three designs for curtains executed by Nicolai Benois for the production at La Scala, Milan in 1949 (Sotheby & Co)

familiar that one tends to overlook the Prokofiev hallmarks. In his autobiographical notes, he devotes little space to it. He writes:

There was a big demand for children's music and in the spring of 1936 I started a symphonic tale for children entitled *Peter and the Wolf*, op. 67, to a text of my own. Every character has its own motif played each time by the same instrument: the duck was played by the oboe, the grandfather by the bassoon, etc. Before each performance the instruments were shown to the children and the themes played for them; during the performance the children heard these themes repeated several times and learned to recognise the timbres of the different instruments. In this lay the educational purpose of the fairy-tale. The text was read during the pauses in the music which was disproportionately longer than the text – for me the story was important only as a means of inducing the children to listen to the music. I composed the music quickly, approximately within one week, and another week was spent on the orchestration.

Peter and the Wolf came to the concert stage from the Central Children's Theatre. Natalia Satz takes up the story:

I've been thinking for a long time that new symphonies ought to be written for children. I wanted to start cultivating musical tastes in children from the first years of school, a love for and an understanding of music . . . I decided to get Prokofiev interested in this idea, and to see him as the author of the first such symphonic fairy-tale. I rang him up and asked if I could come over to talk about a most important matter. He heard me out very attentively, and then said: 'I like the concreteness with which you set forth your ideas.' Evidently, I did get him interested . . . He called me up a few days later and said that he should like to see me as

he had some thoughts to share about a symphony for children. He came to my place, and we sat talking till late, until the last tram, making up all sorts of plots – he with the help of music, and I with words. We came to the conclusion that images had to be found that would be easily associated with the sound of different instruments. The first one which occurred to me was the flute – a little bird. I said so and immediately regretted it, fearing Sergey Sergeyevich's reaction to the banality of my suggestion. But what he said was:

'A flute-bird we'll certainly have. It's quite all right for us to use the children's primitive concepts as well. The most important thing is for us to find a common language with them.'

We decided that in a symphonic fairy-tale for the youngest listeners the images should be striking and utterly unlike one another in character.

'I think it's a good idea to have different animals and birds playing a part in the symphony, but there definitely must be at least one human being,' I said.

Sergey Sergeyevich nodded in agreement, and said: 'If we cast one instrument for the "role" of each animal or bird, we'll have to have something like a string quartet to play the human being because, of course, there'll be more facets to his character.' Carried away, he continued: 'Yes, yes, we've got to begin with concrete, impressive and, above all else, contrasting images. A wolf – a bird, good – evil, big – small. Striking characters, pronounced and different musical timbres, and every character with a leitmotif of his own.'

We wanted the plot to be thrilling and packed with events, otherwise children would not be able to concentrate and sit still for even the twenty or twenty-five minutes into which we meant to fit the whole fairy-tale.

Four days later, Prokofiev brought the piano score of *Peter and the Wolf*. There was a gathering of children in the room next door, and I asked Sergey Sergeyevich to come there and play his newly-born composition. The children listened to it with unflagging attention. And at their request he had to play the concluding march three times.

Boris Asafiev was among those grown-ups who found it politic to speak with exaggerated enthusiasm about this 'modest' work:

. . . And you ask yourself, do we not have here the elements of a new Soviet symphonic style free from both intellectual self-analysis and a tragic view of reality?

According to the composer, the first performance, at a Moscow Philharmonic matinée concert on 2 May 1936, 'was rather poor and failed to attract much attention'. More recently, the piece has enjoyed universal popularity – and not solely among children. It is a work which seems blessed with eternal youth.

Less marketable than this was the 'adult' *Russian Overture*, op. 72, the last of Prokofiev's three concert overtures. As if to compensate for the chamber character of previous entries, this rumbustious showpiece was scored for large orchestra: piccolo and three flutes, three oboes and cor anglais, three clarinets and bass clarinet, three bassoons and double bassoon, eight horns, four trumpets, three trombones and tuba, timpani, bass drum, snare drum, tambourine, cymbals, triangle, castanets, tam-tam, xylophone, glockenspiel, two harps, piano and strings. Although Prokofiev thinned down these requirements in his revised version of 1937, the work remained something of a rarity. Nestyev finds most of it gratuitously garish and the rest of it a shade anaemic. Undeniably episodic, the *Overture* none the less builds to a tumultuous climax, dashing recklessly from theme to theme – some original, others 'direct quotations from folk music' according to Nestyev. The exuberance is infectious, the neglect unaccountable.

In 1936, preparations began for two major jubilees – the 20th anniversary of the Revolution and the centenary of the death of Pushkin. For the latter occasion, Prokofiev undertook to provide incidental music for stage adaptations of *Eugene Onegin* and *Boris Godunov* and a film version of *The Queen of Spades*. All three had famous operatic settings, and Prokofiev wrote of his determination to communicate something of 'the true spirit of Pushkin' to contemporary audiences:

. . . But none of my Pushkin pieces was ever produced. The music lay for a long time on the shelf and was gradually incorporated in other compositions. Only three songs of mine (op. 73) were performed during the Pushkin centenary, my only concrete contribution to the occasion.

Eugene Onegin was eventually given a first performance in 1980! And it was not until 1984 that UK listeners were able to sample Prokofiev's music for *Boris Godunov* (in the context of a performance of Pushkin's historical drama broadcast on BBC Radio 3 on 8 March).

The Cantata for the Twentieth Anniversary of the October Revolution was equally unlucky, though, as a sincere attempt to approach the moving target of 'Socialist Realism', it was perhaps bound to fail. Unlike some later Prokofiev *pièces d'occasion*, the *Cantata* is in no sense a hack job carried out at the behest of political masters. Prokofiev began work on the score in Paris and his response to texts by Marx, Lenin and Stalin is unexpectedly passionate. No pious platitudes here. The sixth movement, *Revolution*, is particularly gripping; its choirs sound off in alternation, exchanging snatches of Lenin's text faster and faster until the music erupts into an astonishing series of effects – a superimposed accordion band, a spoken announcement over loudspeakers, fire alarms ringing, sirens wailing. This is not 'safe' music: hence its failure to receive a single performance in Prokofiev's lifetime. Found guilty of 'vulgar leftist tendencies' (Nestyev), it could be put down as a dry run for *Alexander Nevsky* and forgotten. Then, in 1966, came rehabilitation. And, in 1967, a gramophone recording – understandably shorn of movements eight and ten, *Stalin's Vow* and (*Stalin's*) *Constitution*. Back-pedalling furiously, Nestyev acclaimed the work as a unique masterpiece.

Prokofiev undertook his last major concert tours in the late 1930s. In December 1936, he was in Western Europe and the United States; in the early part of 1938 he visited Czechoslovakia, France, England and the United States. On the West Coast, he spent much of his time in Hollywood film studios, making a careful study of film music techniques with the thought of applying them to his work in Soviet films:

The cinema is a young and very modern art that offers new and fascinating possibilities to the composer. These possibilities must be utilised. Composers ought to study and develop them, instead of merely writing the music and then leaving it to the mercy of the film people.

Soon after his return to Russia, he was given the chance to try out these ideas when Sergey Eisenstein asked him to work on the score of the film *Alexander Nevsky*. The two men had met many times in the past, but few could have predicted the total success of their collaboration: two artists of genius synchronising their talents so perfectly that a single mind might have been at work.

From their first meeting, Prokofiev and Eisenstein needed few words to understand each other:

The action of the film takes place in the thirteenth century and is built up on two opposing elements: the Russians on the one hand, and the Teutonic knights on the other. The temptation to make use of the actual music of the period was naturally great. But a brief acquaintance with Catholic thirteenth-century choral singing was enough to show that this music has in the past seven centuries become far too remote and emotionally alien to us to be able to stimulate the imagination of the present-day film spectator. We therefore decided not to reproduce it as it sounded at the time of the Battle on the Ice seven centuries ago but to adapt it to the modern ear. The same applies to the Russian music of the period; that too had to be given a modern ring.

Having agreed on the overall character of the music, composer and director turned to the pivotal episode of the film, the 'Battle on the Ice'. On the basis of Eisenstein's sketches and his emotional and structural ideas for the sequence, Prokofiev produced a brilliant 'tone poem' in a matter of days. This was then recorded as

152

a basis for the filming. The emotive force of the next scene, in which a Russian girl walks alone amongst bloodied corpses in search of the body of her lover, was also immeasurably enhanced by its musical setting – an aria of chilling beauty.

Neither collaborator was keen to set the rhythm of a scene at the expense of the other. Eisenstein recalls:

There are sequences in which the shots were cut to a previously recorded music-track. There are sequences for which the entire piece of music was written to a final cutting of the picture . . . in the battle scene where pipes and drums are played for the victorious Russian soldiers I couldn't find a way to explain to Prokofiev what precise effect should be 'seen' in his music for this joyful moment. Seeing that we were getting nowhere, I ordered some 'prop' instruments constructed, shot these being played (without sound) visually and projected the results for Prokofiev – who almost immediately handed me an exact 'musical equivalent' to that visual image of pipers and drummers which I had shown him.

The day's run-throughs ended around midnight. Having noted only the timing of a sequence, Prokofiev would depart, promising

153

new music for the following day at 12 o'clock. And Eisenstein could be sure that on the dot of 11.55, Prokofiev would turn up in his little blue car bringing music that harmonised perfectly with all the subtleties of the montage. Even when it came to recording the sound-track, Prokofiev was actively involved, experimenting with 'immensely dramatic' microphone distortions and requisitioning the Mosfilm bath-tub for its percussive qualities. In 1939, he rearranged the music for more conventional forces. In the form of the cantata, op. 78, *Alexander Nevsky* has become one of the most popular choral works of the century. Shostakovich had mixed feelings:

> 14.1.1941 Leningrad
>
> Dear Sergey Sergeyevich,
>
> . . . I recently heard Stasevich perform your *Alexander Nevsky*. Despite a whole series of wonderful moments, I didn't like the work as a whole. It seems to me that artistic norms of some sort have been breached in it. There's too much physically loud, illustrative music. It seemed to me in particular that many sections end before they get started. The beginning of the battle [on the ice] and the entire song for low female voice made a powerful impression on me. Unfortunately, I can't say the same thing about the rest of it. Nevertheless, I'll be immensely pleased if the work receives a Stalin Prize.* For despite its shortcoming, this work deserves more than many another candidate . . .
>
> I clasp your hand warmly,
> D. Shostakovich

The extraordinary success of this patriotic score reinforced Prokofiev's determination to compose an opera on a contemporary Soviet theme. He had had such a project in mind for about five years when he found the appropriate subject in the summer of 1938: Valentin Katayev's civil war story, *I Am the Son of the Working People*. Meyerhold was to produce and Katayev himself agreed to work on the libretto. Prokofiev was not unaware of the problems:

To write an opera on a Soviet theme is by no means a simple task. One deals here with new people, new emotions, a new way of life and hence many of the forms and devices applicable to classical opera might prove unsuitable. For example, an aria sung by the chairman of a village Soviet could, with the slightest awkwardness on the part of the composer, be extremely puzzling to the listener. The recitative of a commissar making a telephone call may also seem strange.

Inevitably, differences arose between composer and librettist.

*It did not.

155

Katayev's banal conception of the work as Ukrainian folk opera clashed with Prokofiev's 'modern' operatic ideal. As in earlier operatic ventures, he refused to sacrifice the flow of dramatic action to the dictates of fashion. There would be neither rousing marches nor song and dance routines in *Semyon Kotko*. 'I don't need rhymes and arias,' he told Katayev.

While the finished score contains much that is very fine, Prokofiev courts critical disaster with music sporadically dark and dissonant:

Although it would obviously have been more advantageous from the standpoint of immediate success to have filled the opera with melodies of familiar pattern to be repeated on many occasions, I preferred to use a new approach and write new melodies of new pattern and as many as possible. This sort of music may be more difficult to understand at first, but after two or three hearings much will become clear. It is better for the listener to make new discoveries each time than to say, after hearing an opera for the second time, 'Oh, I've heard all that before, there's no use listening to it any more.'

New life, new subject matter call for new forms of expression, and the listener must not complain if he has to exert a little effort to grasp these forms.

The drama itself is distinctly not for export. Rita McAllister comments that it 'rarely raises itself above the level of a bad Western'.

Whatever the opera's shortcomings, its failure was (to say the least) politically expedient, as we shall see. From a low point in relations between Nazi Germany and Communist Russia in 1936-7, a fitful reconciliation had been taking place.

In May 1939, Stalin replaced his internationalist foreign minister Litvinov, a Jew, with the German-leaning Molotov; and, in August, Molotov and Ribbentrop signed the infamous Nazi-Soviet pact. Military action followed, pursued jointly by allies against Poland, unilaterally against Finland and the Baltic States. Until the middle of 1941, Prokofiev's country was to some degree in military, trade and cultural alliance with Nazi Germany, the rest of the West 'in an enemy camp'. Popular Front politics, in which Prokofiev had featured prominently if unconsciously, collapsed overnight. With that collapse went the existing market for creative export – Prokofiev never again travelled abroad. At home too, there were changes. *Semyon Kotko* in particular stood no chance in the improbable but inescapable context of a Moscow-Berlin axis. Shostakovich (the Shostakovich of *Testimony*) explains this with his customary sharpness, contrasting its fate with that of a politically-motivated Wagner production staged contemporaneously at the Bolshoi:

A poster announcing the first Bolshoi production of *Semyon Kotko*. It entered the repertoire as late as April 1970.

[Prokofiev's] opera deals with the occupation of the Ukraine by the Germans in 1918. The Germans are depicted as cruel butchers; when Prokofiev was writing the opera, this corresponded to the political setting . . . *Semyon Kotko* was put into production at the Stanislavsky Opera Theatre by Meyerhold himself. It was his last work in the theatre. In fact, he never finished it; he was arrested in the middle of it, and he was no longer Meyerhold, but 'Semyonich'. That was his alleged underground saboteur's nickname. That's quite ridiculous. It was probably the interrogator who invented the name, having read something about *Semyon Kotko* in the papers.

The director was arrested but the work went on as though nothing had happened. This was one of the terrible signs of the age; a man disappeared, but everyone pretended that nothing had happened. A man was in charge of the work, it had meaning only with him, under his direction. But he was no longer there, he had evaporated, and no one said a word. The name Meyerhold immediately disappeared from conversations. That was all . . .

Prokofiev turned to Eisenstein, his friend. The word 'friend' is used as a convention here, particularly when it's used for two men like Eisenstein and Prokofiev. I doubt that either of them needed friends.

They were both remote and aloof, but at least Prokofiev and Eisenstein respected each other. Eisenstein had also been a student of Meyerhold's, so Prokofiev asked the film director to bring the production of *Semyon Kotko* to completion.

Eisenstein refused. The political climate had changed by then, and in that wonderful era attacks on Germans, if only in an opera, were forbidden. The opera's future looked doubtful. Why get mixed up in a politically dubious venture? So Eisenstein said, 'I don't have the time.' He found time, as we know, for *The Valkyrie*.

The subsequent history of both productions is interesting, very, very

157

Romeo and Juliet: Margot
Fonteyn as Juliet in the 1966
film version of the Royal
Ballet production
(National Film Archive)

interesting. The première of *The Valkyrie* proceeded with all due pomp, and leaders from the Party and the State and the Fascist ambassador all attended. There were rave reviews. In a word, another victory on the arts front. *Semyon Kotko* barely squeaked into the world. Naturally the Germans were gone from the production, replaced by some unnamed occupying force. But nevertheless, the powers-that-be were displeased. Stalin panicked at the thought of angering the Germans. Officials from the People's Commissariat of Foreign Affairs showed up at every rehearsal, frowned, and left, saying nothing. That was a very bad sign . . . And so this half-dead production came to life and no one liked it.

After much acrimonious debate, the opera was dropped from the repertoire, its defenders regarded with suspicion in later years when the merest sympathy with modernism was viewed as a sin.

Prokofiev could at least console himself with the triumphant reception accorded *Romeo and Juliet*. Its long-awaited Soviet première had taken place in Leningrad on 11 January 1940, some time after the world première given – to the considerable embarrassment of Kirov Theatre management – at the provincial theatre of Brno, Czechoslovakia in December 1938. Leonid

Lavrovsky's Soviet version paved the way for choreographers the world over to make their own versions (among them Sir Frederick Ashton, John Cranko, Kenneth MacMillan and Rudolf Nureyev) and so bestow on Prokofiev's score the status of a ballet classic.

This happy outcome had not always seemed inevitable. The ups and downs of the Kirov production were well expressed by Galina Ulanova, the great Soviet ballerina who danced Juliet. She proposed this humorous toast in rhyme after the first night:

> Never was a tale of greater woe,
> Than Prokofiev's music to Romeo.

Even she had had to overcome many reservations before growing into the role now considered her greatest achievement. Like the other dancers, she was afraid not only of the music itself, but also of the composer, who appeared unapproachable and haughty:

I do not remember exactly when I first saw Prokofiev, I only know that at some point during the rehearsals of *Romeo and Juliet* I became aware of the presence in the hall of a tall, somewhat stern-looking man who seemed to disapprove heartily of everything he saw and especially of our artists. It was Prokofiev. I had heard that in the early stages of the production, Lavrovsky and Prokofiev had had some heated arguments about the music. Lavrovsky had told the composer that there was not enough music in the ballet for a full-length production and that he would have to add to it. To which Prokofiev had stubbornly replied, 'I have written exactly as much music as is necessary and I am not going to add a single note. The ballet is complete as it is. You may take it or leave it.' . . .

I exchanged barely more than a few words with Prokofiev until the production was nearing completion when it was decided that a formal introduction ought to be made. I shall never forget that occasion. It took place at one of the final rehearsals of the ballet with orchestra in the Kirov Theatre of Opera and Ballet in Leningrad. On the previous day I had undergone a very painful operation on my gum and appeared at rehearsal with my face bandaged and my eyes red with weeping. That is how Prokofiev first met his future Juliet. And since she was obviously unable to dance that day the rehearsal was postponed . . . We were rehearsing the beginning of Act III . . . when the curtain rises Juliet is sitting on a brocaded couch with Romeo kneeling beside her, his head in her lap. The couch stands at the back of the stage some distance from the footlights and, consequently, from the orchestra as well, and hence we who were acting the parts of Romeo and Juliet could not hear it. Suddenly we were startled by a shout from Lavrovsky:

'Why don't you begin?' 'We can't hear the music,' we replied. Prokofiev, who was present, lost his temper: 'I know what you want!' he shouted. 'You want drums not music!'

We did not take offence. We invited him to come on to the stage and sit beside us. He did so, and throughout the entire scene he sat on that couch, listening carefully to the orchestra without saying a word. But on leaving, he said, still looking very annoyed, 'Very well, I shall rewrite the music here and add something.'*

In such situations, Lavrovsky needed all his negotiating skills, and it is entirely to his credit that the production took shape at all. Despite their professional differences, his friendship with Prokofiev survived and even prospered in the years that followed. Lavrovsky was co-author of the scenario for Prokofiev's last ballet, *The Stone Flower*, and directed its posthumous production. He offers this tribute to the composer:

Prokofiev carried on where Tchaikovsky left off. He developed and elaborated the principles of symphonism in ballet music. He was one of the first Soviet composers to bring to the ballet stage genuine human emotions and full-blooded characters. The boldness of his musical treatment, the clear-cut characterisations, the diversity and intricacy of his rhythms, the unorthodoxy of his harmonies . . . serve to create the dramatic development of the performance.

We might say that the blend of lyric and dramatic impulses in *Romeo and Juliet* produces an epic breadth which can take in its stride those more sardonic characteristics of Prokofiev's pre-Soviet period. Its music is immensely assured, strong without being daring, colourful without being extravagant, and it reflects an emotional involvement so often hidden in earlier works. Much the longest ballet Prokofiev had written, its 52 numbers are mostly closed structural units including the conventional dances and genre episodes. Yet within these constraints Prokofiev breaks new ground with his most cohesive piece of music theatre to date – a richly developed choreographic drama replete with clearly defined musical portraits, vividly realistic scenes and psychologically motivated action. Characters are developed through the deft transformation of their motto themes, and Prokofiev is always alive to the dramatic suggestiveness of orchestration, switching from clean, lucent instrumental textures to harshly evocative effects as the occasion demands. With *Romeo and Juliet* he had transcended the limitations of his earlier experiments in the genre.

Outwardly preoccupied with the stagings of recent or not so recent dramatic pieces, Prokofiev worked simultaneously on a range of new compositions. He planned a cycle of three large-scale piano sonatas, a violin sonata in F minor, a patriotic cantata and,

*A number of Soviet productions have been vitiated by the *unauthorised* coarsening and padding of instrumental textures.

160

from May 1940, two further stage works – the ballet *Cinderella* and an opera, *The Duenna*. Prokofiev was not to be deflected from his operatic quest; instead he executed a retreat from ideology to escapism. Completion of most of these projects was interrupted by the outbreak of war. One necessary exception was *Hail to Stalin* (*Zdravitsa*), op. 85 – written very quickly in time for Stalin's 60th birthday in 1939. Once a favourite of Nestyev's, it can boast one good tune and a suitably inflated peroration.

The Duenna, op. 86 was completed (save for some minor adjustments) by the beginning of 1941. Adapted from Richard Sheridan's buoyant eighteenth-century comedy of manners and set to music as nimble and sparkling as the original dialogue, its première was delayed until 3 November 1946. Neither text nor

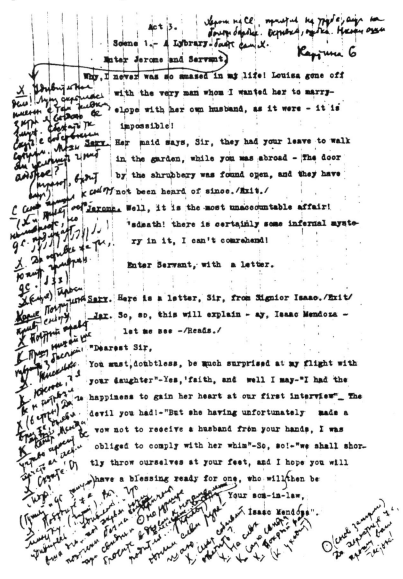

Planning *The Duenna* libretto

161

score disturbed the sensibilities of Party ideologues and, for the first and last time in his career as an opera composer, Prokofiev tasted something close to unqualified success. Then, inexplicably, but not unlike Carl Nielsen's eighteenth-century comedy adaptation *Maskarade*, Prokofiev's *Duenna* failed to catch on internationally.

In Sheridan's play, which is set in Spain, the cause of true love triumphs over an arranged marriage, and those seeking to promote the 'arrangement' are led by the nose into some choice comic situations. Prokofiev felt that he 'had first to decide which element to stress: the comic aspect or the love angle. I chose the latter' – a decision no doubt influenced by the success of *Romeo and Juliet*. *The Duenna*'s comedy is accordingly less grotesque than that of *The Love of Three Oranges*; its characters are recognisably human, its lyricism pronounced.

Based on a skilfully wrought theatrical original, *The Duenna* is perhaps the most structurally convincing of Prokofiev's operas. For once, little or nothing need be added or explained for an audience to enjoy it. Highlights include the magical close of Act 1, in which the night air seems to breathe of love (thanks to the efforts of an offstage string group); the drollery of Act 3 Scene 2, in which Don Jerome and his trio demonstrate some of the disastrous possibilities inherent in amateur music-making; and the sustained lyrical invention of Clara's scene in Act 3 – the emotional heart of a romantic work.

As *The Love of Three Oranges* was to some extent inspired by Prokofiev's developing relationship with Lina, so *The Duenna* reflects his growing involvement with Mira Mendelson, a recent graduate of the Moscow Literary Institute and just 26 years of age in 1941. That year was in every sense a watershed for the composer. In the spring, he suffered the first of a series of heart attacks which dangerously undermined his health. In June, the onset of war was to spell the complete disruption of his family life. Soon, Germany's pact-shattering assault on the Russian heartland grew so intense that the Soviet government initiated radical measures of evacuation to protect senior cultural leaders. Prokofiev, informed of the plan, discussed preparations for the move with his wife, but, when Lina learned that Mira would be included in the evacuation, she decided that she, 17-year-old Sviatoslav, and 12-year-old Oleg had best remain in Moscow.

On the night of 7 August, with a group of prominent Soviet citizens en route for the Caucasus, an impenetrable fog descends on Prokofiev's private life.

Some authorities imply that political dealings were at the root of Prokofiev's change of life-partner – which seems unfair to Mira given her 12 years of devoted care and companionship. She had

after all been acquainted with the composer since late 1938. On the other hand, as Seroff suggests, the times were 'less conducive to romance than they were to survival'. Mira, it is said, had 'strong Party ties', whereas Lina was suspect – even more so than Prokofiev himself. He had before him countless examples of what could happen to individualistic intellectuals in a totalitarian society. Besides being foreign, a crime enough in itself, his wife was still corresponding with her mother in occupied France. Nor did she avoid such contacts in their years apart. After recovering from diphtheria, Lina was again to be seen at Western embassies. In 1945, she accompanied Isaiah Berlin, then a temporary official at the British Embassy, on a trip to the writers' colony at Peredelkino, home of Boris Pasternak.

In February 1947, a decree was issued by the Supreme Soviet removing the right of Soviet citizens to marry foreign nationals, a decree that acted in retrospect. Prokofiev's marriage was suddenly illegal, his children illegitimate. Desperate now, Lina made repeated efforts to get permission to leave Russia with her sons. Prokofiev no longer needed a divorce from her if he wished to marry Mira. Despite Soviet claims to the contrary, it looks as if he did not formalise the new relationship until a civil ceremony on 13 January 1948. On 20 February, Lina was arrested on charges of espionage:

One morning in February 1948 she got a telephone call from a stranger. 'I've just come from Leningrad, and I've brought you a package from your friend.' He gave the name of the person from whom Lina was in fact expecting a package, and continued, 'I'm now at the Leningrad Station. Come quickly. I'll wait for you on the street.'

'Why on the street?' she replied. 'Come to my place, it's close by.'

'No, I'm in a great hurry. I'll be standing on the corner. You'll recognise me by my naval uniform.'

How little she wanted to go! She had the flu, and it was bitter cold outside. But what could she do? She put on her fur hat and a warm fur coat, and went out. When she got to the appointed place, she saw a man in the uniform of a naval officer.

'Lina Ivanovna?'

'Yes.'

And the free citizen of Spain [sic] felt herself pushed toward the pavement where a car was parked. The door swung open . . . two more were in the car.

'Excuse me, I don't understand.'

But the naval officer then shoved her into the car and asked one of the men inside, 'Is this the one?'

'That's her.' It all happened within seconds.

Lina Prokofiev returned to Moscow eight years later. How well the fur coat must have served her in the Siberian labour camps!

(Galina Vishnevskaya)

The detention of relatives and close friends of prominent individuals was a horrifying commonplace of Stalinist terror. It affected politicians and poets – citizens as diverse as V. M. Molotov, whose wife was arrested in 1949 on fictitious charges of spying, and Anna Akhmatova, whose son was repeatedly confined primarily in order to persecute his mother but latterly in the hope of eliciting some propagandist verse. Was Lina's arrest supposed to keep Prokofiev in check?

After some 40 years in the USSR, this remarkable, courageous woman was able to return to the West in 1972. In August 1986 she took part in recording sessions for *Peter and the Wolf*, narrating the story in her idiosyncratic English. She was then aged 88.

Chapter 9

War and Peace

For the rest of 1941, Prokofiev's main concern was the 'Great Patriotic War'. He had been staying at Kratovo, just outside Moscow, when the news came through:

On the warm, sunny morning of 22 June I was sitting at my desk, when suddenly the watchman's wife appeared, looking greatly upset. 'The Germans have invaded us,' she gasped. 'They say they're bombing our cities.' The news staggered me . . . I hurried over at once to see Sergey Eisenstein who lived not far from us. Yes, it was true.

With the implacably advancing alien forces of *Alexander Nevsky* now a reality, overwhelming emotions of patriotism stirred in both men. As the violence intensified, they saw themselves, and increasingly were seen by others, as key guardians of Russian culture. Eisenstein, already immersed in work on *Ivan the Terrible*, drove himself 'at a madman's pace'. Prokofiev, putting *Cinderella* to one side for the moment, embarked on the boldest project of his creative life.

Lina recollects that the idea of an opera based on *War and Peace* was in the air as early as 1935. Some years later, Mira Mendelson began reading the novel aloud to Prokofiev – something she often did to relax him. When she reached the dramatic and touching encounter between Natasha Rostov and the mortally wounded Andrey Bolkonsky, Prokofiev remarked on the scene's 'operatic' quality. On 12 April 1941, he sketched a first brief outline libretto. From the start, he planned to integrate the personal with the epochal. Now, with the attack of Nazi Germany, the balance shifted. The depiction of intimate events and individual destinies served no positive social purpose. The times called for a panoramic national epic:

During this period an idea which had been germinating in my mind to write an opera on Tolstoy's *War and Peace* took decisive shape. Somehow those pages recounting the Russian people's struggle against Napoleon's

Stalin, the war leader
(Fotomas Index)

167

hordes in 1812 and the expulsion of the French armies from Russian soil seemed especially close. It was clear that precisely those pages should lie at the basis of the opera.

Prokofiev lavished unprecedented energy and imagination on this project over a great many years. His faith faltered only as his health worsened and his hopes for a full-scale production were continually thwarted. Mira Mendelson tells us:

During his last years, Sergey spoke almost daily about how he longed for a production of *War and Peace*; it occupied his thoughts constantly, unceasingly.

Prokofiev began the music during his three months' stay in the little town of Nalchik in the Northern Caucasus. Here, as before, he spent a great deal of time with Miaskovsky, exchanging ideas and playing sketches of work in progress. Miaskovsky wrote later that he did not care for Prokofiev's new symphonic suite *The Year 1941*; dutiful but rather casually wrought, it worked better as film music. (Prokofiev's war-related pieces were subsequently denounced by Shostakovich at a plenary session of the Organisation Committee of the Composers' Union held in March 1944.) However, the Second String Quartet, op. 92 won general approval. 'Magnificent music!' Miaskovsky called it.

The Quartet is one of a handful of Prokofiev works based almost entirely on folk tunes. As with the *Overture on Hebrew Themes*, he needed some persuasion before choosing this compositional course:

'Look here,' the chairman of the [Nalchik] Arts Committee said to us, 'you have a goldmine of musical material here that has remained practically untapped. If you take advantage of your stay here to work up this material you will be laying the foundation of a Kabardinian music.' And indeed the material proved to be very fresh and original and before long we all set to work.

Miaskovsky very soon sketched the outline of his 23rd Symphony. I contemplated writing a string quartet. I felt that the combination of new, untouched Oriental folklore with the most classical of classic forms, the string quartet, ought to produce interesting and unexpected results. But when I actually started to work it suddenly occurred to me that since the musical culture of Kabarda was at a low level of development according to European standards, apart from some beautiful folk songs, my quartet might not be understood in Nalchik at all. However the chairman of the Arts Committee to whom I confided my doubts reassured me on this score. 'Write as you feel,' he said. 'If we won't understand your quartet now we will appreciate it later on.'

Nestyev, not impressed by this, fails to find in the work an adequate reflection of 'the new life being created in the republics of the North Caucasus at that time.' [!] Prokofiev's exuberant treatment of folk material he finds unacceptably 'radical'. By the time Prokofiev completed this score (on 3 December 1941), he and the other distinguished refugees had been moved on to Tbilisi in Georgia. He later learned that when the Germans took Nalchik, the arts administrator joined the partisans and was killed in an attack on enemy communication lines.

In the 1920s, Prokofiev had dined in Monte Carlo. At Giardino's restaurant on the top of the hill, one might share a table with Diaghilev, Picasso, Derain, Balanchine, Stravinsky and Nabokov. How different was his life now! The months in provincial Tbilisi were far from easy. The winter was unusually cold and prices very high. Prokofiev was ailing and his poor health soon compelled him to give up concertising. Still the Germans advanced. Still the composer worked unceasingly. 'Am finishing up the last bars of *War and Peace*, thus very shortly I'll be ready to submit to your bondage,' he told Eisenstein in a letter of 29 March 1942. He had already agreed – he could hardly refuse – to compose the score for *Ivan the Terrible*. The prestige project was escalating into a two or even three-part cinematic epic. Also nearing completion was the turbulent and compact Piano Sonata No. 7, op. 83. Miaskovsky considered this 'superbly wild'.

The international success of the Seventh has done little to affect the neglect of its predecessor, the Piano Sonata No. 6, op. 82. One of Prokofiev's most audacious instrumental works, it was the first of the 'war' sonatas to be completed. Sviatoslav Richter recounts how, in the spring of 1940, Prokofiev brought the score to one of musicologist Pavel Lamm's musical gatherings:

Prokofiev entered the room. He came not as a regular, but as a guest – this could be felt. He looked as if it were his birthday, but . . . a little overbearing as well. He brought his sonata and said: 'Well, to work!' At once: 'I'll play.' . . . He was younger than many, but everyone felt that he meant to say: 'Though I am younger, I am as good as any one of you!' His somewhat haughty attitude towards his associates didn't, however, extend to Miaskovsky, to whom he was particularly attentive.

Prokofiev's behaviour was businesslike, professional. I remember how he heeded the advice of Neuhaus, who considered that the bass A couldn't sound for 5 bars, and he rewrote the passage.

It seems to me that he played his sonata twice and left. He played from manuscript and I turned the pages for him.

Prokofiev did not even finish playing but I had already decided that I would play this sonata.

When later, during the war, I heard him play the Eighth Sonata, he already didn't play as well as then.

The remarkable clarity of style and structural perfection of the music

amazed me. I hadn't heard anything like it before. The composer, with barbaric audacity, breaks with the ideals of the romantics and includes the shattering pulse of the twentieth century in his music. This is a magnificent sonata, classically well-balanced in spite of all the sharp corners.

Prokofiev himself gave the official première in a Moscow radio broadcast of 8 April 1940. At once the Sonata aroused contradictory responses. The first movement, with its pounding, percussive opening, was considered 'excessively brutal'. Nestyev finds the charming inner movements, a quick march and a slow waltz, more to his taste. The finale is lean and 'classical' until the reappearance of first movement material rekindles an atmosphere of disquiet, distrust and even dread.

Richter received the music of the Seventh Sonata at the beginning of 1943. He became engrossed in it and learned it in four days:

A concert of Soviet music was being prepared and Prokofiev wanted me to perform his new sonata. He had just returned to Moscow and lived in the National Hotel. I came to play the sonata for him. He was alone. There was a piano in the room, but everything began with the pedal not working and Prokofiev said: 'So what, let's fix it . . . ' We crawled under the piano, fixed something under it, and in a moment bumped foreheads so hard that we saw stars. Sergey Sergeyevich later recalled: 'But we fixed the pedal after all, didn't we!'

. . . The première of the sonata took place in the October Hall of the House of Trade Unions. I was its first performer. The work was extremely successful . . .

Prokofiev was present at the concert and was called on the stage. When almost all the audience had left and mainly the musicians had remained (there were many: I remember Oistrakh, Shebalin . . .), everyone wanted to hear the sonata a second time. The atmosphere was elevated and at the same time serious. And I played well.

The listeners particularly keenly grasped the spirit of the work which reflected their innermost feelings and concerns . . .

Nestyev draws attention to the 'beautiful singing theme' of the central *Andante caloroso*, in contrast to the outer movements, where 'boldness and stunning power' are 'so exaggerated as to make it difficult for the reader to perceive any features of Soviet reality'. Other writers detect here a reversion to obsolete romanticism, a *divertissement* quality out of step with the rest. Francis Poulenc disagrees: 'Ah! marvellous . . . one of those melodies of which Prokofiev has the secret.' All trace of sentimental goo is abruptly swept aside by the furious *Precipitato* finale (in $\frac{7}{8}$), perhaps the most dynamic music ever written by a composer renowned for his dynamic piano style. In March 1943,

171

Ivan the Terrible, Part 1:
Nikolay Cherkasov as Ivan
(National Film Archive)

Prokofiev was awarded the Stalin Prize, second degree, for this, his most radical sonata.

In May 1942, Prokofiev travelled to Alma-Ata, a town not far from the Chinese border where evacuated members of the major Soviet film studios were hard at work on morale-boosting projects. Here began the first stage of his collaboration with Eisenstein on *Ivan the Terrible*, work that resumed in Moscow two years later when the director prepared the final cut of Part 1. After an angry dispute over music intended for the sequence of the oath-taking, Eisenstein provided Prokofiev with more detailed sketches and all went well. The bulk of the score was in fact composed after the film had been shot. The composer Dmitri Kabalevsky recorded his amazement that Prokofiev's extremely logical and precise way of working in these circumstances, metronome and chronometer to the fore, 'in no way hampers his creative thinking; he writes film music with the same inspiration and passion that goes into his other compositions'.

On 18 January 1945, the first part of *Ivan the Terrible* was released to general acclaim, the unhurried majesty of the film action superbly complemented by Prokofiev's forceful and dramatic film score. Chaplin sent a telegram extolling it as 'the greatest historic film that has ever been made'. But not everyone

172

liked it. Stravinsky's diary for 27 November 1959 contains the entry:

Luncheon here in Gladstone [Hotel, New York] with Bill Brown. Went with him to see, in Museum of Modern Art, the most stupid and provincial Russian film *Ivan the Terrible*, first part, with very embarrassing music of the poor Prokofiev.

None of the music was arranged for concert performance by the composer himself; instead, he incorporated its best moments into other works. Long after Prokofiev's death however, the scholar Abram Stasevich perpetrated an *Ivan the Terrible* oratorio which *is* occasionally heard, despite its interminable length and undue reliance on spoken narration.

During the summer months of 1942, Prokofiev worked on a one-movement cantata, the *Ballad of an Unknown Boy*, to a text by Pavel Antokolsky:

It is based on the moving story of the boy whose mother and sister were killed by the fascists and who avenges their death by hurling a grenade into a fascist staff car during the enemy's retreat from his native town. The name and fate of this boy have remained unknown, but word of his heroic exploit has swept both front and rear, rousing others to feats of heroism. I wanted the music to reflect the tragic mood of the text in a

Eisenstein shooting
Ivan the Terrible
(National Film Archive)

173

swift-moving, dramatic cantata. As I wrote it, I pictured the boy's broken childhood, the cruelty of the enemy, boundless courage and imminent victory.

Unfortunately the result is earthbound and episodic. The march theme of the invading Nazis is repeated endlessly – after the fashion of the famous invasion theme of Shostakovich's Seventh Symphony but to even less effect. The Cantata received only a single performance on 21 February 1944. No one liked it. 'N.Ya.M. only mumbled something about it politely through his moustache,' Prokofiev wrote. '*The Boy*, I'm sorry to say, has been trampled to death.'

While living in Alma-Ata, Prokofiev planned to compose an opera based on Kazakh folk material, but other, more pressing duties intervened. *War and Peace* had to be finished, which meant more than simply completing the orchestration. In July 1942, he received the predictable advices of the Moscow Committee on Arts Affairs, whose endorsement would have to precede the work's acceptance for production by any of the state opera houses. Prokofiev embarked on a revision that strengthened the obvious contemporary analogies (Napoleon/Hitler; Kutuzov/Stalin), boosted the mass heroics of the *War* element, and played down the genre episodes which depicted the aristocracy in time of *Peace*. He had been heartened by the determined advocacy of Samuel Samosud, conductor at the Bolshoi. After a special January hearing at which Prokofiev himself sat at the piano and tried 'without much felicity' to negotiate both the vocal and instrumental parts, Samosud wrung from his directorate the promise of a production by the end of the year. He and Prokofiev sought to involve Eisenstein in the project as a sort of unofficial stage director designate. He seemed the ideal man to bring originality and freshness to the obligatory scenes of the people's heroism. For the tableauesque 'Moscow Aflame', he had already suggested the addition of the episode in which actors from the French theatre flee the fire in make-up and costume. It was his idea also to give a 'more belligerent' send-off to 'The French retreat', something Prokofiev realised in the 'howling and whistling' of an orchestral prelude.

At the beginning of October 1943, Prokofiev and Mira returned to Moscow, this time to remain. Triumphant Russian armies had pushed the front far to the west, the tide of the war had turned and preparations for *War and Peace* were moving forward. Or so Prokofiev assumed. In fact, the delayed reunion of the Bolshoi company frustrated plans for a full-scale production. Prokofiev informed Eisenstein of the change in a letter of 17 November 1943. Apparently a concert performance under Samosud was

David Oistrakh
(EMI/Lauterwasser)

planned for December. Then, with the première almost a reality, backstage politics dashed Prokofiev's hopes as so often in the past. Samosud was relieved of his duties at the Bolshoi and *War and Peace* was dropped. In Leningrad, it was the same story: the Kirov postponed production for an indefinite period. Prokofiev could only tell Eisenstein that the new director there was supposed to revive the 'traditional' repertoire: 'to pacify me, they'll produce *Cinderella*,' he added.

Completing that ballet had been Prokofiev's major task for the second half of 1943, much of it spent at Perm in the Urals. The relaxed atmosphere of this beautiful region finds a parallel in the charming Flute Sonata, op. 94, 'the sunniest and most serene of [Prokofiev's] wartime compositions' (Nestyev). The composer explains:

I had long wished to write music for the flute, an instrument which I felt had been undeservedly neglected. I wanted to write a sonata in delicate, fluid classical style.

Ironically, the piece is better known today as a Violin Sonata: No. 2 in D, op. 94 bis*, an arrangement made at the request of David Oistrakh:

*The formidable Violin Sonata No. 1, sketched as early as 1938, did not emerge until after the war.

175

When I first heard his Sonata for Flute, shortly after it was written, it occurred to me that it would sound very well on the violin. I felt that this beautiful piece of music ought to live a fuller and richer life on the concert stage. I approached the composer with the suggestion that he write a violin version of it. Prokofiev was interested in the suggestion. We arranged to meet and talk the matter over. It was the first time I had seen Prokofiev at work and it was a revelation to me: I had never believed it possible to work with such speed and efficiency. He asked me to make two or three versions of each passage in the score that required editing, numbering each one carefully. As I submitted the pages to him, he marked the version he considered suitable and made a few pencil corrections here and there. Thus in no time the violin version of the sonata was ready.

In either format, Prokofiev reveals once again the inexhaustible melodic gift that makes him unique among twentieth-century musicians. Shostakovich hailed the Sonata as 'a perfectly magnificent work'.

The orchestration of *Cinderella* was not accomplished until the late spring of 1944. No doubt Prokofiev lavished special care on it. It is certainly one of the most original features of a generally enchanting score. The composer goes for a deliberately unnatural, 'silvery' sound balance – not at all easy to bring off in performance when the strings are called upon to demonstrate expressive warmth at the very extremes of the register. The many exposed and high-lying violin lines have been known to sound tinny; the unusual melodic writing for cellos, basses and low wind *can* turn muddy and graceless. But it is only in such grossly overloaded passages as the climax of the Act 2 *pas de deux* that the writing itself must be blamed.

Given the lighter subject matter, Prokofiev makes *Cinderella* less opulently romantic than *Romeo and Juliet*. Nestyev strains to interpret Cinderella herself as a realistic heroine of democracy. Prokofiev's own comments recognise the drama for what it is – a dream, and a suitably balletic one:

What I wished to express above all in the music of *Cinderella* was the poetic love of Cinderella and the Prince, the birth and flowering of that love, the obstacles in its path and finally the dream fulfilled.

The fairy-tale offered a number of fascinating problems for me as a composer – the atmosphere of magic surrounding the Fairy Godmother, the twelve fantastic dwarfs that pop out of the clock as it strikes twelve, and dance *chechotka* (a kind of tap dance) reminding Cinderella that she must return home; the swift change of scene as the Prince journeys far and wide in search of Cinderella; the poetry of nature personified by the four fairies symbolising the four seasons – spring, summer, autumn and winter – and their companions. The producers of the ballet, however, wanted the fairy-tale to serve merely as a setting for the portrayal of flesh-

The Royal Ballet production of *Cinderella* at the Royal Opera House, Covent Garden: Cinderella leaves for the Ball (Zoë Dominic)

and-blood human beings with human passions and failings. N. D. Volkov and I gave much thought to the dramatic aspect of the ballet. The music has three basic themes: first theme – Cinderella, the abused and ill-treated; second theme – Cinderella, chaste, pure, pensive; third, broad theme – Cinderella in love, radiant with happiness. I tried to convey the different characters through the music – the sweet, pensive Cinderella, her timid father, her ill-tempered stepmother, her selfish, capricious sisters, the passionate young Prince – in such a way that the spectators could not but share their joys and sorrows.

Apart from the dramatic structure, I was anxious to make the ballet as 'danceable' as possible, with a variety of dances that would flow from the pattern of the story, and give the dancers ample opportunity to display their art. I wrote *Cinderella* in the traditions of the old classical ballet, it has pas de deux, an adagio, gavotte, several waltzes, a pavane, passepied, bourrée, mazurka and galop. Each character has his or her variation.

It was not until after the war that Ulanova began work on the leading role:

I tried to persuade Prokofiev to give Cinderella the beautiful theme of the Fairy Godmother, but all my efforts were unavailing. Prokofiev was a man for whom art was sacred and he was incapable of making any compromises. He had created that melody for the Fairy Godmother, that was her theme as he saw it and felt it, and nothing on earth could have induced him to give it to any other character.

The fact that we 'fell in love' with *Cinderella* at first sight and that much of it was clear to us from the very outset, or at any rate much sooner than in the case of *Romeo and Juliet*, showed how well we had learned to understand Prokofiev's music . . .

177

When this, his best ballet, was staged in the Bolshoi Theatre the composer was already seriously ill and unable to attend rehearsals. Only rarely, when his health permitted, did we see him at performances.

This was possibly just as well. Yuri Fayer, the conductor, incurred Prokofiev's intense displeasure by reinforcing the fragile textures specified in the score.

Prokofiev spent the summer of 1944 in the large country retreat run by the Composers' Union at Ivanovo, to the west of Moscow. Nestyev speaks of the comradely warmth between the composer and his colleagues in residence there. Other accounts have him snubbing Shostakovich, teasing Kabalevsky and refusing to acknowledge the likes of Khrennikov. Whatever the truth of these reports, Prokofiev must have found it hard to accept the disproportionate influence wielded by those he considered his 'musical inferiors'.

This was, of course, one of the most insidious elements of Stalin's cultural revolution. With artist, critic and administrator directly employed by the state, the distinction between artistic assessment and party discipline had blurred so that the cultural worker sometimes assumed the role of inquisitor or informer. Those who had risen to the top of the cultural bureaucracy wished,

Composer and bureaucrat Tikhon Khrennikov, Chairman of the Composers' Union from 1948, acclaimed by Soviet youth (Novosti)

178

not unnaturally, to protect their position rather than encourage the truly talented people under their control. Similarly, those who aspired to ascend the ladder were unwilling to take risks which might endanger their prospects. Artists given every incentive *not* to innovate were thus condemned to follow established models. Rather than evolving a new culture, the system served to preserve the worst features of the old, creating a cultural élite as morally compromised as the political leadership and with the same vested interests in the preservation of the status quo. In the West, the cult of the commonplace was a response to popular taste, inspired by greed: in the Soviet Union, it was the result of official preference. Lenin had attacked as hypocrisy the notions of 'absolute freedom' voiced by 'bourgeois individualists':

There can be no real and effective 'freedom' in a society based on the power of money . . . Are you free in relation to your bourgeois publisher, Mr Writer, in relation to your bourgeois public, which demands that you provide it with pornography . . . ?

Yet, in contemporary Western societies, the artist who wished to rise above the level of that 'pornography' had usually been 'free' to do so and starve or prosper in the attempt. Prokofiev had long ago exchanged this set of constraints for the Soviet alternative. Certainly, he does not appear to have relished Union business, but then he was reluctant to spend time on anything not directly related to his own creative plans.

At Ivanovo he completed the Piano Sonata No. 8, op. 84 – the last of the 'war' trilogy begun in 1939. In a number of respects, the Eighth stands slightly apart from its predecessors. The explosive intensity and inexorable drive have relaxed. Instead, the music bears a stylistic kinship with the theatre pieces Prokofiev was working on at the time. The opening *Andante dolce* idea is not so very different from Natasha's theme in *War and Peace*, except that Prokofiev's distinctive harmonic colouring is here more obtrusive, dislocating the melodic line so as to suggest, in Soviet analytical parlance, some dazed survivor greeting the aftermath of war. As in the Sixth and Seventh Sonatas, the central movement is a comparatively tranquil interlude, here a subdued *Andante sognando*, something like a minuet. The *Vivace* finale starts off as a typical Prokofiev *toccata* but includes the now almost customary reminiscences of the first movement. For Nestyev, the extended central episode, with its grotesquely heavy tread, evokes an image of 'heroic troops resolutely marching ahead, ready to crush anything in their path'. Richter finds the work as a whole:

. . . the richest of all of Prokofiev's sonatas. It has a complex inner life with profound contrapositions. At times it seems to freeze, as if listening

179

to the inexorable march of the times. The sonata is somewhat heavy to grasp, but heavy with richness – like a tree heavy with fruit.

By the time of its official première, Prokofiev had also turned out the *12 Russian Folksongs*, op. 104. Today, these delightful settings are among the more familiar items in his extensive vocal catalogue.

On 13 January 1945, Prokofiev was in Moscow to conduct the première of a new symphony. Sviatoslav Richter again:

I will never forget the first performance of the Fifth Symphony in 1945, on the eve of victory . . . This was Prokofiev's last performance as a conductor. I sat close to the stage, in the third or fourth row. The Grand Hall was probably lighted as usual, but when Prokofiev stood up, it seemed as if the light poured directly on him from somewhere up above. He stood like a monument on a pedestal.

And then when Prokofiev mounted the podium and silence set in, artillery salvos suddenly thundered.

Emil Gilels, who gave the first public performance of the Piano Sonata no. 8 at the suggestion of the composer (29 December 1944) (Novosti)

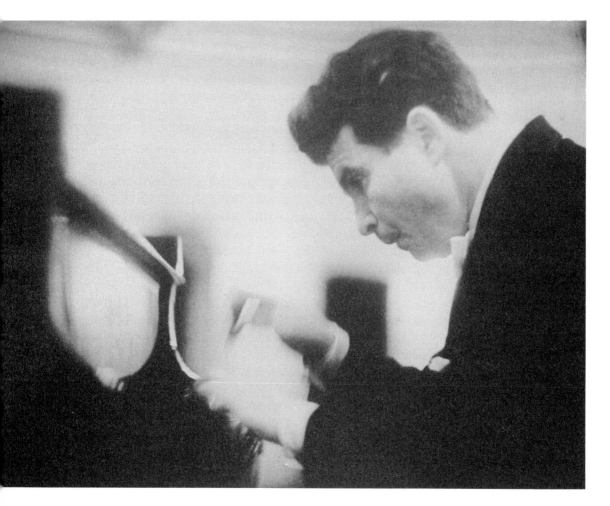

The opening bars of
Prokofiev's Fifth Symphony
in his expanded piano score

His baton was already raised. He waited, and until the cannon fire ceased, he didn't begin. There was something very significant, very symbolic in this. A sort of common borderline had come for everybody . . . and for Prokofiev as well.

From its opening bars, the new music seemed to capture the mood of a nation on the brink of victory. That said, the Fifth is no conscious 'War' Symphony; some of its themes date back to the 1930s. A work of stature and dignity, it represents Prokofiev's most thoughtful and considered symphonic effort to date:

I wrote my Fifth Symphony in the summer of 1944 and I consider my work on this symphony very significant both because of the musical material put into it and because I returned to the symphonic form after a sixteen-year interval. The Fifth Symphony completes, as it were, a long period of my works. I conceived it as a symphony of the greatness of the human spirit.

181

The work was well received both at home and abroad – by Kabalevsky, who predictably stressed its profoundly national character, and by Olin Downes of the *New York Times*:

The Symphony is certainly one of the most interesting, and probably the best, that has come from Russia in the last quarter-century. It is unquestionably the richest and most mature symphonic score that the composer has produced. There are new spiritual horizons in the serenity of the opening movement and wonderful developments that come later . . .

We must assume that Israel Nestyev was busy castigating those Western 'aesthetes' who dared imply that the Symphony 'too openly appeals to the masses'. In any event, he seems to have missed the genuinely favourable Western comment. No matter. A bit of eager editing and the lukewarm notice in the journal *Musical America* is transformed into a hymn of praise. [The words in brackets are omitted in the processed version which appears in his Prokofiev biography.]:

The eagerly awaited Fifth Symphony of Prokofiev burst [more] like [a bon-bon than] a bombshell upon the musical horizon of New York . . . It is difficult, without understating, to describe [*original*: This is not written to disparage] a work so beautifully orchestrated, so cleverly linked together, so packed with wit and invention.

The Fifth needs no special pleading. According to Nestyev, the way in which its musical material is developed is more theatrical than symphonic:

. . . it is the shifting of various moods and scenes that predominates here, rather than the development and modification of themes. In most cases, the themes are not subjected to any substantial transformation, but simply painted in different tonal colours, varied, or set forth in new combinations. At times the work seems to be not so much a traditional symphony as an exciting symphonic drama.

For Western commentators, the Symphony's principal virtue is its *rejection* of dramatic/programmatic schemes. What matters is its disciplined control of musical relationships within the traditional four-movement plan. The material is far more integrated than in the three previous symphonies. Rhetorical devices and rhythmic motifs apparently designed to move the action along turn out to be closely interrelated; subordinate ideas are developed rather than dropped. In short, Prokofiev has attempted a 'real' symphony.

Opposite
Prokofiev on the podium

The first movement, following the example of Shostakovich, is

182

more *Andante* than *Allegro*, drawing together the musical threads to culminate in a triumphant burst of glory. Prokofiev's dense orchestration only enhances the monumental effect.

The second movement is a perfectly proportioned scherzo derived from material originally intended for *Romeo and Juliet*. Launched with insistent strings, its music is hard-edged and precise with perhaps an unconscious hint of ragtime. The equally invigorating trio section provides a touching contrast, its bright-eyed quality enhanced by Prokofiev's characterful harmonic sleights of hand. The return of the scherzo is unexpectedly sinister and macabre, but then the movement as a whole recalls the demoniacal wit of the young Prokofiev without lapsing into shallow balleticism.

The *Adagio* introduces one of the composer's most haunting melodies over the kind of 'pulsing' accompaniment familiar from the slow movement of the Second Violin Concerto. If the forthright simplicity of much of the rhetoric here looks forward to later works, the introduction to the finale looks back to an immediate past. Nestyev at least hears no irony here:

. . . the main theme of the first movement reappears like a reminiscence; here the composer once more reminds the listener of the principal idea of the Symphony – the theme of man's spiritual grandeur and heroic strength.

Whatever the intention, the main *Allegro* theme takes off with abundant good humour. Prokofiev avoids both empty nobility and naïve optimism in its working out. Simple exuberance generates fierce motoric energy (reminiscent of the Seventh Sonata) and the dénouement is uniquely exhilarating.

A few days after the triumphant première of this, his opus 100, Prokofiev slipped, struck his head and suffered severe concussion. Rushed unconscious to hospital, his blood pressure elevated dangerously. For some months he seemed barely able to hold on, as Kabalevsky remembers:

Prokofiev lay absolutely motionless. From time to time he ceased to recognise those around him and lost consciousness . . . It seemed this was the end.

Chapter 10

Autumnal

At the beginning of the 1950s, the Swiss composer Arthur Honegger, profoundly disillusioned with musical life in the West, formulated the following statement:

The profession of a composer is peculiar in that it is the principal activity and occupation of a man who exerts himself to produce wares for which no one has any use.

Compare Prokofiev in 1937:

The time is past when music was written for a handful of aesthetes. Today vast crowds of people have come face to face with serious music and are waiting with eager impatience. Composers: take heed of this; if you repel these crowds they will turn away from you to jazz or vulgar music. But if you can hold them you will win an audience such as the world has never before seen. But this does not mean that you must pander to this audience. Pandering always has an element of insincerity about it and nothing good ever came of that. The masses want great music, great events, great love, lively dances. They understand far more than some composers think, and they want to deepen their understanding.

Of course, it can be argued that Prokofiev's vision remained just that – a dream out of step with grimmer Soviet realities, that to take Soviet cultural promises at anything approaching face value was itself a gross miscalculation. And yet, viewed as a whole, Prokofiev's Soviet period stands up as an illustration of the possibilities of the popular in modern music. The new Russian music of the Stalin years had to be simpler in form and texture than the more alienated product permitted in the Twenties, but for Prokofiev this was not necessarily a disadvantage. Some of his foreign period works are marked by a degree of elaboration which can easily sound contrived. If the Soviet authorities did not respond to everything in Prokofiev's oeuvre, they were eager

Prokofiev at his country
house

enough to mobilise an élite group of pieces in support of their own
theories. (*Alexander Nevsky*, *Romeo and Juliet*, *Zdravitsa* and the
Fifth Symphony – these were among the 'model' compositions
cited by Prokofiev himself in his own defence in 1948.) Small
wonder that the composer never really understood his official
critics. What was there to understand? Stalin or no Stalin, he had
always relied upon his innate musicality, pursuing his synthesis of
melodic impulse and modern idiom with a minimum of
intellectual posturing and a maximum of wit and humour.

By the late 1940s, this was no longer possible for two main reasons. First, there was Prokofiev's deteriorating health: he survived the immediate crisis of January 1945, but recurrent headaches and periods of critically high blood pressure plagued him for the rest of his life. More and more, he was forced to ration his energies. Illness sapped the old fund of drive and irony and slowed what had always been an exceptional rate of composition. A second factor was the creeping reaffirmation of pre-War cultural policies. With the onset of the Cold War, Zhdanov was moving through literature, theatre and film to reach a pitch of hysteria with his 'musical court martials' of 1948.

As in 1936, the catalyst was Stalin's dissatisfaction with a recent Soviet opera. Vano Muradeli's *The Great Friendship* was a musically mediocre proposition, consciously designed to flatter the dictator's native Georgia. Its fatal flaw was a plot which glorified Commissar Ordzhonikidze, an old Georgian Bolshevik forced into suicide during Stalin's purges. Following Zhdanov's 'informal' but deliberately divisive three-day composers' conference, held in January 1948, the Central Committee of the Party promulgated its decision 'On Muradeli's opera *The Great Friendship*' on 10 February. This spiteful document, no more than a pretext for the vilification of Prokofiev, Shostakovich, Miaskovsky, Khachaturian and nearly all the leading composers of the day, was ritualistically endorsed by groups of penitent musicians assembled at Composers' Union branches all over the country. The new order was confirmed at the First All-Union Congress of Composers held, amidst an avalanche of public pressure, from 19 to 25 April. The light music lobby was only too happy to sustain the assault on a small group of highbrow composers. Many of Prokofiev's earlier works were effectively proscribed, his privileged status gone for good.

The campaign against musical 'formalism' became a dominant issue of public life. It even generated its own literary sub-genre. The hero of Osip Cherny's novel *Sneghin's Opera* composes a 'formalist' music drama which flops because the proletariat has no use for it. Sneghin asks his wife and her home help (i.e. 'the people') whether there is any room for individualistic tragedians in contemporary music. 'No,' says the Stalinist spouse, 'one must be a great conscious artist and not fuss about your own self.' With self-expression identified with the tragic element and both deemed inappropriate to the era, Cherny sends the composer to a Party meeting where he listens to criticism, sees the light, rejects his past and comes home a convinced 'Socialist Realist'. *Ilya Golovin*, Sergey Mikhalkov's drama of 1949, tells the story of a composite Prokofiev/Shostakovich figure one of whose symphonies is criticised by the Party even as it wins acclaim from American

Andrei Zhdanov, specialist in cultural repression (Novosti)

broadcasters. In the end, Golovin rejects the compliments of rotten capitalists and turns to the masses for inspiration, publishing scores in a popular style. The result? 'Standing Room Only' signs at every performance.

Stranger than fiction was the spectacular débâcle of a real live opera, *From All One's Heart* by Herman Zhukovsky. Its libretto exposed idealised life on a collective farm to all the rigours of an

188

inoffensively folkish musical backdrop: everything seemed to be in order. The opera reached the Bolshoi on 16 January 1951 and received favourable reviews from the usual journals. On 15 March 1951, it was awarded the Stalin Prize third class for 1950 and Zhukovsky received 25,000 roubles. Suddenly, on 19 April, *Pravda* published a blistering criticism of every aspect of the production. In their increasingly mindless attempts to satisfy Party diktat, those appointed to be critical had momentarily subordinated every critical faculty to the blind urge toward ideological purity. On 11 May, the Stalin Prize committee recommended that the Prize be revoked.

In our own times, the cultural dimension of the 'Zhdanovschina' (Zhdanov's Terror) has continued to fascinate. David Pownall's *Master Class* (a most unusual stage-play first performed at Leicester in January 1983) starts from the conceit that Stalin personally bullied Prokofiev and Shostakovich into writing 'real' music. At the piano, the make-believe dictator leads an exhausting session of composition by committee.

The truth was less sensational. Whereas Miaskovsky made no formal reply to the 'charges', Prokofiev sent Khrennikov a dignified apologia. Too ill to resist, he was at last forced to run for cover, reduced to writing what most of his colleagues had been writing for years: music that was nothing in particular and therefore presumably could not offend the boss, music that could not be 'wrong'. For the first time in Prokofiev's career, the melodious becomes the merely bland. With Soviet musicology at pains to present this final period as a 'last flight' of autumnal inspiration, the music itself shows an inevitable falling off. As Prokofiev himself understood, all art must retain its autonomy if it is to 'function'. What militates against its universality is not individuality but anonymity.

From 1948 to 1951, not a year went by without the loss of a close friend – first Eisenstein, then Asafiev, Miaskovsky and Lamm. Had it not been for the children, and the contacts with a mostly younger group of executant musicians – Samosud, Oistrakh, Rostropovich, Richter and Vedernikov – Prokofiev would have found himself very much alone in this period. Kabalevsky was as much 'minder' as friend and Shostakovich visited rarely. Prokofiev's later works were prepared for publication by another visitor Levon Avtomyan. After 1949, Prokofiev and Mira 'seldom went anywhere', preferring the rural seclusion of Nikolina Gora, the Prokofiev home since June 1946.

The death of Miaskovsky on 8 August 1950 was a particularly grievous blow. Their last exchange of letters dates from the previous spring with Prokofiev issuing an urgent summons to his old friend:

189

Nikolay Miaskovsky,
Prokofiev's closest friend
(Novosti)

Miaskovsky's last letter to
Prokofiev

23 April 1950

Dear Seryozhechka, congratulations on your 59th birthday! I embrace
you heartily and hope to see you soon at Nikolina Gora in the best of
health.

Forgive me for the parcel, it might not suit your taste; but for some
reason I took a fancy to it at once. We were all delighted with your
Bonfire.

Warm regards to Mira Alexandrovna.

With all my heart
N. Miaskovsky

Enraptured with Cinderella!

Prokofiev's reply:

16 May 1950

Dear Nikolay Yakovlevich,

I embrace you with all my heart. I think of you all the time. Come to
Nikolina Gora as soon as possible.

Your
S.P.

190

The two ailing composers had regularly spent their holidays together. Mira tells us how they liked to wander through the forests around Nikolina Gora:

Sometimes during such walks in the woods [Sergey] would pick mushrooms, following in the footsteps of his friend Nikolay Yakovlevich Miaskovsky to whom Sergey Sergeyevich gave the title of 'master of mushroom sport'. After Miaskovsky died, Sergey Sergeyevich often used to return to the forest path where he and Nikolay Yakovlevich last strolled together in July 1950.

Whatever the losses, whatever the disappointments, Prokofiev never gave up the thing that meant most to him – his work:

Sergey Sergeyevich could not conceive of a single day without work. With his remarkable singleness of purpose he could work under any circumstances – all he needed was a piano and a desk. But he composed music even when there was neither piano nor desk – in trains, in ships' cabins and in hospital wards. He worked in all moods – in moments of spiritual elation and at times when he felt weary and depressed; when he felt so energetic and vigorous that even his doctors would be satisfied; and when he had to alter his entire mode of life in order to be able to compose at all . . .
. . . The illness which overshadowed the last years of his life did not lessen his capacity for work; on the contrary, because of it all his physical and mental energies were concentrated on his art. This is one of the reasons why his autobiography, which he very much wanted to write, remained unfinished. That was perhaps the only allowance he made for illness and he greatly regretted it. He willingly sacrificed many of life's pleasures for the sake of what was to him the supreme joy – the joy of creation. He had always considered a day spent without work as a day wasted, and in the latter period nothing upset him more than to be forced by his doctors to lay aside his work if only for a short time. On such days when asked how he felt he would reply bitterly, 'I am only vegetating,' and though usually pleasant and gentle in his manner he would become irritable and depressed.
In the spring of 1950, while in hospital, he wrote me that he had been trying to persuade his doctors to permit him to work 'at least twice a day for half an hour at a time . . . ' Later, when he was convalescing in a sanatorium, he told me, 'At last I feel like a normal human being again: they have allowed me to work twenty minutes a day.' Twenty minutes! How pitifully little for one who never counted the time devoted to the music that was the very breath of life to him!

Accompanied by Mira, Sviatoslav Richter twice visited the composer in his Kremlin Hospital ward:

He was alone, and somehow completely grown soft. The tone of his voice was extremely offended. He said: 'They won't let me write . . . The doctors won't allow me to write . . . '

Mira Alexandrovna soothed him. 'Seryozhenka . . . Seryozhenka.' As you would talk to a sick child – soothingly and monotonously.

He complained that they kept taking his paper away, but that he wrote and hid the small paper napkins under his pillow . . . Then we visited him a second time, a month later. Prokofiev was getting better. He was allowed to write. He joked, related something. He was sweet, pleasant and serene. He accompanied us to the stairs and when we reached the bottom, he waved good-bye to us . . . with his foot. There was something boyish about him, as if a naughty schoolboy were before us.

In June 1945, Prokofiev had been well enough to attend Samosud's three concert performances of scenes from *War and Peace*. As Prokofiev's personal physician fretted, first-nighters cheered their great compatriot so recently near to death. Not long afterwards, Samosud was offered the artistic directorship of Leningrad's Maly Opera Theatre. He accepted the post on one condition – that he be permitted to stage the opera. In this version, *War and Peace* was to be a two-evening affair, thirteen scenes in all. As soon as Prokofiev's health permitted, he and Samosud embarked on a second revision of the score. At length, Prokofiev produced the two additional sections: 'A ball given by a courtier of Catherine the Great' and 'The war council at Fili'. Both were outstandingly successful. The first came easily, giving the composer an excuse for a succession of captivating dance numbers in the style of *Cinderella*. The second was not composed until 1947. As the central pivot for Part Two, it would have to focus on Field-Marshal Kutuzov. Samosud was anxious to provide the character with a great climactic aria encapsulating the spirit of Russian patriotism. Prokofiev was less than enthused. The search for the right music turned into a protracted argument. 'As I remember, there were at least eight versions . . .' Samosud recalls.

'Just what is it you want?' Prokofiev demanded on one occasion.

'That it be an aria such as in *Susanin* or *Igor* – central, eloquent, crucial.'

'I can't *do* that . . . '

'Then write a better one. You've got to.'

At length, Prokofiev handed Samosud a sheet on which he had scribbled down one of the melodies from his *Ivan the Terrible* film score. 'This, it seems, is what you wanted.' As the rewritings continued, the flowing, very 'Russian' theme of Kutuzov's aria became a principal leitmotif of the opera.

The music for Part Two of *Ivan* was assembled between June and November of 1945. At much the same time, Prokofiev began a Ninth Piano Sonata, sketched out a Sixth Symphony, and

Ivan the Terible, Part 2
(National Film Archive)

polished off the *Ode to the End of the War*, op. 105. Borrowing its thematic material from the unpublished *Revolution* cantata, he scored the work for an experimental combo which excluded violins, violas, and cellos in favour of eight harps, four pianos, a bloated wind section and a battery of percussion. As for Eisenstein's film, criticism of its 'ideological conception' had been mounting steadily. While Eisenstein recuperated from a near-fatal heart attack, working on his memoirs as Prokofiev advised, Stalin saw the film and disliked it intensely. *Ivan the Terrible*, Part Two was banned for twelve years. The material that had been shot and edited for Part Three was simply destroyed.

Although Prokofiev's own health gave continued cause for concern, his condition had stabilised by May 1946 and he was permitted to travel to Leningrad for his first glimpse of Samosud's production of 'Lyric-Dramatic Scenes after Tolstoy's novel *War and Peace*'. The evening began with Scene 1, 'At the Rostov estate', and ended with Scene 8, 'Before the Battle of Borodino'; the imposing choral Epigraph was omitted. A remarkable hit with the public, the production was given 105 times during the season 1946-7. There seemed no good reason not to proceed with plans to produce Part Two of the opera.

After the première of Part 1 of *War and Peace*, composer and cast congratulate musical director Samuel Samosud, flanked by Prokofiev and Mira. (Novosti)

The summer season of 1946 was notable for another overdue triumph, the completion of the Violin Sonata No. 1 in F minor, op. 80 – one of the greatest of Prokofiev's non-orchestral works. David Oistrakh takes up the story, for it is 'his' sonata:

I remember the day in the summer of 1946 when I drove out to Prokofiev's country house in Nikolina Gora to hear a new violin sonata he had written (it figures as No. 1 in the list of his works). 'You must come,' he said over the phone. 'Nikolay Yakovlevich has also written a violin sonata. So you will have a chance to hear two new sonatas at the same time.'

I arrived punctually at the appointed hour. Before long, Miaskovsky who lived nearby, joined us, and we sat down to listen to Prokofiev's sonata. If I am not mistaken Miaskovsky was also hearing it for the first time. Before beginning to play, Prokofiev enumerated all the movements, after which he played the whole sonata through without pausing. It made a powerful impression, in spite of the fact that his performance was somewhat 'shy'. One felt that this was truly great music, and indeed for sheer beauty and depth nothing to equal it had been written for the violin for many a decade. Miaskovsky had only one word for it: 'A masterpiece,' he said. 'My dear fellow, you don't realise what you have written!' he kept saying to Prokofiev. He was obviously deeply moved.

194

The English National Opera
production of *War and Peace*:
three scenes from the revival
of October 1975.

The Bolshoi production of
1959 is still in the repertoire
and on disc, but ENO's
version, first aired in 1972, is
the fullest ever staged. An
eclectic pageant, it retains an
element of Stalinist panto
while allowing us to follow
the individual destinies of
Natasha, Andrey and Pierre
without ruinous excisions.

(1) Felicity Lott as Natasha,
Tom McDonnell as Andrey
(Donald Southern)

Then Nikolay Yakovlevich was to play his sonata. However it was decided to make a short break during which Miaskovsky went to his home, while Prokofiev showed us (my son and myself) around his garden . . .

Later when I and my partner L. N. Oborin, the pianist, were learning to play the sonata we visited the composer many times and he gave us a great deal of invaluable advice. One could see that this work was very dear to him. He took obvious pleasure in working at it with us, making suggestions concerning both the character of the movement and the inner meaning of the music itself. For instance, about one passage of the first movement where the violin plays passages running up and down the scale, he said that it should sound 'like the wind in a graveyard'. After remarks of this kind the whole spirit of the sonata assumed a deeper significance for us. Never have I been so completely absorbed in a piece of music. Until the first public performance I could play nothing else, think of nothing else.

During the following winter, Prokofiev's health worsened again. Too ill to observe at first hand the preparations for Part Two of *War and Peace*, he nonetheless continued to write. He managed to complete the Symphony No. 6, op. 111, on 18 February 1947 and sketched ideas for a cello sonata even as he worked on late revisions to the 'war' scenes. The dress rehearsal did not take place

(2) Derek Hammond Stroud
as Napoleon
(Donald Southern)

until July. Even then, he was unable to join the audience – an audience studded with apprehensive functionaries from the Committee on Arts Affairs and the Composers' Union. Zhdanov's clamp-down was only six months away. How might Stalin himself react to Prokofiev's audacious vision of Russian history? The times were not propitious and the theatre opted for postponement. There would be further 'closed' premières but nothing more. Nothing but bureaucrats suggesting ruinous cuts, administrators reluctant to go out on a limb and a composer desperate to see his work performed. Eventually as Samosud confirms:

Prokofiev's desire to see *War and Peace* was so urgent, so compelling, that he was prepared to go literally to any lengths of editorial changes, abbreviations, or cuts if only it would be produced.

On 11 October, the Leningrad Philharmonic opened its new season with the unveiling of the Sixth Symphony. Yevgeny Mravinsky conducted and Prokofiev was able to join him on the platform to acknowledge a polite ovation. If the immediate response was not hostile, this was merely the calm before the

196

(3) Harold Blackburn as
Kutuzov
(Donald Southern)

storm. In 1948, the work was targeted for special censure. Even today the Sixth is seldom recognised for what it is, the finest work of Prokofiev's Soviet period and arguably his masterpiece.

To some extent the Symphony was inspired by the war years. As the composer told Nestyev:

Now we are rejoicing in our great victory, but each of us has wounds which cannot be healed. One has lost those dear to him, another has lost his health. This must not be forgotten.

The Sixth is a commemoration of the dead, weighed down with the self-searching of the living. As if the problems of his personal life were not sufficient, Prokofiev must have been increasingly worried about his art. As Nicolas Nabokov wrote:

All these years he thought he was doing exactly the kind of work his government wanted; that is, writing simple and easily 'consumable' music . . . Suddenly he began to doubt his own interpretation of the government's decrees and to wonder what he should do next . . . his remaining artistic integrity quite naturally revolted against the very idea

197

of conformity for conformity's sake, a conformity which was not based on his own beliefs and ran counter to his artistic freedom.

All the more remarkable then that the Sixth should represent a step forward, plumbing unsuspected emotional depths with true symphonic discipline. The broad canvas – three movements in 43 minutes – may owe something to the example of Shostakovich. But the sound world it creates is wholly individual, 'sharp and ringing, like the dripping of snow in spring' (Galina Vishnevskaya).

After a stark, decisive call to attention, the first movement proper begins with a surprisingly lyrical tune. The second theme (oboes) is similarly unexpected, subdued and chant-like with an otherworldly quality intensified by its remoteness from the original key. The powerful central section has a rare sense of purpose and an almost Mahlerian cut and thrust as the unlikely lyrical theme gradually amasses epic strength. Throughout, the sense of climax is masterly. But there can be no final triumphant resolution as in the corresponding movement of the Fifth. Dark instrumental colours cloud the otherwise positive sound of the final chord.

There is no scherzo. The central movement is a full-scale *Largo* as weighty as the first. The opening, anguished and grating, has an emotional intensity rarely encountered in Prokofiev's work. The first theme too seems laden with grief. Nestyev is once again found throwing stones, complaining that the movement is 'devoid of contrast'. In fact the second theme, first heard on the cellos, is less intense, more freely lyrical. The flow is interrupted by a stormy episode which superficially recalls the 'Midnight' scene from *Cinderella* and similar passages in *Semyon Kotko*. It serves here to anticipate the distinctive sonorities of the finale. The middle section, tenderly nostalgic, includes a serenade for the horns, while the last part of the movement provides a telescoped reappraisal of the opening material in reverse order. The coda itself is a not quite serene ending.

After this, the breezy innocence of the Finale comes as a shock. We are back in the world of the *Classical Symphony*, except that the unflagging *Vivace* is punctuated by snatches of a clumsy peasant-dance stomping crudely in the bass. The second idea is another witty inspiration, although there is perhaps something unsettling about the tuba's off-beat interjections. The music continues in good-humoured, mock-classic vein. At one exuberant point, horns and strings combine both themes. And yet there is a growing sense of disquiet. The music loses its way and peters out. As in recent sonatas, Prokofiev suddenly turns aside. There is to be no optimistic resolution as favoured by Soviet officialdom. Instead the composer reserves a postscript for himself. With the return of the plaintive, chant-like theme from the first movement and the explosion which follows, the Symphony turns finally and unmistakably to tragedy. Another pause, and the *Vivace* returns, but the stomping theme is all that is left – a thudding, mechanistic whirlwind which abruptly collapses in a heap. In musical terms, the Symphony reaches its goal, but to describe this passage as a triumphant flourish is to miss the point. As Volkov has Shostakovich say of his own Fifth Symphony:

It's as if someone were beating you with a stick and saying, 'Your business is rejoicing. Your business is rejoicing,' and you rise, shakily, and go marching off muttering, 'Our business is rejoicing, our business is rejoicing.' What kind of apotheosis is that?

The effect of suffering on *Stravinsky's* artistic beliefs was that he determined to keep his art and his life as separate as possible rather than seeking a musical outlet for his feelings – a philosophy defined by T. S. Eliot's aphorism:

The more perfect the artist, the more completely separate in him will be the man who suffers and the mind which creates.

The deepening of Prokofiev's musical imagination at this point throws the composers' aesthetic differences into greater relief. When Olin Downes of the *New York Times* welcomed the new Symphony, Stravinsky wrote to Nabokov on 15 December 1949:

I heard Prokofiev's Sixth Symphony. Nothing justifies its dullness and it shows neither aesthetic nor technical novelty. This is clear to everyone except comrade Olin Downes.

Even *Musical America*, the journal which characterised the Fifth as a 'bon-bon', found something to praise in the Sixth:

Perhaps because the work is a kind of autobiographical confession, it is loose in structure and repetitious, and the gorgeous effects of scoring seem to tempt the composer to excess. Nevertheless, there is no resisting the passion, sincerity, and drive of large sections of the work.

In the autumn of 1947, Prokofiev completed his Piano Sonata No. 9, op. 103, the work begun two years before and dedicated to Sviatoslav Richter. Prokofiev had shown Richter the sketches, saying: 'I have something interesting for you. This will be your sonata . . . Only don't think it will be for effect . . . ' As Richter remembers:

199

Truly, at first glance it seemed quite simple, I was even a little disappointed. [Later] on his [60th] birthday Prokofiev was ill again. A concert was arranged in the Composers' Union two days before and he listened to it over the phone. I played the Ninth Sonata for the first time. This sonata is radiant, simple, and even intimate. I think that in some respects it is a domestic sonata. The more you hear it, the more you come to love it and feel its magnetism. The more perfect it seems. I love it very much.

A domestic sonata from the rebellious student of the 'Evenings of contemporary music'! Nothing could contrast more strongly with the characteristic music of Prokofiev's youth:

The new tone, more relaxed, quieter, more limpid, can be attributed to the change in character of an ill and ageing man, who has exchanged his youthful energy for a more contemplative attitude to life. But it is perhaps also the successful achievement of the Soviet music to which he was tending, the end of the quest for a 'new simplicity'.

(Claude Samuel)

The Sonata's conclusion provides a calm, Olympian close to Prokofiev's kaleidoscopic cycle of nine.

1947 also saw the composition of the Sonata in D major for Solo Violin(s), op. 115. An entirely characteristic miniature despite the constraints of the medium, Nestyev finds it 'unusually thin when played by unaccompanied violin alone. Only if it were possible to hear this composition played by an ensemble of violinists in unison, as the composer intended, could one properly evaluate it.' [!]

In November 1947, the Russian people were called upon to celebrate 30 years of Soviet power. Prokofiev responded with the anaemic *Festive Poem* (*Thirty Years*) for symphony orchestra, op. 113 and the cantata *Flourish Mighty Land*, op. 114 – 'spirited, gay and quite fresh' according to Miaskovsky. When Zhdanov's axe fell, Prokofiev was hard at work on a new opera, *The Story of a Real Man*, op. 117. The Kirov Theatre had enthusiastically welcomed the idea of an opera based on the heroic exploits of airman Alexey Meresyev – a sort of Soviet Douglas Bader – and Prokofiev must have hoped that the project would restore him to favour as he worked on through 1948. 'Clear melodies and the simplest harmonic language possible – these are the other elements which I shall strive for in this opera,' he said. On 3 and 4 December respectively, *The Story of a Real Man* and *War and Peace* were given 'closed' previews in Leningrad theatres. Prokofiev insisted on attending, but neither work was accepted for production. *The Story of a Real Man* was eventually premièred (albeit in bowdlerised form) at the Bolshoi Theatre on 8 October 1960. It shows the quality of Prokofiev's creative thought at a low ebb.

Many of the works composed in these last years fail to match up to Prokofiev's own high standards. With theatrical venues denied him, Prokofiev turned again to music for children. For the children's radio division he wrote first the symphonic suite *Winter Bonfire*, op. 122. Miaskovsky's diary for 10 April 1950 contains this sympathetic entry: 'Recently heard Pr's charming children's suite to verses by Marshak on the radio. Very imaginative and witty.'

Prokofiev: a photographic portrait of 1951 (Novosti)

201

The collaboration with Marshak also hatched an overtly propagandist oratorio of the airwaves entitled *On Guard for Peace*, Prokofiev's op. 124:

I can still see Sergey's anxious expression on waking in the middle of the night before the first performance of the oratorio *On Guard for Peace*, wondering whether he had succeeded in putting into the work what he wanted to express . . .

After the virulent attacks to which the composer had been subjected in the press, one can understand the real significance of Mira Mendelson's reminiscence.

It was the same story before the first 'audition' of the Seventh Symphony at the Composers' Union. Prokofiev had written 'a simple symphony, for young listeners'. Even so, he feared that he might be misunderstood. Kabalevsky recalls:

We found him ill in bed. He questioned us anxiously about the audition and brightened up at once when he heard that it had been successful. Again and again he asked us about it, as if he feared we had only been trying to pacify him, 'Isn't the music rather too simple?' he asked, but he was not doubting the correctness of his search for a new simplicity; he merely wanted to be reassured that his creative quests had been understood and appreciated.

The Seventh is an endearing though not noticeably symphonic composition. It lacks drive and conflict and attempts to make up for it with a display of sophisticated orchestration. There is no doubt that Prokofiev *was* worried about the direction of his art. He was listening, perhaps more than necessary, to the advice of Stalinist intellectuals, among them Alexander Fadeyev, leader of the Writers' Union in the wake of Zhdanov's literary purge. He was putting his name to vacuous essays and statements concocted by Party hacks. He was churning out threadbare, functional music for broadcasting purposes: the sole distinction of *The Volga Meets the Don*, op. 130 was that it was 'the only symphonic work dedicated to this historic event', i.e. the opening of a canal. He was easily persuaded to add the conventional final flourish to the wistful close of his new Symphony. (Rostropovich tells us that he did it for the Stalin Prize money and wanted the new ending suppressed after his death.) Worst of all, the broad flowing themes of yesteryear were beginning to unravel into something bland and intermittently banal.

The first open concert performance of the Seventh proved to be Prokofiev's last public appearance. Painfully aware of his colleague's failing health, Shostakovich penned this moving tribute the very next day:

12.X.1952. Moscow

Dear Sergey Sergeyevich,

Warm congratulations on your wonderful new symphony. I listened through it yesterday with great interest and enjoyment from first to last note. The Seventh Symphony has turned out to be a work of lofty accomplishment, profound feeling, and enormous talent. It is a genuinely masterful work. I am not a music critic, therefore I shall refrain from more detailed comments. I am simply a listener who loves music in general and yours in particular. I regret that only the fourth movement by itself was played as an encore. The whole thing should have been played. For that matter, new works ought to be played twice officially, and the third time for an encore. It seems to me that S. A. Samosud performed the Seventh Symphony superbly.

I wish you at least another hundred years to live and create. Listening to such works as your Seventh Symphony makes it much easier and more joyful to live.

I warmly clasp your hand. Greetings to Mira Alexandrovna.

Yours. D. Shostakovich

The best of Prokofiev's post-1948 music is a product of the faithful friendship and close collaboration of Mstislav Rostropovich. The Cello Sonata, Op. 119 might seem over-sweet or diffuse by the exalted standards of the F minor Violin Sonata. But the relaxed form of utterance is unforced and, in its own way, rewarding. The piece has much in common with the Ninth Piano Sonata and was well received when publicly performed by Rostropovich and Richter. The young cellist was even more heavily involved in the preparation of the *Sinfonia Concertante* (more properly Symphony-Concerto), op. 125. In this expansive reworking of the Cello Concerto, op. 58, he not only edited the solo part to exploit more fully the technical possibilities of the instrument, but also assisted with the scoring. He certainly made things immensely difficult for soloists less gifted than himself.

On 18 February 1952, Rostropovich introduced the work with the Moscow Youth Orchestra under the brave (because inexperienced) direction of Sviatoslav Richter. The reception was cool, as well it might be. Nestyev explains:

In the Symphony-Concerto, just as in the Sixth Symphony and the last piano sonatas, the old and the new in Prokofiev stand side by side. The old manifests itself chiefly in the harshness of timbre and harmony and in the deliberately disjointed character of certain passages . . . But these particular passages, which displeased some members of the audience at the première . . . must not be construed as the predominant stylistic elements of the work. On the contrary, it is the broad and idiomatic singing themes . . . that are the most prominent features of this composition.

Today it comes as a relief to recognise some of the old Prokofiev bite, the piquant orchestral timbres, the mischievous disregard for convention.

Some critics retain a similar regard for Prokofiev's last ballet score, *The Stone Flower*. Based on one of Bazhov's colourful folk legends from the Ural mountains, the project took shape from the autumn of 1948. The choreographer was to be Lavrovsky, 'who had done such a splendid job' with *Romeo and Juliet*. The piano score was completed between September 1948 and March 1949 – at a time when illness prevented the composer from working more than an hour a day. As so often in the past, it was the production itself which failed to materialise. According to Lavrovsky:

The music was sharply criticised at a number of auditions. It was said to have little in common with the artistic imagery of Bazhov's tales, that it was gloomy, heavy, and difficult to dance to. A great many hasty, inconsiderate, and indeed tactless, judgments were passed. Prokofiev chafed at the delay in the production and felt hurt. At this time his health took a turn for the worse . . . Unfortunately I could do nothing to bolster his spirits, in fact I was compelled to conceal much from him for fear of affecting his health.

Many months later, as Mira recalls:

. . . the theatre asked Sergey Sergeyevich to make additions to the score. They wanted him, as Sergey Sergeyevich put it, 'to make the dramatic parts louder, which means to coarsen the texture of the score'. Grateful as he was to the theatre for the superb productions of the ballets *Romeo and Juliet* and *Cinderella*, he could not agree to this request. The orchestration of *The Stone Flower* had been based on the logical development of the plot, the characters, the nature of the dance; the theatre's request would have meant revising the whole conception, and this upset him very much. He declared that it 'gave him no rest'.

'Unfortunately', says Kabalevsky,

. . . having obtained the composer's consent 'in principle', the theatre took the liberty of revising the score on their own after his death. A comparison of both scores – the author's and the one 'edited' by the theatre – will show how much more subtle and colourful is Prokofiev's music.

The Stone Flower is not the only Prokofiev ballet score to have been adulterated by 'hussars of orchestration' on the Bolshoi staff. But, by the end of his life, Prokofiev was apparently willing to do the same job himself. Lavrovsky reports:

. . . Rehearsals began. Prokofiev livened up at once. More than two years

205

had passed since he had written the music. We had altered and revised much of the material in the light of some of the criticism. Prokofiev rewrote a good deal, for example, the duet of Katerina and Danila in the fourth act.

It was this duet that occupied Prokofiev at the end:

Prokofiev was sitting over the orchestral score of the duet. He seemed quite well, was absorbed in his work . . . I spent the rest of the day staging the duet, and that evening I called up Prokofiev to tell him about it . . . Mira Alexandrovna answered the phone and in a barely recognisable voice told me that Sergey Sergeyevich was dead.

Twentieth-century music has been so full of self-conscious attitudes, so often a vehicle for ideas and manifestos which themselves have little to do with art, that it is refreshing to come back to a composer who wrote music simply – out of an irrepressible feel for the medium. Even during these last painful months, the struggle to create was paramount:

A few days before the end, completely exhausted by a severe attack of influenza, Sergey Sergeyevich asked me to inscribe the titles of these works in the list of his compositions we had compiled in 1952. Deeply distressed (for I knew that many of these works had been barely begun), I endeavoured to assure him that we would have plenty of time to do that later on when the work was finished. But he was so insistent that to humour him I sat down at once and entered the following titles at his dictation:
'Op. 132–Concertino for violoncello and orchestra, in three movements.
'Op. 133–Concerto No. 6 for two pianos and string orchestra, in three movements.
'Op. 134–Sonata for violoncello solo, in four movements.
'Op. 135–Fifth Sonata for piano, new version, in three movements.
'Op. 136–Second Symphony, new version, in three movements.
'Op. 137–Tenth Sonata for piano in E flat.
'Op. 138–Eleventh Sonata for piano.'
Only one of these works, the new version of the Fifth Piano Sonata, was completed before he died.

(Mira Mendelson)

Other struggles are recalled in Ilya Ehrenburg's carefully worded tribute of 1955:

He renounced the [Western] world that had made him famous; he wanted to work for his own people and for the future. He suffered many trials, but he never lost heart, never gave up the fight, and he died young in spirit, uncompromising, true to himself to the end. He was a great man

Opposite
Prokofiev's last work, the sketch for his Piano Sonata no. 10

10-я соната.

and future generations will not be able to understand that difficult and glorious time which we still have the right to call our own without listening carefully to Sergey Prokofiev's music and pondering over his remarkable fate.

Joseph Stalin, the man most directly responsible for this 'remarkable fate', died at 9.50 pm on 5 March 1953. It was on the same evening, at approximately 9.00 pm, that Prokofiev himself died of a massive brain haemorrhage. The death of the composer went unreported for some days. *Sovetskaya Muzyka* carried their obituaries in the April 1953 issue – Stalin's on page 1, Prokofiev's on page 117.

In those days, when life itself seemed locked in expectation of further horrors, someone striding through a corridor in the [Bolshoi] theatre flung out the words, 'Sergey Prokofiev is dead'. The news swept through the theatre, and hung in the air like an impossibility. Who had died? Another person besides Stalin could not have dared to die. Stalin alone had died, and all of the people's feelings, all the grief of loss, should belong to him alone.

. . . The streets of Moscow were blocked off, and traffic had come to a standstill. It was impossible to find a car, and it cost a tremendous effort to move Prokofiev's coffin from his apartment across from the Moscow Art Theatre to a tiny room in the basement of the Composers' House on Myausskaya Street for a civil funeral.

All of the hothouses and florists' shops had been emptied for the Leader and Teacher of All Times and All Peoples. Nowhere could one buy even a few flowers to place on the coffin of the great Russian composer. In the newspapers, there was no room for an obituary. Everything was Stalin's – even the ashes of Prokofiev, whom he had persecuted. And while hundreds of thousands of people trampled one another in the frenzy to get to the Hall of Columns so as to bow one last time to the superman-murderer, the dark, dank basement on Myausskaya Street was almost empty – the only people present being Prokofiev's family and friends who happened to live nearby and could break through the police barriers.

(Galina Vishnevskaya)

Catalogue of Works

Op. 1   Piano Sonata no. 1 in F minor (1907 rev. 1909); Moscow, 21 February [6 March] 1910

2   Four Études for piano: (I) D minor, (II) E minor, (III) C minor, (IV) C minor (1909); Moscow, 21 February [6 March] 1910 (only three performed)

3   Four Pieces for piano: (I) *Story*, (II) *Badinage*, (III) *March*, (IV) *Phantom* (1907-8 rev. 1911); St Petersburg, 28 March [10 April] 1911

4   Four Pieces for piano: (I) *Reminiscence*, (II) *Élan*, (III) *Despair*, (IV) *Suggestion Diabolique* (1908 rev. 1910-12); St Petersburg, 18 [31] December 1908

5   Sinfonietta in A major for orchestra (1909 rev. 1914-15); Petrograd, 24 October [6 November] 1915. Later revised as op. 48

6   *Dreams*, symphonic poem for orchestra (1910); St Petersburg, 22 November [5 December] 1910 (student performance)

7   Two poems for women's voices and orchestra, words by K. Balmont: (I) *The White Swan*, (II) *The Wave* (1909-10); St Petersburg, February 1910 (only *The White Swan* performed)

8   *Autumnal*, sketch for orchestra (1910 rev. 1915, 1934); Moscow, 19 July [1 August] 1911

9   Two poems for voice and piano, words by A. Apukhtin and K. Balmont (1911); St Petersburg, 15 [28] March 1914 (only one performed)

10   Concerto no. 1 in D flat major for piano and orchestra (1911-12); Moscow, 25 July [7 August] 1912

11   Toccata in D minor for .piano (1912); Petrograd, 27 November [10 December] 1916

12   Ten *Episodes* for piano (1906-13); Moscow, 23 January [5 February] 1914 (only three performed)

12b   *Humoresque Scherzo* for four bassoons (1915); London, 2 September 1916. (Transcription of op. 12 no. 9)

13   *Maddalena*, opera in one act, libretto by M. Lieven (1911-13); BBC, 25 March 1979 (orchestrated by E. Downes)

14   Piano Sonata no. 2 in D minor (1912); Moscow, 23 January [5 February] 1914

15   *Ballade* for cello and piano (1912); Moscow, 23 January [5 February] 1914

16   Concerto no. 2 in G minor for piano and orchestra (1912-13 rev. 1923); Pavlovsk, 23 August [5 September] 1913

17   Five *Sarcasms* for piano (1912-14); Petrograd, 27 November [10 December] 1916

18   *The Ugly Duckling* for voice and piano (1914); Petrograd, 17 [30] January 1915. Based on Andersen's fairy tale. Also exists in a version for voice and orchestra

19   Concerto no. 1 in D major for violin and orchestra (1916-17); Paris, 18 October 1923
20   *Scythian Suite* (from *Ala and Lolli*) (1915); Petrograd, 16 [29] January 1916.
21   *The Buffoon (Chout)*, ballet in six scenes, scenario by S. Prokofiev after A. Afanasyev (1915 rev. 1920); Paris, 17 May 1921
21b   *The Buffoon (Chout)*, symphonic suite from the ballet (1920); Brussels, 15 January 1924
22   *Visions Fugitives*, 20 pieces for piano (1915-17); Petrograd, 15 April 1918
23   Five poems for voice and piano, words by V. Goryansky, Z. Gippius, B. Verin, K. Balmont, N. Agnivtsev (1915); Petrograd, 27 November [10 December] 1916 (only four performed)
24   *The Gambler*, opera in four acts, libretto by S. Prokofiev after the story by Dostoyevsky (1915-17 rev. 1927-8); Brussels, 29 April 1929
25   Symphony no. 1 in D major, 'Classical' (1916-17); Petrograd, 21 April 1918
26   Concerto no. 3 in C major for piano and orchestra (1917-21); Chicago, 16 December 1921
27   Five poems, words by Anna Akhmatova (1916); Moscow, 5 [18] February 1917
28   Piano Sonata no. 3 in A minor (1907 rev. 1917); Petrograd, 15 April 1918
29   Piano Sonata no. 4 in C minor (1908 rev. 1917); Petrograd, 17 April 1918
29b   *Andante* for orchestra (1934); 13 February 1958. Transcribed from op. 29
30   *Seven, they are seven*, cantata for tenor, chorus and orchestra, words by K. Balmont (1917-18 rev. 1933); Paris, 29 May 1924
31   *Old Grandmother's Tales*, four pieces for piano (1918); New York, 7 January 1919
32   Four Pieces for piano: (I) Dance, (II) Minuet, (III) Gavotte, (IV) Waltz (1918); New York, 30 March 1919
33   *The Love of Three Oranges*, opera in four acts with prologue, libretto by S. Prokofiev after the play by Carlo Gozzi (1919); Chicago, 30 December 1921
33b   *The Love of Three Oranges*, symphonic suite from the opera (1924); Paris, 29 November 1925
33ter March and Scherzo from *The Love of Three Oranges*, transcription for piano (1922)
34   *Overture on Hebrew Themes* in C minor for clarinet, piano and string quartet (1919); New York, 26 January 1920
34b   *Overture on Hebrew Themes* for symphony orchestra (1934); Moscow, 30 November 1934. New version of op. 34
35   Five songs without words for voice and piano (1920); New York, 27 March 1921. No. 2 also exists in a version for voice and orchestra
35b   Five melodies for violin and piano (1925). Arrangement of op. 35
36   Five poems for voice and piano, words by K. Balmont (1921); Milan, May 1922
37   *The Fiery Angel*, opera in five acts, libretto by S. Prokofiev after the story by V. Bryusov (1919-23 rev. 1926-7); Paris, 25 November 1954 (complete concert performance)
38   Piano Sonata no. 5 in C major (1923); Paris, 9 March 1924. Later revised as op. 135
39   Quintet in G minor for oboe, clarinet, violin, viola and double bass (1924); Moscow, 6 March 1927. (Incorporates music from the unpublished ballet *Trapeze*)
40   Symphony no. 2 in D minor (1924-5); Paris, 6 June 1925
41   *Le Pas d'Acier* (Steel Step), ballet in two scenes, scenario by G. Yakulov and S. Prokofiev (1925-6); Paris, 7 June 1927
41b   *Le Pas d'Acier*, symphonic suite from the ballet (1926); Moscow, 27 May 1928
42   'American' Overture in B flat major, for 17 performers (1926); Moscow,

7 February 1927

42b 'American' Overture in B flat major, for full orchestra (1928); Paris, 18 December 1930. New version of op. 42

43 *Divertissement* for orchestra (1925-9); Paris, 22 December 1929

43b *Divertissement* for piano (1938). Transcribed from op. 43

44 Symphony no. 3 in C minor (1928); Paris, 17 May 1929

45 *Things in themselves* (*Choses en soi*), two pieces for piano (1928); New York, 6 January 1930

46 *The Prodigal Son*, ballet in three scenes, scenario by B. Kochno (1928-9); Paris, 21 May 1929

46b *The Prodigal Son*, symphonic suite from the ballet (1929); Paris, 7 March 1931

47 Symphony no. 4 in C major (1929-30); Boston, 14 November 1930. Later revised as op. 112

48 Sinfonietta in A major for orchestra (1929); Moscow, 18 November 1930. Revision of op. 5

49 Four *Portraits*, symphonic suite from the opera *The Gambler* (1931); Paris, 12 March 1932

50 String Quartet no. 1 in B minor (1930); Washington, 25 April 1931

50b *Andante* from Quartet in B minor, arranged for string orchestra (1930)

51 *Sur le Borysthène* (*On the Dnieper*), ballet in two scenes, scenario by S. Lifar and S. Prokofiev (1930-1); Paris, 16 December 1932

51b *Sur le Borysthène*, symphonic suite from the ballet (1933); Paris, 1934

52 Six transcriptions for piano (1930-1); Moscow, 27 May 1932. Transcribed from opp. 46, 35, 50, and 48

53 Concerto no. 4 in B flat major for piano (left hand) and orchestra (1931); West Berlin, 5 September 1956.

54 Two Sonatinas for piano: (I) E minor, (II) G major (1931-2); London, 17 April 1932 (only the second one performed)

55 Concerto no. 5 in G major for piano and orchestra (1931-2); Berlin, 31 October 1932

56 Sonata for two violins in C major (1932); Moscow, 27 November 1932

57 *Symphonic Song* for orchestra (1933); Moscow, 14 April 1934

58 Concerto for cello and orchestra in E minor (1933-8); Moscow, 26 November 1938. Later revised as op. 125

59 Three Pieces for piano (1933-4); Moscow, 1935

60 *Lieutenant Kijé*, suite based on the film score (1934); Moscow, 21 December 1934 (radio performance)

60b Two songs from *Lieutenant Kijé*: (I) *The Little Grey Dove is Cooing*, (II) *Troika* (1934)

61 *Egyptian Nights*, symphonic suite from the incidental music to the play (1934); Moscow, 22 December 1938

62 *Pensées*, three pieces for piano (1933-4); Moscow, 13 November 1936

63 Concerto no. 2 in G minor for violin and orchestra (1935); Madrid, 1 December 1935

64 *Romeo and Juliet*, ballet in four acts, scenario by S. Radlov, A. Piotrovsky, L. Lavrovsky and S. Prokofiev (1935-6); Brno, 30 December 1938

64b *Romeo and Juliet*, first symphonic suite from the ballet (1936); Moscow, 24 November 1936

64ter *Romeo and Juliet*, second symphonic suite from the ballet (1936); Leningrad, 15 April 1937

65 *Music for Children*, 12 easy pieces for piano (1935); Moscow, 11 April 1936

65b *A Summer's Day*, symphonic suite for small orchestra (1935 arr. 1941); Moscow, 1946 (radio broadcast). Transcribed from op. 65 nos. 1, 9, 6, 5, 10, 11 and 12

66 Six mass songs for voice and piano: (I) *Partisan Zheleznyak*, (II) *Anyutka*, (III) *The Fatherland is Growing*, (IV) *Through Snow and Fog*, (V)

Beyond the Hill, (VI) *Song of Voroshilov* (1935)

67 *Peter and the Wolf*, symphonic tale for narrator and orchestra, text by S. Prokofiev (1936); Moscow, 2 May 1936

68 Three children's songs for voice and piano: (I) *Chatterbox*, (II) *Sweet Song*, (III) *The Little Pigs* (1936); Moscow, 5 May 1936 (*Chatterbox* only)

69 Four marches for military band (1935-7); 1937 (first march only)

70 *The Queen of Spades*, music for the unrealised film (1936)

70b *Boris Godunov*, music for Meyerhold's (unrealised) production of Pushkin's drama (1936); Moscow, April 1957

71 *Eugene Onegin*, music for Tairov's (unrealised) production of the play after Pushkin (1936); BBC, 1 April 1980

72 *Russian Overture* for symphony orchestra (1936, rev. for reduced orchestra 1937); Moscow, 29 October 1936

73 Three romances for voice and piano, words by Pushkin: (I) *Pine Trees*, (II) *Roseate Dawn*, (III) *Into Your Chamber* (1936); Moscow, 20 April 1937

74 *Cantata for the Twentieth Anniversary of the October Revolution* for symphony orchestra, military band, accordions, percussion and two choirs, text from writings and speeches of Marx, Lenin and Stalin (1936-7); Moscow, 5 April 1966

75 *Romeo and Juliet*, ten pieces for piano (1937); Moscow, 1937

76 *Songs of Our Days*, suite for soloists, chorus and orchestra (1937); Moscow, 5 January 1938

77 *Hamlet*, music for the play (1937-8); Leningrad, 15 May 1939

77b *Gavotte* from the music for *Hamlet* for piano (1938); Moscow, 22 November 1939 (radio performance)

78 *Alexander Nevsky*, cantata based on the film score for mezzo-soprano, chorus and orchestra, text by V. Lugovskoy and S. Prokofiev (1939); Moscow, 17 May 1939

78b Three songs from *Alexander Nevsky*, words by V. Lugovskoy: (I) *Arise, people of Russia*, (II) *Mark ye bright falcons*, (III) *And it happened on the banks of the Neva* (1939)

79 Seven mass songs for voice and piano (1939)

80 Sonata no. 1 in F minor for violin and piano (1938-46); Moscow, 23 October 1946

81 *Semyon Kotko*, opera in five acts, libretto by V. Katayev and S. Prokofiev after a story by V. Katayev (1939); Moscow, 23 June 1940

81b *Semyon Kotko*, symphonic suite from the opera (1941); Moscow, 27 December 1943

82 Piano Sonata no. 6 in A major (1939-40); Moscow, 8 April 1940 (radio performance)

83 Piano Sonata no. 7 in B flat major (1939-42); Moscow, 18 January 1943

84 Piano Sonata no. 8 in B flat major (1939-44); Moscow, 30 December 1944

85 *Zdravitsa (Hail to Stalin)*, cantata for chorus and orchestra on folk texts (1939); Moscow, 21 December 1939

86 *The Duenna (Betrothal in a Monastery)*, opera in four acts, libretto by S. Prokofiev, verses by Mira Mendelson, after the play by Sheridan (1940-1); Leningrad, 3 November 1946

87 *Cinderella*, ballet in three acts, scenario by N. D. Volkov (1940-4); Moscow, 21 November 1945

88 Symphonic march in B flat major for orchestra (1941)

89 Seven mass songs for voice and piano (1941-2); Nalchik, November 1941 (nos. 3 and 4 only)

89b March in A flat major for military band (1941). Based on op. 89 no. 2

90 *The Year 1941*, symphonic suite for orchestra (1941); Sverdlovsk, 21 January 1943

91 *War and Peace*, opera in five acts with a choral epigraph, libretto by S. Prokofiev and M. Mendelson after Tolstoy (1941-3 rev. 1946-52);

Leningrad, 12 June 1946 (first version, first eight scenes only); Leningrad, 31 March 1955 (second version, 11 scenes); Moscow, 8 November 1957 (revised performing version in 13 scenes)

92 String Quartet no. 2 in F major (on Kabardinian themes) (1941); Moscow, 5 September 1942

93 *Ballad of an Unknown Boy*, cantata for soprano, tenor, chorus and orchestra, words by P. Antokolsky (1942-3); Moscow, 21 February 1944

94 Sonata for flute and piano in D major (1943); Moscow, 7 December 1943

94b Sonata no. 2 in D major for violin and piano (1943 arr. 1944); Moscow, 17 June 1944. Transcription of op. 94

95 Three pieces for piano from *Cinderella* (1942)

96 Three pieces for piano (1941-2). Transcriptions from *War and Peace* and the film *Lermontov*

97 Ten pieces for piano from *Cinderella* (1943)

97b *Adagio* from *Cinderella* for cello and piano (1944); Moscow, 19 April 1944 (radio performance)

98 National Anthem of the Soviet Union and National Anthem of the R.S.F.S.R. (1943, 1946). Unpublished sketches

99 March for band in B flat major (1943-4); Moscow, 30 April 1944 (radio performance)

100 Symphony no. 5 in B flat major (1944); Moscow, 13 January 1945

101 *Romeo and Juliet*, third suite for orchestra (1946); Moscow, 8 March 1946

102 Six pieces for piano from *Cinderella* (1944)

103 Piano Sonata no. 9 in C major (1947); Moscow, 21 April 1951

104 Twelve Russian folk songs for voice and piano (1944); Moscow, 25 March 1945

105 *Ode to the end of the War* for eight harps, four pianos, wind, percussion and double basses (1945); Moscow, 12 November 1945

106 Two duets, arrangements of Russian folk songs for tenor and bass with piano (1945)

107 *Cinderella*, first suite for orchestra (1946); Moscow, 12 November 1946

108 *Cinderella*, second suite for orchestra (1946)

109 *Cinderella*, third suite for orchestra (1946); Moscow, 3 September 1947 (radio performance)

110 *Waltzes Suite* for orchestra (from *War and Peace*, *Cinderella* and *Lermontov*) (1946); Moscow, 13 May 1947

111 Symphony no. 6 in E flat minor (1945-7); Leningrad, 11 October 1947

112 Symphony no. 4 in C major (1947). Revised version of op. 47

113 *Festive Poem (Thirty Years)* for orchestra (1947); Moscow, 3 October 1947

114 *Flourish Mighty Land*, cantata for chorus and orchestra, text by E. Dolmatovsky (1947); Moscow, 12 November 1947. Written for the 30th anniversary of the October Revolution

115 Sonata for Solo Violin(s) in D major (1947); Moscow, 10 March 1960

116 *Ivan the Terrible*, music for the films: Part I, 1942-4; Part II, 1945. Arranged as oratorio by A. Stasevich in 1961

117 *The Story of a Real Man*, opera in four acts, libretto by M. Mendelson and S. Prokofiev after the novel by Boris Polevoy (1947-8); Leningrad, 3 December 1948 (closed perf.); Moscow, 8 October 1960 (staged)

118 *The Stone Flower*, ballet in four acts, scenario by L. Lavrovsky and M. Mendelson after the story by P. Bazhov (1948-53); Moscow, 12 February 1954

119 Sonata for cello and piano in C major (1949); Moscow, 1 March 1950

120 Two Pushkin Waltzes for orchestra (1949); Moscow, 1952 (radio performance)

121 *Soldiers' Marching Song*, words by V. Lugovskoy (1950)

122	*Winter Bonfire*, suite for narrators, boys' chorus and orchestra, text by S. Marshak (1949-50); Moscow, 19 December 1950
123	*Summer Night*, suite for orchestra from the opera *The Duenna* (1950)
124	*On Guard for Peace*, oratorio for narrators, mezzo-soprano, mixed chorus, boys' chorus and orchestra, text by S. Marshak (1950); Moscow, 19 December 1950
125	Sinfonia Concertante (Symphony-Concerto) in E minor for cello and orchestra (1950-1 rev. 1952); Moscow, 18 February 1952 (in original form as 'Second Cello Concerto'). Revision of op. 58
126	*Wedding Suite* for orchestra from *The Stone Flower* (1951); Moscow, 12 December 1951
127	*Gypsy Fantasy* for orchestra from *The Stone Flower* (1951); Moscow, 18 November 1951
128	*Ural Rhapsody* for orchestra from *The Stone Flower* (1951)
129	*The Mistress of Copper Mountain*, suite for orchestra from *The Stone Flower*. Unrealised
130	*The Volga meets the Don*, festive poem for orchestra (1951); Moscow, 22 February 1952 (radio performance)
131	Symphony no. 7 in C sharp minor (1951-2); Moscow, 11 October 1952
132	Concertino for cello and orchestra in G minor (1952). Unfinished work; completed by Rostropovich and Kabalevsky
133	Concerto for two pianos and string orchestra. Unfinished
134	Sonata for unaccompanied cello in C sharp minor. Unfinished
135	Piano Sonata no. 5 in C major (1952-3); Alma-Ata, 2 February 1954. Revision of op. 38
136	Symphony no. 2 in D minor. Projected revision of op. 40; unrealised
137	Piano Sonata no. 10 in C minor (1953). The sketch for this sonata was Prokofiev's last work
138	Piano Sonata no. 11. Unrealised.

OTHER WORKS

Arrangements
'O, no John!' (English folksong), arr. for voice and orchestra (1944)
Organ prelude and fugue in D minor by Buxtehude, arr. for piano (1920)
Waltzes by Schubert, transcribed as a suite for piano, two hands (1920)
Waltzes by Schubert, transcribed as a suite for two pianos, four hands (1923). Revision of the earlier suite

Incidental Music
Kotovsky, music for the film (1942)
Lermontov, music for the film (1941)
Partisans in the Ukrainian Steppes, music for the film (1942)
Tonya, music for the film (1942)

Operas
Khan Buzay, opera (1942). Incomplete.
Distant Seas, opera (1948). Incomplete.

Bibliography

It would be presumptuous to believe that so unusual a personality and so prolific a composer as Sergey Prokofiev could be dispensed with in a single volume. The historical, sociological and cultural background is immensely complex, and it has been difficult to telescope discussion of the composer's style without resorting to unhelpful generalisations. Prokofiev himself wanted his music to strike us as instinctive, spontaneous and heartfelt. Nevertheless, his output can and ought to be examined in order to elucidate its highly original harmonic vocabulary, its unique blend of ancient and modern in technique and aesthetic. Unhappily, much of the work listed below (all available in English) must be read with extreme caution. In *Silk Stockings*, the Cold War Cole Porter musical which had commissars clutching copies of 'Who's Still Who?', a bureaucrat is informed of Prokofiev's death and observes: 'I didn't even know he was arrested.' The highly combative polemic of Olkhovsky's *Music under the Soviets: the agony of an art* is matched by the thinly disguised pro-Soviet propaganda of Moisenko's *Realist Music*. Two sides of a coin at last being withdrawn from circulation.

Prokofiev: General

Austin, William: 'Prokofiev', in *Music in the 20th century* (London: Dent, 1966)

Blok, V., ed.: *Sergey Prokofiev: materials, articles, interviews* (Moscow: Progress Pubs., 1978)

Brown, Malcolm: *Prokofiev – a critical biography* (in preparation)

Bush, Geoffrey: 'People who live in glass houses', *The Composer*, 37 (Autumn, 1970)

Cazden, Norman: 'Humour in the music of Stravinsky and Prokofiev', *Science and Society*, 18 (1954)

Eisenstein, Sergey: 'P-R-K-F-V', in: I. Nestyev: *Sergei Prokofiev: his musical life*, (New York: Knopf, 1946)

Hanson, Lawrence & Elizabeth: *Prokofiev. The prodigal son: an introduction to his life and work in three movements* (London: Cassell, 1964)

Harris, Roy: 'Roy Harris salutes Sergei Prokofiev', *Musical America*, 81 (May, 1961)

Lambert, Constant: 'Prokofieff', *The Nation*, xlvii (September, 1930)

McAllister, Rita: 'Some days in the life of Sergei Sergeievich', *Music and Musicians*, xix (March, 1971)

    'Sergey Prokofiev', in: *The New Grove Dictionary of Music and Musicians* (London: Macmillan, 1981)

    'Sergey Prokofiev', in: *Russian Masters 2: Rimsky-Korsakov, Skryabin, Rakhmaninov, Prokofiev, Shostakovich* (The Composer biography series) (London: Macmillan, 1986)

Moreux, Serge: 'Prokofieff: an intimate portrait', *Tempo*, 11 (Spring, 1949)

Nabokov, Nicolas: *Old friends and new music* (London: Hamish Hamilton, 1951)

Nestyev, Israel: *Sergei Prokofiev: his musical life* (New York: Knopf, 1946)
Prokofiev (London: OUP, 1961)

Poulenc, Francis: *My friends and myself* (London: Dobson Books, 1978)

Prokofiev, Sergey *et al*: 'Prokofiev's correspondence with Stravinsky and Shostakovich', in M. H. Brown & R. J. Wiley, *eds.*: *Slavonic and Western music: essays for Gerald Abraham* (Russian Music Studies: 12) (Ann Arbor, Michigan: UMI, 1985)

Prokofiev, Sergey *ed*. D. H. Appel: *Prokofiev by Prokofiev: a composer's memoir* (New York: Doubleday, 1979)
Prokofiev by Prokofiev: a composer's memoir [abridged edition] (London: Macdonald and Jane's, 1979)

Robinson, Harlow: *Sergei Prokofiev: a biography* (London: Robert Hale, 1987)

Samuel, Claude: *Prokofiev* (London: Calder and Boyars, 1971)

Seroff, Victor: *Sergei Prokofiev: a Soviet tragedy* (London: Frewin, 1969)

Shlifstein, Semyon, *ed.*: *Sergey Prokofiev: autobiography, articles, reminiscences* (Moscow: Foreign Languages Publishing House, [1961])

Szigeti, Joseph: 'The Prokofiev I knew', *Music and Musicians*, xi (June, 1963)

Prokofiev: Individual Works

Ashley, Patricia: Prokofiev's piano music: line, chord, key (diss., U. of Rochester, 1963)

Auric, Georges: 'A new Prokofiev concerto', *The Listener*, 16 (December, 1936)

Austin, William: 'Prokofiev's Fifth Symphony', *Music Review*, xvii (August, 1956)

Bennett, Clive: 'Prokofiev and Eugene Onegin', *Musical Times*, cxxi (April, 1980)
'Unstaged dramas', *The Listener*, 111 (March, 1984)
Prokofiev dramatic music (BBC Music Guide) (London: in preparation)

Brown, Malcolm: 'Prokofiev's Eighth Piano Sonata', *Tempo*, 70 (Autumn, 1964)
The symphonies of Sergei Prokof'ev (diss., Florida State U., 1967)
'Prokofiev's War and Peace: a chronicle', *Musical Quarterly*, lxiii (July, 1977)

Corsaro, Frank & Sendak, Maurice: *The Love for Three Oranges* (London: Bodley Head, 1984)

Del Mar, Norman: 'Confusion and error', *The Score*, 21 (October, 1957)

Downes, Edward: 'Prokofiev's War and Peace', *Opera*, 23 (October, 1972)

Drew, David: 'Prokofiev's demon', *New Statesman*, 72 (September, 1966)

Henderson, Lyn: 'How The Flaming Angel became Prokofiev's third symphony', *Music Review*, xl (February, 1979)

Henderson, Robert: 'Busoni, Gozzi, Prokofiev and The Oranges', *Opera*, 33 (May, 1982)

Jefferson, Alan: 'The Angel of Fire', *Music and Musicians*, xiii (August, 1965)

Keldysh, Yuri: 'Sergei Prokofiev's last opera', *Soviet Literature* (June, 1960)

Layton, Robert: 'Serge Prokofiev (1891-1953)', in R. Simpson, *ed.*: *The Symphony*, vol. 2 (Harmondsworth: Penguin, 1967)
'Prokofiev and the sonatas', *The Listener*, 77 (January, 1967)
Prokofiev symphonies and concertos (BBC Music Guide) (London: in preparation)

Lloyd-Jones, David: 'Prokofiev and the opera', *Opera*, 13 (August, 1962)

McAllister, Rita: 'The Fourth Symphony of Prokofiev', *The Listener*, 78 (July, 1967)
'Prokofiev's early opera Maddalena', *Proceedings of the Royal Musical Association*, xcvi (1969-70)
'Natural and supernatural in The Fiery Angel', *Musical Times*, cxi (August, 1970)

The operas of Sergei Prokofiev (diss., U. of Cambridge, 1970)

'Prokofiev's Tolstoy Epic', *Musical Times*, cxiii (September, 1972)

'Prokofiev's Maddalena: a première', *Musical Times*, cxx (March, 1979)

Mitchell, Donald: 'Prokofieff's Three Oranges: a note on its musical-dramatic organisation', *Tempo*, 41 (Autumn, 1956)

Nestyev, Israel: 'Music inspired by the genius of Lenin (a Prokofiev cantata)', *Soviet Literature* (April, 1969)

Palmer, Christopher: 'Film composing and Prokofiev', *Crescendo International*, 15 (March/May, 1977)

Roseberry, Eric: 'Prokofiev's piano sonatas', *Music and Musicians*, xix (March, 1971)

Soviet Music and Musical Life

Abraham, Gerald: *Eight Soviet composers* (London: OUP, 1943)

Arbatsky, Yuri: 'The Soviet attitude towards music', *Musical Quarterly*, xliii (July, 1957)

Asafiev, Boris: *Russian music from the beginning of the 19th century* (Ann Arbor, Michigan: Edwards, 1953)

  A book about Stravinsky (Russian Music Studies: 5) (Ann Arbor, Michigan: UMI, 1982)

Bakst, James: *A history of Russian-Soviet music* (New York: Dodd, Mead & Co., 1966)

Brown, Malcolm *ed.*: *Russian and Soviet music: essays for Boris Schwarz* (Russian Music Studies: 11) (Ann Arbor, Michigan: UMI, 1984)

Brown, Malcolm: 'The Soviet Russian concepts of "Intonazia" and "Musical Imagery"', *Musical Quarterly*, lx (October, 1974)

Krebs, Stanley: *Soviet composers and the development of Soviet music* (London: Allen & Unwin, 1970)

Lipovsky, Alexander: *Lenin Prize winners: Soviet stars in the world of music* (Moscow: Progress Pubs., [1967])

McQuere, Gordon *ed.*: *Russian theoretical thought in music* (Russian Music Studies: 10) (Ann Arbor, Michigan: UMI, 1983)

Moisenko, Rena: *Realist music* (London: Meridian, 1949)

Olkhovsky, Andrei: *Music under the Soviets: the agony of an art* (London: Routledge, 1955)

Polyakova, Lyudmila: *Soviet music* (Moscow: Foreign Languages Publishing House, [1961])

Schwarz, Boris: *Music and musical life in Soviet Russia, 1917-1970* (London: Barrie & Jenkins, 1972)

Slonimsky, Nicolas: 'Soviet music and musicians', *Slavonic Review*, 22 (December, 1944) 'The changing style of Soviet music', *Journal of the American Musicological Society*, iii (Autumn, 1950)

Vishnevskaya, Galina: *Galina: a Russian story* (London: Hodder & Stoughton, 1985)

Volkov, Solomon: *Testimony: the memoirs of Dmitri Shostakovich* (London: Hamish Hamilton, 1979)

Werth, Alexander: *Musical uproar in Moscow* (London: Turnstile Press, 1949)

Widdicombe, Gillian: 'Three friends', *The Observer* (November, 1977)

Soviet Culture and Politics

Barber, John: 'The establishment of intellectual orthodoxy in the USSR', *Past and Present*, 83 (May, 1979)

Barna, Yon: *Eisenstein* (London: Secker & Warburg, 1973)

Berlin, Isaiah: *Personal impressions* (Oxford: OUP, 1982)

Billington, James: *The icon and the axe: an interpretive history of Russian culture* (New York: Knopf, 1966)

Deutscher, Isaac: *Ironies of history: essays on contemporary Communism* (London: OUP, 1966)

Ehrenburg, Ilya: *Memoirs* (London: MacGibbon & Kee, 1961-6)

Eisenstein, Sergey: *The film sense* (London: Faber, 1963)

Fitzpatrick, Sheila: 'Culture and politics under Stalin: a reappraisal', *Slavic Review*, 35 (June, 1976)

Gorki, Maxim: *Literature and life: selected writings* (London: Hutchinson, 1946)

Grey, Camilla: *The Russian experiment in art* (London: Thames & Hudson, 1962)

Hingley, Ronald: *Russian writers and Soviet society* (London: Weidenfeld & Nicolson, 1979)

James, C. Vaughan: *Soviet socialist realism: origins and theory* (London: Macmillan, 1973)

Lenin, V. I.: *On literature and art* (Moscow: Progress Pubs., 1967)

Mandelstam, Nadezhda: *Hope against hope* (Harmondsworth: Penguin, 1975)
Hope abandoned (Harmondsworth: Penguin, 1976)

Medvedev, Roy: *Let history judge* (London: Macmillan, 1972)

Nettl, J. Peter: *The Soviet achievement* (London: Thames & Hudson, 1967)

Slonim, Marc: *Soviet Russian literature 1917-1977* (London: OUP, 1977)

Tucker, Robert: *The Soviet political mind* (London: Allen & Unwin, 1972)

Zhdanov, Andrei: *On literature, music and philosophy* (London: Lawrence & Wishart, 1950)

Acknowledgements and References

Acknowledgements are due for quotations from the following sources:

G. Abraham: *The Tradition of Western Music* (London, OUP, 1974); Y. Barna: *Eisenstein* (London, Secker & Warburg, 1973); I. Berlin: *Personal Impressions* (Oxford, OUP, 1982); J. Billington: *The Icon and the Axe: an Interpretive History of Russian Culture* (New York, Knopf, 1966); A. Blok, trans. J. Lindsay: *The Twelve and the Scythians* (London, Journeyman Press, 1982); V. Blok, ed.: *Sergey Prokofiev: Materials, Articles, Interviews* (Moscow, Progress Publishers, 1978); M. Brown: 'Prokofiev's War and Peace: a chronicle' (*Musical Quarterly*, July 1977); M. Brown and R. J. Wiley, eds.: *Slavonic and Western Music: Essays for Gerald Abraham* (Russian Music Studies: 12) (Ann Arbor, Michigan, UMI, 1985); D. Drew: 'Prokofiev's demon' (*New Statesman*, Sept. 1966); V. Duke: *Listen Here* (New York, Obolensky, 1963); A. Grechaninov: *My Life* (New York, Coleman-Ross, 1952); S. D. Krebs: *Soviet Composers and the Development of Soviet Music* (London, Allen & Unwin, 1970); V. I. Lenin: *On Literature and Art* (Moscow, Progress Publishers, 1967); V. Mayakovsky, trans. M. Hayward: *The Bedbug and Selected Poetry* (New York, Meridian Books, 1960); R. McAllister: 'Natural and supernatural in *The Fiery Angel*' (*Musical Times*, Aug. 1970) and 'Sergey Prokofiev' in *The New Grove Dictionary of Music and Musicians* (London,

Macmillan, 1981); D. Mitchell: 'Prokofiev's *Three Oranges*: a note on its musical-dramatic organisation' (*Tempo*, Autumn 1956); N. Nabokov: *Old Friends and New Music* (London, Hamish Hamilton, 1951); I. Nestyev: *Prokofiev* (London, OUP, 1961); H. Ottaway: sleeve notes for *The Five Piano Concertos* and *Violin Concertos nos. 1 & 2* (London, Decca Record Company, 1975/7); F. Poulenc: *My Friends and Myself* (London, Dobson Books, 1978); S. Prokofiev, ed.: D. H. Appel: *Prokofiev by Prokofiev* (New York, Doubleday, 1979); E. Roseberry: *Shostakovich: his Life and Times* (Tunbridge Wells, Midas Books, 1982); C. Samuel: *Prokofiev* (London, Calder & Boyars, 1971); B. Schwarz: *Music and Musical Life in Soviet Russia* (London, Barrie & Jenkins, 1972); V. Seroff: *Sergei Prokofiev: a Soviet Tragedy* (London, Frewin, 1969); S. Shlifstein, ed.: *Sergey Prokofiev: Autobiography, Articles, Reminiscences* (Moscow, FLPH, 1961); N. Slonimsky: 'Soviet music and musicians' (*Slavonic Review*, December 1944); I. Stravinsky and R. Craft: *Memories and Commentaries, Expositions and Developments* and *Dialogues and a Diary* (London, Faber, 1960/2/8); [Stravinsky], ed. R. Craft: *Stravinsky: Selected Correspondence Vol. 1* (London, Faber, 1982); V. Stravinsky and R. Craft: *Stravinsky in Pictures and Documents* (New York, Simon & Schuster, 1978); G. Vishnevskaya: *Galina: a Russian Story* (London, Hodder & Stoughton, 1985); S. Volkov: *Testimony: the Memoirs of Dmitri Shostakovich* (London, Hamish Hamilton, 1979).

In addition, I would like to thank the following for their kindness and courtesy in placing so much material at my disposal:

Boosey & Hawkes Music Publishers Ltd, EMI Records Ltd, English National Opera, Rob. Forberg – P. Jurgenson Musikverlag, National Film Archive, Novosti Press Agency, Sotheby & Co., Westfield College Library, Westminster Central Music Library.

Every effort has been made to trace copyright holders for the illustrative material used in the book. Apologies are extended to those whom it has not been possible to contact.

Finally, this book could not have been written without the invaluable assistance of, Elizabeth M. Thomson, Beryl Lester, Sue Harris, Frances Rae, Robert M. Walker, family and friends.

David Gutman
London, 1987

Index

Illustrations are indicated by **bold** type.

221

222